Praise for *Executive Pre*

"In today's dog-eat-dog world where degrees from the finest schools, high cognitive abilities, and superior technical skills are merely threshold competencies, it becomes increasingly important for career success to stand out from the pack and project a leader image that others look up to and want to follow. In this second edition of Harrison Monarth's bestselling book *Executive Presence*, he shows leaders and those who want to become one, step-by-step, how to develop a strong personal brand that inspires and wields a positive influence. Packed with insights from leading neuroscientists on how to regulate emotions in pressure-cooker situations, coaching advice on getting buy-in for one's most ambitious ideas, and guidance on resolving conflict during difficult conversations and crafting strategic stories that lead others to action, *Executive Presence* is a highly engaging read by one of today's top executive coaches that should be on every leader's desk."

> —Francesca Gino, Professor of Business Administration at
> Harvard Business School Behavioral Scientist, author,
> *Rebel Talent* and *Sidetracked*

"We live in a reputation economy. What you think of yourself is irrelevant compared to what other people think of you, and that is especially true if you want to be a leader. This book provides an authoritative guide to shaping how others see you and emerge as a leader. Don't read it unless you want to be one!"

> —Dr. Tomas Chamorro-Premuzic, Chief Talent Scientist at
> ManpowerGroup, Professor of Business Psychology,
> Columbia University, author, *Why Do So Many Incompetent
> Men Become Leaders?* and *The Talent Delusion*

"*Executive Presence* was a classic, a must-read for those wanting to expand their influence and position themselves as leaders. But this newly updated edition is even more useful. Incorporating provocative insights from the expanding field of neuroscience, Harrison Monarth offers readers proven practices for exerting influence and managing perceptions, even as we act on our basic values and demonstrate confidence in our core strength.

Highly specific and engaging, Monarth's new opus is the ideal coaching tool–whether you're coaching others or yourself."

—SALLY HELGESEN, author, *How Women Rise* (with Marshall Goldsmith), *The Female Advantage*, *The Web of Inclusion*, and *The Female Vision*

"Self-awareness is a foundational skill for any leader looking to develop a strong executive presence. Harrison's book provides readers with actionable strategies to help them positively engage and influence organizational stakeholders at all levels. Whether you are a high-potential manager or seasoned executive, this book is a must-read."

—DR. TASHA EURICH, *New York Times* bestselling author, *Insight* and *Bankable Leadership*

"A significant part of successful leadership is the ability to project an image that conveys credibility and inspires people. In this must-read second edition of *Executive Presence*, Harrison breaks down the mystery behind this elusive concept. Chapter by chapter he shares the specific behaviors, skills, and characteristics that help aspiring executives and leaders at all levels stand out from their equally smart peers and gain influence far beyond their formal authority. Best of all, Harrison's expert coaching shows that anyone with a desire to succeed can build executive presence, no matter where they start!"

—DORIE CLARK, author of *Reinventing You* and *Stand Out*, and adjunct professor, Duke University Fuqua School of Business

"Harrison Monarth's sprightly book *Executive Presence* departs from the mainstream of self-help literature in three important ways: (1) it concerns how to get ahead in one's career as opposed to learning how to feel better about oneself; (2) it is evidence-based as opposed to being based on personal intuition and experience; and (3) it focuses on improving how a person is perceived by others (i.e., improving a person's reputation) as opposed to increasing self-understanding."

—DR. ROBERT HOGAN, Chairman and President of Hogan Assessments

Executive
PRESENCE

The Art of Commanding Respect Like a CEO

SECOND EDITION

HARRISON MONARTH

Mc Graw Hill

New York   Chicago   San Francisco   Athens
London   Madrid   Mexico City   Milan
New Delhi   Singapore   Sydney   Toronto

1 2 3 4 5 6 7 8 9   BNG   24 23 22 21 20 19

ISBN   978-1-265-61325-9
MHID   1-26-561325-7

McGraw-Hill Education books are available at special quantity discounts to use as premiums and sales promotions or for use in corporate training programs. To contact a representative, please visit the Contact Us pages at www.mhprofessional.com.

To Asli

Contents

Foreword

Harrison Monarth's *Executive Presence* is essential reading for anyone desiring to rise up out of obscurity in our corporate existence. From the moment we step into our offices, and all the day long until sleep mercifully shuts our cares away, we are immersed in combat. Either we will wreak our will—prevail—or we will fail. Mr. Monarth writes with clarity and zest. He is in full command of his materials. Not only does he never permit psychosociological claptrap to clutter his prose; he transcends it, keeping his thinking bright and clear. Among his several major theses—all useful—is his paramount contention about "social intelligence." Our relations with subordinates, peers, and superiors in the corporate battleground are critically a matter of perception—our own, about the impact that our arguments per se may be having on other people, but also of the instant judgments that are being formed about us on an irrelevant personal basis. Sun Tzu could not have put the terms of engagement more subtly. We must understand our vulnerability. We are neither superior to the impact of our personalities nor independent of how they may be perceived. The battle is won or lost not so much because of the cogency of our position but often because of the chords that our manner of speaking, dress, deportment, or attitude strike on the sympathies of others. Social intelligence is the critical factor in any contest of wills. I am grateful to Mr. Monarth for his wisdom."

    —REID BUCKLEY, writer, speaker, educator, author,
      An American Family—The Buckleys

Acknowledgments

I WANT TO thank my literary agent, Rita Rosenkranz, for her continued support, from the first book to this one. Many years ago she took a chance on an unknown author and I'm certain I owe a good amount of my success to her foresight. My thanks also to Amy Li and my long-time editor Donya Dickerson at McGraw-Hill who felt that the time is right for a second edition of *Executive Presence*, ten years since the first edition had been published. I owe much gratitude to Frank Flaherty, adjunct professor of journalism at NYU and brilliant editor whose thoughtful editing of my manuscript kept my verbosity in check. My thanks go also to Terri Peterson, professor of political science at Lehman College in New York, who provided excellent research at sometimes impossibly short notice; and, of course, most particularly, to my beloved wife, Asli, who chose a life in fashion, but who would have made an excellent editor had she decided to go that route. Her relentless support and encouragement kept me going throughout the many long days and short nights when work and life made it difficult to focus on writing. And finally, this updated edition would not exist without the experiences I've gained coaching some of the most brilliant leaders and executives from organizations all over the world. The many insights we've gained in our sessions together hopefully help others navigate their own challenges and chart an inspiring path to success.

Introduction

A Primer on Executive Presence

SHORTLY AFTER THE first edition of this book was published in 2009, a senior talent management executive from pharmaceutical giant Merck called to inquire about our Executive Presence coaching programs. She and her colleagues had identified a group of internal leaders who needed to work on their executive presence, she said, and she wanted us to coach them. Then she paused for a moment and asked, "But . . . what is it?"

This reminded me of a now famous phrase, expressed in a written opinion by a U.S. Supreme Court justice in a 1964 pornography case (*Jacobellis v. Ohio*) about what is and what isn't obscene material. "I know it when I see it," Justice Potter Stewart wrote, conceding that while he wouldn't be able to intelligently define such material, he nonetheless was able to form an opinion on a case-by-case basis.

Similarly, the Merck executive and a legion of other corporate managers are now wrestling with the full import of the phrase "executive presence," which has become a buzzword since I wrote the first edition of this book. Several other authors have attempted to define the term, with most centering their ideas on some mix of communication skill, appearance, and a set of extroverted behaviors. And while these are important components of executive presence, I believe the concept is more complex than that. I've worked with managers, emerging leaders, and executives for decades—both within organizational hierarchies and as an outside coach and leadership consultant—and the insights I've gained into the qualities integral to executive presence go far beyond speaking well, looking good, and acting with confidence.

Here are some other aspects of executive presence that I've discovered in the trenches: It's about being in control of your emotions when you're under stress. It's about putting the people around you in a positive and productive state of mind. It's about projecting the warmth and strength that foster trust and credibility. It's about leaving absolutely no doubt about the value you contribute to others and your organization. It's about knowing how to influence others for mutual gain. It's about practicing excellent judgment in interpersonal and professional situations. It's about actively monitoring and managing your reputation. And it's about understanding how to build a powerful personal brand.

In this revised and updated edition of *Executive Presence: The Art of Commanding Respect Like a CEO*, I've provided detailed guidance for developing these and many other capabilities.

You'll get the type of straightforward, pragmatic coaching advice I have shared for the past two decades with more than 60 Fortune 500 CEOs and thousands of senior leaders globally, both in intensive one-on-one executive coaching engagements and in leadership development workshops. These client organizations include GE, Deloitte, MetLife, PepsiCo, Chanel, General Motors, Walkers Shortbread, the U.S. Air Force, the Nature Conservancy, Water.Org, Hewlett-Packard, Hilton Worldwide, Cisco, Standard & Poor's and Procter & Gamble, to name a few.

Of course, it isn't just senior leaders who need guidance on conveying a consistent and formidable executive presence. In my work I also encounter many talented and hardworking high-potential managers who contribute solid value to their organizations, but somehow get stuck at a certain level while their (sometimes less talented and less hardworking) peers seem to snag the career-boosting assignments and high-powered sponsors. Enhancing the executive presence of the former, underappreciated group of executives often provides the leverage they need to get their careers moving again. More broadly, above a certain level of the corporate hierarchy, knowledge, expertise, brainpower, diligence, and credentials from the finest schools are not enough for continued career success. Those attributes simply earn you entry into a game where all the players are smart and have three letters after their name. In such rarefied fields, it is, again, executive presence that can make all the difference.

In fact, over the last few years, a series of surveys has highlighted just how crucial executive presence is to both successful leadership and career advancement.

For example, in a paper published by Gavin R. Dagley and Cadeyrn J. Gaskin in *Consulting Psychology Journal*, the American Psychological Association cited research, finding that 89 percent of nearly 400 senior executives and professional development managers credited executive presence with helping people get ahead at work. Nearly 80 percent said that limited executive presence could hold people back.

The authors of the APA paper also conducted their own study, surveying professionals who'd been exposed to vast numbers of executives and who were in part responsible for those executives' development and advancement. The most interesting findings were the distinctions that these experienced professionals made between executive presence characteristics deemed most important in initial encounters and those that weigh more heavily over time. The five characteristics that signaled strong executive presence in initial encounters included status and reputation, physical appearance, projected confidence, communication ability, and engagement skills. The five traits found to be more important over time were interpersonal integrity, values-in-action, intellect and expertise, the ability to deliver outcomes, and the willingness to use coercive power when appropriate.

The Center for Talent Innovation, a nonprofit think tank, surveyed 268 senior executives at large corporations on executive presence, and a majority of them cited gravitas as one of its core characteristics, a characteristic that particularly helps people climb the organizational ladder. (Among other things, gravitas was defined in the survey as remaining confident and calm under pressure, acting decisively, displaying integrity and courage, and demonstrating emotional intelligence.)

What is clear from these and other studies is that executive presence isn't simply *one* characteristic that you're either blessed with or lack in spades. It's rather a mix of mindset, skills, and behaviors that you can learn, acquire, and hone and then wield to boost your impact beyond any formal authority you may have. What is also clear is that executive presence is something that is perceived by *others*—not determined by *you*. This means that, to sway and manage the all-important perceptions of others, you must gain strategic self-awareness of the competencies and characteristics you need to develop for a potent executive presence, and then you need to engage in constant self-monitoring of those skills and traits.

This revised and updated edition of *Executive Presence* features several brand-new chapters. For instance, in the new Chapter 2, you will find tools to help you detect any blind spots and unhelpful behaviors that impair your executive presence. In Chapter 3, we will explore various emotion-regulation strategies, backed by the latest findings in neuroscience, to help you stay calm and composed in any high-pressure situation. And in Chapter 10, you'll learn how strengths that normally bolster executive presence can become liabilities in high-pressure situations—when self-confidence morphs into arrogance, for instance—and how to rein in those runaway qualities.

Besides the wholly new material, each of the original chapters has been substantially updated and revised, with fresh examples, new research, and revealing insights from coaching sessions with leaders who needed to improve their executive presence or risk diminishing their effectiveness or even derailing their careers.

For instance, you'll learn about the CEO of a social media firm who had a reputation as a "people pleaser" and who needed to develop his ability to hold people accountable to regain the confidence of his board and enterprise leadership team. You'll learn about a director at a global consumer goods company who needed to overhaul the laid-back, somewhat passive style that led senior executives to doubt his readiness for a global leadership role. You'll explore why a VP of technology at a health insurance firm had to change certain behaviors that led to complaints from peers and direct reports about his abrasive interpersonal style. And you'll learn how an introverted senior manager discovered that she needed to overcome her reluctance to network both internally and externally in order to get on the radar of decision makers who could promote her to the C-suite.

In addition, I've packed this new volume with science-backed strategies and proven techniques that you can put into practice almost immediately to strengthen your executive presence. You'll discover why low-status leaders are often ignored, but also how you can benefit from conveying low, medium, or high status, depending on the interpersonal context. You'll appraise different methods to get buy-in from others for your ideas, as well as methods to motivate people to take action. In the updated chapter on strategic storytelling, you'll explore the three types of story that every leader must master to successfully influence others, and you'll assess which story-telling structures best match your specific objective—whether it is building trust and credibility, or inspiring others with a compelling vision, or sharing knowledge in a way that it "sticks." And you'll discover how best to build your personal brand—offline and online—with different strategies for generation X, gen Y (the millennials), and gen Z, which by itself made up 25 percent of the U.S. population as of 2015, according to *Forbes* magazine.

Over all, in order to land in the front ranks of your equally smart and ambitious colleagues, you must construct a compelling and authentic executive presence, with the enormous advantage that you can carry it with you everywhere. Yes, executive presence is a complex mix of ingredients, but our understanding of it has now matured to the point where you no longer need to guess at its essential components. My hope is that you feel inspired to study and master the ideas and strategies I've laid out in this revised and updated edition of *Executive Presence: The Art of Commanding Respect Like a CEO*, so that you can gain an important edge in your quest to become a leader in your chosen field.

Want to Measure Your Executive Presence?

My free Executive Presence Indicator is a self-assessment designed to give insight into your strengths as well as opportunities for improvement as they relate to executive presence. This survey is designed for leaders, high potentials and other professionals who are ready to propel their careers forward.

Take the assessment today at executivepresenceindicator.com.

The Natural Laws of Perception

How People Perceive You

WHEN KAREN ABRAMSON became CEO of Wolters Kluwer Tax & Accounting, she learned quickly that she was under a magnifying glass. In a 2014 interview with the *New York Times*, she revealed how surprised she was at the little things people around her started watching. "If I were seen having a conversation with somebody in the hallway, people assumed they were my best friend, though it was the first time I had talked to them all month." Even her clothing drew scrutiny. After staff meetings she'd get feedback and suggestions on her style—including her lipstick color. "The first couple of times it happens, you feel very insecure, but then you learn to move on with your life," Abramson told the *Times*.

Of course, astute leaders like Abramson know quite well that to simply "move on with your life" without considering the myriad perceptions we create along the way, many of them unintended, is bound to present some speed bumps on the road to leadership effectiveness. When Abramson discovered that people would act on an offhand comment she'd made, she became more careful. When she learned that her trademark blunt communication style led to unintended consequences, she softened it.

While you may have more flexibility in terms of self-expression at the senior level of management, the flip side is that people assign more weight to your messages, and as Abramson learned, may jump to conclusions and into action.

Executive presence is anchored in what others perceive, not what we intend to communicate. To paraphrase Robert Hogan, cofounder of Hogan Assessments: Others marry us, hire us, fire us, promote us, lend us money, and follow us, not because of what *we* think of ourselves, but because of what *they* think of us.

I often see firsthand how a blind spot to this crucial distinction threatens to upend the careers of otherwise talented and smart individuals.

One leader I worked with, Ross, the charismatic head of public affairs at a global public relations firm, was well connected and was reliable in bringing new business to the firm. He also considered himself the kind of manager who developed his team members, giving them opportunities to learn and grow and stretch beyond their comfort zone. But that's not how his direct reports and peers perceived his delegation of tasks. These comments on his management style were typical: "His instinct is to delegate, but [he] doesn't always do it in the most effective way; his instinct is to forward things to somebody without discussion and not necessarily keeping track of what *he's* supposed to do and whether it's his responsibility or somebody else's. *Everything* is delegated. Can be frustrating sometimes. He is perceived as not being willing to do the work; he doesn't like to get his hands dirty."

Another client of mine was Danielle, a senior vice president in risk management for a global insurance firm. Danielle's biggest strengths were her business acumen, her critical thinking skills, and her drive, which enabled her to see and seize opportunities within the business. She was perceived as someone who was driving the business forward rather than being passive. She also had excellent relationships with her direct reports, who loved her. But Danielle had a major blind spot. While she thought she was well positioned for a more senior executive role in an upcoming round of promotions, her bosses disagreed. They felt she needed to work on enhancing relationships with regional presidents and other individuals at more senior levels than she; that she needed to work on managing up; that she needed to get comfortable connecting with regional VPs and be more proactive in building those relationships. Danielle's networking efforts had mostly focused on her operational network, consisting of the individuals whom she needed to engage to get the work done. In the process she lost sight of the importance of the type of personal and strategic networking that would have put her on the radar of key decision makers at more senior levels.

Both Ross and Danielle were strong contributors to the success of their respective companies. But their blind spots kept them from reaching their full potential. From what I've seen in my coaching practice, their predicaments are common. One biopharma CEO I coached viewed himself as "consensus seeking" while his leadership team saw him as indecisive. The VP of technology for a consumer products company considered himself "laid-back" while others interpreted his behavior as a lack of engagement. The director of provider relations at a regional health plan saw herself as a "humble leader," but many of her colleagues saw her as a pushover who lacked confidence. All these executives expressed some dismay at how others got it wrong. But as we already know, their intentions weren't what mattered. The perceptions of others did.

To develop our executive presence and understand our true impact on others, we must have a clear idea of the good, the bad, and the ugly of how we're perceived. Self-awareness of our strengths and weaknesses is the key to this understanding, and I've devoted the entire next chapter to helping readers develop this ability.

Perceptions of Executive Presence

Some people don't merely enter a room; they take possession of it. Their relaxed confidence is reflected in their walk, their posture, and the ease with which they engage others. Their eye contact is steady and their smile sincere. They're socially appropriate in dress and conversation, and everyone they meet can't help but *feel* their presence. Yet if that were all there is to executive presence, you'd be holding a pamphlet instead of a book right now.

Instead, authentic executive presence is a fluid combination of certain characteristics, behaviors, skills, and personality traits that all add up to a personal power that inspires and engages people. But while executive presence is complex, it is also attainable. Over two decades of coaching high-potential managers and leaders in the Fortune 500, I've found that anyone with a desire to change and grow can indeed develop this presence in all its facets.

My appreciation of what constitutes executive presence was formed in several ways: years of conversations with senior leaders about what executive presence looks like and the qualities they need to see in emerging leaders; close observation of respected leaders who bring out the best in others; research in the social sciences and leadership literature; and the failures of leaders who had talent and cognitive ability but nonetheless faltered due to an unwillingness to listen to feedback and adapt their behavior.

I've distilled my perspectives on executive presence into 5 categories and 17 distinct yet interdependent traits and abilities that I believe to have the biggest impact on this critical quality (see Figure 1.1).

Communication: Mastering difficult conversations, engaging others, telling strategic stories, inspiring and persuading
Competence: Having intellect and expertise, delivering results, acting decisively
Personal brand: Having status and reputation, projecting calm under pressure, possessing a compelling physical appearance, projecting confidence, having interpersonal integrity
Courage: Holding people accountable, speaking truth to power
Political savvy: Networking and building alliances, managing up, generating buy-in and support

(handwritten annotation: "↳ I love to see")
(handwritten annotation: "manage up")

Figure 1.1   The Traits of Executive Presence

We'll be discussing all of them throughout this book.

It's worth noting that we all have different executive presence profiles; we're stronger in some areas and weaker in others. Similarly, our strengths may naturally emerge in some situations and waiver or even vanish at other times, perhaps when we're under stress. For instance, you may give excellent presentations to peers and direct reports but bungle the same task in front of a more senior audience. Or you may be perceived to have executive presence in initial encounters due to your strong engagement skills and conversational savvy, but you may lose that distinction over time when others perceive—rightly or wrongly—that you're mostly style over substance. The reverse may also be true, where your humble demeanor may initially be interpreted as timidity, but after some exposure it is viewed as a "quiet strength" that is an integral component of your leadership effectiveness.

The Path from Observation to Action

An easy way to understand how perceptions are formed and how people reach faulty conclusions is called the ladder of inference (Figure 1.2), a concept developed by organizational psychologist Chris Argyris. Made popular in *The Fifth Discipline Fieldbook: Strategies and Tools for Building a Learning Organization*, by systems scientist Peter Senge, this theory describes the journey that our general thinking process takes in leading us from observable reality—or facts—to our decisions and actions.

In this "ladder," each rung represents a different stage in the reasoning process. It looks something like this:

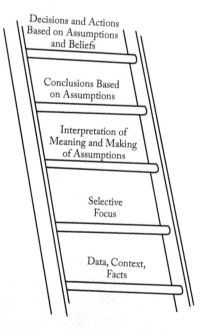

Figure 1.2   The Ladder of Inference

1. We start with observable reality—the raw data, the context, and other "facts."
2. We then selectively focus on certain aspects of this observable reality—the facets that catch our eye, often based on our interests, biases, beliefs, and prior experiences.
3. Then we try to make sense of what we perceive and make assumptions based on this meaning.
4. Next, we draw conclusions based on our assumptions that either reinforce our beliefs or alter them.
5. Finally, we make decisions and take actions based on what we believe to be true.

As you can see, the ladder of inference can be a useful checklist for determining whether our reasoning is based on verifiable facts or the subconscious influence of our beliefs and preexisting assumptions. It also shows clearly how easy it can be for people to climb up to certain conclusions that may lead to undesirable consequences. An example involving one of my clients illustrates this point.

When Jeremiah was promoted to executive managing director at a major financial services company, his leadership team almost doubled in size. In his former role, he valued loyalty and socialized with his team members in meetings, at lunch, and after hours; this approach lifted morale and created a strong team esprit de corps. But when he continued this behavior with his original team members after his promotion, he created the perception that he had an inner circle, a cadre of favorites, which alienated the new team members. This caused strife between the camps and throttled collaboration. While the warm friendships Jeremiah forged with members of his original, smaller team helped create a collegial atmosphere, this approach is rarely sustainable with larger teams, as perceived inequities will inevitably arise in terms of personal chemistry, attention, and distribution of rewards and resources.

The new team members' conclusion that Jeremiah had an inner circle and their resistance to cooperating with these "teacher's pet" colleagues affected more than the productivity of Jeremiah's team. It also cast a shadow over his judgment as a leader; after all, a leader's main job is to be inclusive and harness the talents and skills of *all* his people.

Jeremiah's troubles remind us that we are constantly on display and that our behaviors are up for interpretation, for better or worse. Also, if we are in a leadership position, the results are often magnified.

Other Factors That Influence Perceptions

While we can't very well control what others think of us, it can be helpful to understand some of the more powerful filters through which we all process incoming data that color our perceptions.

1. Stereotypes

To gauge the strength of stereotypes, consider an exercise that has been adopted by organizational psychologists in workshops across the globe. "Draw a leader" was the simple instruction that Tina Kiefer, a professor of organizational behavior at the University of Warwick in the United Kingdom, gave to a room full of male and female executives. The results, regardless of gender, were that the executives would reliably draw pictures of males every time, attributing such equally imaginary leadership qualities to their creations as "Vision," "Decisive," "Charisma," and "Listens."

Yet in a study on leadership effectiveness that was published in APA's *Journal of Applied Psychology* in 2014, "Women were seen as more effective leaders than men in middle management, business and education organizations." The same study found that women were also seen as more effective in senior management positions, as rated by others.

Researchers from Florida International University analyzed over five decades of data and found that while men would generally rate themselves higher in leadership effectiveness, ratings by others often found women to be the more effective leaders across a variety of leadership contexts.

One way to combat "Man = Boss" stereotypes is to expose people to more women leaders and use strategic storytelling strategies to highlight their many contributions and achievements in general, and specific to an organization. Gender, of course, is just one of the stereotypes that executives may confront; ethnicity and race and many other traits have also prompted unjustified generalizations that these tactics can help to blunt.

2. Beliefs

Belief systems represent a view of the world, the ideas that a person holds as true and unquestionable, spanning everything from religion, cultural norms, and political affiliations to educational experiences, child-rearing, and leadership styles. Our various biases and learned preferences are the product of a lifetime of emotional and intellectual evolution, and they rest in part on things that are not provable. Then, when we encounter ideas, we're drawn to the ones that support our current beliefs, selectively focusing on the confirming evidence and dismissing the contradictory evidence. Conversely, when we encounter ideas that violate our preexisting beliefs, we often bend over backward trying to disprove them.

Strategically, this means it's often best to concentrate one's efforts on influencing people who are on the fence about an issue, rather than people whose heels are dug in. New research may help in this regard. A study led by Princeton University showed that weakly held beliefs based on misinformation can be weakened or even rendered insignificant by repeatedly exposing the holder to correct information *that is related to the misinformation.* While the study centered mostly on such scientific topics as allergies, nutrition, and health, we might extrapolate the strategy to everyday management challenges. Say, for instance, that a leader is viewed as tough and difficult to work for. By repeatedly sharing accurate information and examples about her that illustrate that she has high standards but treats people fairly, those on the fence about the leader's management style will grow more likely to remember the positive information and less likely to believe the negative stories. The key is to make sure the new information is related in nature to the misinformation and based on objective data, as opposed to just someone's opinion.

3. Values

Closely aligned with belief systems is the filter of personal values. Indisputably, most people like people who share their values and are wary or even downright hostile to those who don't. Unscrupulous politicians exploit this tendency, pitting us against each other by underscoring our differences rather than emphasizing our shared values to bring us closer together. An organization runs more smoothly when workers share its values—or at least abide by them during working hours. "Cultural fit" is often a criterion in the search for future company leaders, not least because those at the top set the tone for what's expected, what's rewarded, and what's punished.

Yet despite best efforts to ensure that values are aligned, organizational life is often rife with interpersonal dust-ups triggered by clashing values. If, for example, you're pushing a web developer to go live with a site that is still experiencing some functionality problems, but the developer stakes his reputation on everything running smoothly, then the conclusion he'll reach in a nanosecond about your request is that you are very wrong! We are constantly faced with such challenges to our values. Sometimes, depending on how strongly we hold certain values, we may make concessions. Think of the senior executive who promotes a fellow Harvard alumnus over a more qualified candidate from a different alma mater. Although the senior executive values fairness and merit, he feels no harm will result if once in a while he lets emotional attachments tip the scale to favor a *conflicting value*. Nevertheless, generally speaking, our values frame our perceptions and guide us through all kinds of moral challenges. And if they don't, they may not be values at all. To quote the inimitable philosopher Jon Stewart: "If you don't stick to your values when they're being tested, they're not values. They're hobbies."

4. First Impressions

The power of first impressions has been so well documented that the utterance of the cliché about not getting a second chance can turn the utterer into Captain Obvious. And while we all know that the perceptions we create in initial encounters can have an outsized impact on how a relationship unfolds—if one does, that is—we're often not sure what to do when it didn't go so well. Because, you know, that *second chance* thing.

But don't give up. First of all, new research from a series of joint studies by Cornell, Harvard, Yale, and the University of Essex reveals that most of us tend to think we did worse in initial encounters and conversations than we actually did. We think that our conversation partners like us less than we like them, and that the moments when others formed their opinions about us were generally more negative than the moments when we formed our opinions about them. We're so wrapped up in our own worries about what we should say or do that we often miss signals of others' positive affections toward us, the studies show. What to do? When you encounter someone for the first time, remember that we tend to view our performance negatively, and also remember that your counterparts in these meetings are themselves often plagued by the same insecurities and critical self-assessments. If you do these things, you will be able to relax a bit at these initial meetings, and by being relaxed and less focused on yourself, you really will make a better first impression than if you were anxious and in your head.

What if, though, an initial encounter really didn't go so well; in fact, we barely blundered our way through? There's bad news here but also good news, according to research by a team of psychologists from Canada, Belgium, and the United States. The bad news, as noted above, is that perceptions based on negative first impressions tend to stick like glue. Even when we have that second chance, any positive new perceptions we create are limited to the context in which they're formed. For instance, say you made a poor first impression on a new colleague when you interrupted her several times during her presentation. After some time, you run into her again—at a company-sponsored community fund-raiser, say—and you end up having a pleasant chat, and your colleague realizes that you're actually a nice person. Unfortunately, though, your colleague's new, positive perception about you is limited to contexts like the fund-raiser event. The original negative perception about you will continue to dominate in all other contexts.

The good news? Forewarned is forearmed. If you have made a bad first impression, identify as many different contexts as possible in which you can create positive impressions that will help to weaken that negative initial impression. As one of the study's researchers explained: "What is necessary is for the first impression to be challenged in multiple different contexts. In that case, new experiences become decontextualized and the first impression will slowly lose its power." But if all you do is rely on the occasional friendly chat in the lunchroom to counter a bad first impression, you'll only spin your wheels and miss valuable opportunities to build your executive presence.

We never run out of opportunities to make first impressions in life: There are the job interviews, client pitches, investor presentations, contract negotiations, meeting your new boss and colleagues for the first time, speaking at conferences—the list is endless. And that's just at work. Each opportunity comes with its unique risks and rewards; do well, and you're off to a good start with other opportunities sure to follow. Botch the whole thing, however, and the best that will happen is *nothing*. The worst runs the gamut from getting fired or not hired to being ignored, rebuked, cold-shouldered, or labeled a dud. To avoid such fates, I recommend keeping three simple yet powerful ideas in mind whenever you make your debut before a new audience: warmth, strength, and value.

Warmth, Strength, and Value Create Powerful First Impressions

Warmth

The first tool for making a powerful first impression and forging an emotional connection is *warmth*. Warmth fosters trust and puts people in the receptive frame of mind known to psychologists as an *approach* state, as opposed to an *avoid* state. Those opposite states stem from the ancient part of our brain, which is constantly scanning for pain or pleasure, for threat or reward. We want to know very quickly, from the moment we become aware of someone else, Is this person friend or foe? Can this person help me or hurt me?

Genuine warmth and the ability to engage others with socially appropriate behavior is one of the keys that can unlock the gates to mutual trust and liking. People are constantly asking themselves three things: What's happening? What's going to happen next? And how am I being treated? The answer to that last question is particularly important because people are highly protective of their status—i.e., how they view themselves in a group and how they're seen by others. Being treated coldly or indifferently makes people feel rejected, which triggers a threat response in the brain that makes us shun new experiences—the *avoid* state. In fact, neuroscience research has shown that feelings of rejection affect the same areas of the brain that are involved in the processing of physical pain, which can often make us withdraw or lash out in anger. By showing warmth and sharing part of ourselves in initial encounters, we enable others to let their guard down as they assess our motives and intentions.

There are myriad ways to demonstrate warmth: by engaging rather than appearing passive, by relaxing our expression, by flashing a genuine smile (the so-called Duchenne smile that wrinkles the corners of the eyes), by nodding and displaying open body language and gestures. As the encounter proceeds, you can further demonstrate interest by asking the person questions about things that are important to him or her and by sharing something about yourself that will create trust and help the person relate to you. Remember, we're drawn to those who share our values and avoid those who don't.

↳explain

Strength

Showing *strength* is a second tool for making effective first impressions. Such a display will boost perceptions of our competence and credibility, which also help gain the attention and trust of others. Strength is conveyed by the way you carry yourself, posture, tone of voice, eagerness to engage, and confidence. Even if you're nervous, you must appear outwardly calm, or you'll raise suspicions about your competence and readiness. Research has shown that strong reputations, significant achievements, and impressive networks are associated with executive presence, especially in initial encounters. The challenge is to demonstrate all this without being accused of braggadocio. But do not be so wary of that accusation that you say too little. When others are trying to gauge whether you can be trusted and are someone they want to affiliate with, you can benefit by association when you link yourself to people, organizations, and institutions that they trust and respect. Statements like "The way we solved these problems at Google . . . ," or "After I finished my MBA in Boston, I decided to . . . ," or "Mary Barra (CEO of General Motors) once asked me how . . ." can signal your achievements and associations without triggering your hearer's gag reflex. Humility in recounting any such nuggets is important, but if it is to lead to more, it must be balanced with strength to give you solid footing in these initial encounters. What's important to remember is, don't do any of this to build yourself up or make yourself feel important. The entire purpose is to let the people in your audience know they are safe with you: They will not be wasting their time. They will be getting top value from you.

Value

Value is the third component of a powerful first-impressions strategy. But don't be misled by one popular value theory, deemed the "elevator speech" approach. I understand the intention behind it—be concise in getting your point across; speak no longer than the duration of a short elevator ride. But the elevator metaphor is clumsy and as such often misinterpreted. What "point" are we talking about? Your idea for something? Your suitability for a job or assignment? Your ability to solve a problem? Better than wasting your time on crafting an elevator speech, think about how you can illustrate your *value* to a person, team, or organization. And say it for as long as it takes to say it, whether that's 10 seconds or 2 minutes. By value I mean *outcomes*. What is the outcome you can effect? What is the end result we'll get if we associate with you? What value do you contribute to the organization?

[handwritten marginalia: emphasize the outcome]

I've heard senior leaders say about someone they have known for a long while, "I still have no idea what he does." Why? Because we frequently lose people at "Hello." We flub the opportunity to communicate our value right from the start—the *meaning* of what we bring to the table, the outcome—so that people can know our purpose instantly and whether we're someone they want on their team, or we're someone worth listening to, or we're someone who might be a good fit for a particular role.

Imagine that you had to introduce yourself to your peers, vendors, and customers at a conference for technology executives. A company whose public communication strategy I've long admired is Emerson Technologies, so I'll use one of its award-winning advertising campaigns and imagine that campaign as an introduction in the following example.

[handwritten marginalia: great example]

Say an Emerson employee introduced himself like this: "My name is Bob Shaw. I'm the senior VP of engineering for Emerson's digital scroll compressor technology for refrigerated food transport. Happy to be here." This wouldn't tell you much. It would go in one ear and out the other. And you'd likely forget you ever met this person.

But suppose he continued, "What this means is that my team helps companies like Dole protect and preserve the world's most popular fruit—

bananas—with precise shipping temperatures over thousands of miles of ocean travel to ensure fresh arrival at local stores."This part of his statement sits squarely in the spirit of Emerson's advertising campaign. [It explains clearly the outcome of his work and the value to his customers and the end consumer: ripe yellow bananas, ready for consumption.]

This sort of clarity and communication of value and outcome stimulates the reward center in our brain, because from a neuroscience perspective, our brains crave clarity and certainty, and those qualities make people more real to us and boost our perception of their presence. But most of us would just stop at the first part of the introduction—name, role, function, and maybe tenure at the company, none of which is very useful in terms of helping someone perceive value.

There are many other ways you can illustrate value. One is by offering a sort of proof of concept—evidence of your success or achievements, either organizationally or personally. Maybe you can mention how many units you've shipped, or how many orders you've processed, or the prestigious awards you've received, or the number of lives you've saved. When people perceive the value you've contributed to others, it's much easier to imagine what you could do for them.

In the battle between reality and perception, perception wins every time. Therefore, if we keep in mind what's important to others and the myriad ways their perceptions may be influenced, we can make informed decisions that add to rather than subtract from our executive presence.

In Chapter 2 we'll explore how you can develop your self-awareness, which is the quality on which most of your success as a respected communicator and leader will ride.

2

Self-Awareness

Understand Yourself Better to Understand Your Impact on Others

WHEN 109 EMERGENCY room doctors at four different hospitals were asked to estimate how often they prescribe opioids compared with their peers, 65 percent of them underestimated their prescribing rates, according to a yearlong study by the University of Colorado School of Medicine and the University of Massachusetts Medical School.

Considering that prescription opioids contributed to 64,000 drug-overdose deaths in 2016 alone, better self-awareness by doctors writing these prescriptions may literally save lives. Indeed, once the surveyed ER physicians saw their actual data, opioid prescription rates dropped over the following 12 months. The study's authors deduced that the doctors were jolted into changing their behavior after seeing the difference between their self-awareness and the reality of their actions.

Of course, doctors are not the only people with a skewed perception of their traits and behaviors. Ninety-four percent of college professors believe they have above-average teaching skills, according to David Brooks, conservative political and cultural commentator for the *New York Times*. And as far as the rest of us go, well, just ask your friends how good a driver they think they are.

Blind spots. We all have them.

And while ours may not contribute to a national health crisis, they may be doing us harm in the way we manage our careers and perceive the impact we have on others. That's why honing accurate self-awareness is critical in developing an executive presence that is credible with all audiences.

In this chapter I explore what I call "dynamic self-awareness," a multilayered approach that involves both getting to know yourself and making sense, via good feedback, of how well you do in constantly changing environments.

Just as we can learn the intricacies of, say, project management for the implementation of a new software system—set schedules, hold meetings with stakeholders, get requirements from all impacted business units, keep everyone working toward a deadline—we can also learn how to examine our own preferences, biases, values, beliefs, and behaviors in order to see the links between how we feel, how we think, how we act, and, most important, how our behaviors affect others. Dynamic self-awareness is about uncovering and recognizing blind spots and unhelpful behaviors that can limit executive presence.

A Closer Look at Self-Awareness and Why It Matters

Importance of self-awareness

Enter the term "self-awareness" into Google, and you'll get somewhere around 340 million (yes, that's *million!*) results. Look for it in the standard business school curriculum, however, and you may have to do some digging. Columbia Business School offers some material on self-awareness development as part of its Leadership Lab, which is a series of extracurricular activities that span the entire MBA experience, and also includes assessments and one-on-one coaching. Chicago Booth School of Business offers LEAD (leadership effectiveness and development), a program that, according to the university, is designed to enhance participants' self-awareness and interpersonal effectiveness. And the University of Michigan's Ross School of Business offers a three-hour elective leadership development program "with an emphasis on self-understanding and learning," according to the school website. Most often, we found that the concept of self-awareness is buried somewhere in the copy of various MBA program descriptions as opposed to being presented as a stand-alone module that's worthy of study or even mastery.

However, this scarcity of self-awareness in the business school curriculum doesn't mean the topic is not getting any attention from the academic community.

Harvard Business School professor Bill George, for instance, defines self-awareness as "the skill of being aware of our thoughts, emotions, and values from moment to moment." Organizational psychologist Tasha Eurich breaks the concept down a bit further, distinguishing between *internal* and *external* self-awareness, that is, between an awareness of our own state of being and that of how others view us. Beyond this is what Robert Hogan, a psychologist and cofounder of Hogan Assessments, calls *strategic self-awareness*, which is the kind of self-awareness you need to compete successfully in your business. Combining and tending to these different forms of self-awareness creates a dynamic self-awareness that is both useful on its own merits and, again, key to developing your executive presence.

So why does self-awareness matter? Because a lack of it can lead us to misjudge our own behavior, or at least the effect it has on others' evaluations of us. For example, I worked with one client, Carlos, a high-potential leader at a U.S.-based global consumer goods company, whose collaborative style and interpersonal sensitivity were prized by his colleagues. However, his reluctance to speak up in meetings, especially with more senior leaders present, made him appear disengaged. He also seemed unwilling or unable to "clearly articulate a point of view and then defend it," according to his boss. Carlos was surprised by this assessment. The way he tells it, he just didn't want to add to what he considered "the noise" in these meetings, where, according to him, "people talk a lot but don't really say anything." In fact, as a native Spanish speaker with limited conversational fluency in English, Carlos had some difficulty participating in the lively verbal back-and-forth that is common to many American and European business meetings, but he had convinced himself that his reticence was the appropriate response to others' verbosity. And while you may have found yourself nodding at Carlos's sentiment about people's tendency to often talk much but say little, you may also agree that Carlos's lack of self-awareness of how his behavior was actually perceived by his colleagues prevented him from conveying the executive presence his bosses expect in a future senior leader.

Lack of self-awareness can also mean that we think we're more skillful than we are. Professors Justin Kruger and David Dunning, authors of the famous study "Unskilled and Unaware of It," point out that many people are unable to figure out where their knowledge ends: "Indeed, in many social and intellectual domains, people are unaware of their incompetence, innocent of their ignorance." In other words, they don't know what they don't know. The "Dunning-Kruger effect" is a term often used to ridicule the happily clueless, but there is hope. Dunning himself has observed that there are ways to overcome the ignorance of one's ignorance.

In the following sections I'll give examples from my own executive-coaching experiences of how a lack of self-awareness can hinder advancement and how getting feedback can increase self-awareness. Feedback is crucial to all forms of self-awareness, be it from self-reflection to informal observations from colleagues to formal assessments. I'll also provide the concrete steps you can take to obtain the feedback you need to enhance your own self-awareness and build your executive presence.

A Look Inside Yourself

Being curious about yourself is the first step in developing the skills for a dynamic self-awareness. This is not simply a matter of filling out an online assessment of your preferences and tendencies and discovering that you "work constructively and calmly under stress and pressure" or "are hesitant to take on new challenges." Self-awareness is about more than recognition of your preferences: It is a complex interaction of reflection, keen observation, and experience.

Tasha Eurich and her team of researchers observe that internal self-awareness "represents how clearly we see our own values, passions, aspirations, fit with our environment, reactions (including thoughts, feelings, behaviors, strengths, and weaknesses), and impact on others." It's the ability to recognize what we believe in, what we want, and how we behave.

McKinsey principal Nate Boaz and consultant Erica Ariel Fox divide the results of such inward examination into "profile awareness" and "state awareness." Profile awareness involves a recognition of your own thoughts and behaviors, while state awareness "is the recognition of what's driving you at the moment you take action." Boaz and Fox note that the latter is different from "state of mind": "State awareness involves the real-time perception of a wide range of inner experiences and their impact on your behavior."

As such, state awareness is harder to master than profile awareness. Astute senior executives may be fully aware that their dark side comes out under pressure—whether that is yelling at people or making impulsive decisions—but then catch themselves too late in the act to do anything about it, other than eat crow or issue mea culpas.

In a nutshell, profile awareness is awareness of your general tendencies, while state awareness requires specific, on-the-spot awareness.

Consider my coaching client Jim, a senior executive at a global automotive manufacturer. Jim was generally held in high esteem by his colleagues and considered a likely successor to the CEO, who was scheduled to retire within a couple of years. Jim's development opportunities in preparation for the CEO role were to improve his emotional resilience—in particular, his ability to demonstrate empathy and manage conflict productively.

While Jim's self-assessment in a 360-degree feedback survey showed that he was mostly aware of his tendencies (profile awareness) to respond emotionally in certain situations, his ability to recognize this behavior in the moment it occurred (state awareness) was much lower and led to 360-degree feedback comments such as:

- "His forcefulness tends to seem like intimidation and makes him appear not to welcome dispute."
- "Listen more and don't be so defensive when someone has a different view."
- "Practice a relaxed face when listening. His natural face is intense when listening because he is engaged and is thinking, but for those who do not know him he may appear angry."

The CEO summarized the view of many of Jim's colleagues when he observed: "Jim is emotionally transparent, which I generally believe to be a good thing. However, when he is unhappy or displeased with an individual or situation, he can be emotional [and] thereby intimidate an individual or group, which tends to truncate discussion. This behavior is not intended to intimidate, but given his position and organizational credibility, it can stifle open and honest communication by the team."

Jim was aware that conflict management, emotional awareness, and behavioral self-control were challenges for him—he scored himself low in these areas in a self-assessment—but he lost track of his emotions and behaviors in critical situations: a clear case of lacking state self-awareness. Jim rose to the top levels of his organization because he was smart, dedicated, hardworking, and extremely knowledgeable about his industry, but as with so many otherwise highly capable leaders, his upward mobility was stymied simply because he lacked critical self-awareness in the moments when it counted most.

As his boss had noted, Jim's behavior "can stifle open and honest communication by the team," which is the opposite of what a leader should do. Diverse viewpoints and innovative ideas, freely expressed, are what leaders need to encourage in order to operate effectively and make informed decisions. In our coaching sessions, Jim learned about and better appreciated the effect his behaviors had on his peers and direct reports, and he used that knowledge to put people in more productive mental states.

Neuroscientist Evian Gordon's work on the "threat and reward response" sheds light on the neurological reactions that are triggered in social situations. A person who is made socially anxious, for example, may freeze up as his or her brain switches into survival mode.

"This impairs analytic thinking, creative insight, and problem solving," Gordon reasoned. "In other words, just when people most need their sophisticated mental capabilities, the brain's internal resources are taken away from them."

I'll talk more about the brain's role in emotion regulation in the next chapter, but note the role that neurological processes play in state awareness—and how easy it is for our minds to get away from us.

There are ways to prevent ourselves from "losing our minds" in this way, and these strategies begin with a basic understanding of ourselves and how we respond to our environment—that is, with internal self-awareness.

Most of us think of ourselves as reasonably self-aware—we're great husbands and fathers, standout wives and mothers, excellent drivers, and benevolent leaders, if you just ask us. But as we've seen from the example of the ER doctors and college professors at the beginning of this chapter, we may be just a tad delusional. Underlying this delusion may be the natural discomfort we feel at the unwelcome possibilities emerging from an honest assessment of those personal traits that we perceive as embarrassing or less than admirable. If you want to become more self-aware, however, feedback—that which you give yourself, and that which you get from others—is crucial to that awareness.

So how do you check your inner profile? Be mindful, reflect and identify, and integrate.

Be Mindful

The first step of mindfulness, is, paradoxically, to deliberately empty your mind by dismissing distracting thoughts and feelings, while the second requires you to pay attention to what is happening in the moment. David Rock, founder of the NeuroLeadership Institute, notes that the ability both to pay attention to what you're thinking and to observe what's going on *Be present* around you "requires both serenity and concentration; in a threatened state, people are much more likely to be 'mindless.'" It's when you're most caught up in the moment that you're likely to be *least* aware of what's happening.

I'll talk more about mindfulness and training your brain in the next chapter. Until then, note that some people engage in regular mindfulness training, which involves specific kinds of exercises to focus your attention, while others find meditation a good way to disentangle themselves from daily aggravations. The point is to clear from your mind the distractions that can obscure your view of yourself and your situation.

Reflect and Identify

If mindfulness is the process of clearing away the clutter, reflection leads you to consider your values and characteristics. Posing a few questions may help, such as:

- **Values.** What do you value in yourself, your family and friends, and your colleagues? Do you live by a particular ethical or religious code? How do you live out your values in practice? How do you respond when someone violates your code? What if you violate your own code? Have your values changed over the years? How?

- **Decision making.** How do you make decisions? Do you listen to your intuition? Or do you need all the facts before making the call? Do you weigh available options and decide on your own, or do you let others decide on a course of action? Do you tend to strive for consensus, or are you comfortable deciding even in light of dissenting views?

- **Emotions.** Are you able to identify your emotions while you're experiencing them? What emotions are you most comfortable expressing? Least? What information do you get from your emotions? Are you able to manage them when in difficult circumstances? Do your emotions affect how you approach certain situations?

- **Goals.** What are your personal and professional goals? Are they in sync with each other? What progress have you made in achieving those goals? Are you prevention focused or promotion focused in your approach to your goals and desires? That is, are you more likely to protect what you already have or to take risks to gain something more?

- **Social behavior.** How do you behave around others? Are you comfortable meeting new people? Are there clear differences in how you act in different areas of your life? Do you have to like someone to work well with the person? What is your approach to working with subordinates? Peers? Superiors?

This is not an exhaustive list of questions, of course, but these and questions like them can help you identify what makes you tick.

This is important, because the questions you ask, as well as how you ask them, matter. Eurich argues that introspection done wrong can actually hinder self-awareness. Too often we ask ourselves "why" questions about our emotions, attitudes, and behavior, she writes, but research has shown "that we simply do not have access to many of the unconscious thoughts, feelings, and motives we're searching for. And because so much is trapped outside of our conscious awareness, we tend to invent answers that *feel* true but are often wrong." We want answers and so jump to a conclusion that makes sense on the surface but doesn't hold up under scrutiny.

Instead, Eurich counsels that "we should ask *what*, not *why*. 'What' questions help us stay objective, future-focused, and empowered to act on our new insights." Questions of "why" trap us, but "what" questions can get us the information we need to move on.

What vs Why [handwritten note]

might disagree [handwritten note]

While these questions can help you to identify your values, characteristics, and automatic behaviors, it can also be valuable to take psychometric tests to sort out your personality traits. Finally, organize this information: write down and prioritize your goals, say, or note if your values are compatible or in conflict with one another. The point is to gather as much productive information as you can and shape it into self-knowledge.

like doing this [handwritten note]

Integrate

Mindfulness, reflection, and identification all influence different aspects of your internal self-awareness, but to attain full self-awareness requires an integration of those three practices. You have to connect who you are with what you believe and want and how you act in various situations, all of which require regular and pointed self-examination. Cultivating self-awareness is not a one-time event; for it to take hold, you have to make it a habit. Even this is not enough, however. That's because any integration is incomplete without the kind of feedback that you can only get from others.

External Self-Awareness

As important as awareness of your own thoughts and actions is, if your self-perception is at odds with how others see you, you're operating in the dark.

Eurich's definition of external self-awareness is succinct: "understanding how other people view us." Do others see in us the same values, passions, aspirations, and behaviors that we see in ourselves? If not, why not? This is important, because Eurich notes that those whose self-image lines up with the image others have of them are more likely to get along better with those others and have more productive working relationships with them.

Unlike internal self-awareness, where you can do much of the work on your own, developing external self-awareness *requires* feedback from others—be it from a mentor, informally from your colleagues or customers, or via a more formal 360-degree assessment.

Unfortunately, while many people like to say "I welcome criticism," in fact most of us do not welcome it at all. Writer Kristin Wong highlighted a series of experiments in which participants would rather talk to people who had a high opinion of them than talk to those who had an accurate one. As one of the authors of the study noted, "Individuals tend to enjoy their own relationships more with people they believe see them in desirable ways." In short, we'd rather be inaccurately praised than accurately perceived.

Interesting point

Yet it is also true that most of us don't want to be "caught out," cluelessly thinking we're killing it while our coworkers are shaking their heads at our ill-fated efforts. One colleague of mine admits that she simply "hates being wrong—*hates* it. But the only thing worse than being wrong is not knowing that I'm wrong."

And that's where feedback comes into play. A trusted mentor, a boss who has your best interest at heart and wants to see you succeed, even a colleague whom you may find a bit prickly but whose straightforwardness you value—they can all be great resources in providing you with a different perspective, if not valuable constructive criticism. The point is, you want to turn to people whose feedback you can trust and who you know will be honest in their assessment of you. This can also be a good way of building up your tolerance for such instruction: If you can get good feedback from a trusted source or advisor, then you're more likely to see the upsides of feedback overall.

One note of caution when asking colleagues for targeted feedback: Unlike a mentor or boss who's invested in your success, colleagues may be less comfortable giving an overall assessment than they would in offering specifics, so you have to ask questions of limited scope. If you worked on a project with someone whose feedback you'd find valuable, ask the person how he or she thought it went—what specifically worked well and what could have been even better. By asking with humility and without the slightest hint at indignation—that includes wrinkling your nose, furrowing your brow, or squinting your eyes—you stand a much better chance of mining feedback gold as opposed to receiving anodyne observations that help no one, least of all you.

Finally, you should find out if your company offers formal 360-degree evaluations. This usually involves bringing in an outside consultant or executive coach—we do lots of 360-degree surveys for client companies—who specializes in such assessments and provides an in-depth report of how your managers, peers, direct reports, and other colleagues see you. In a 360-degree feedback process, you are asked to select somewhere between 15 and 25 colleagues whom you trust to provide honest feedback on your strengths and development opportunities. The latter used to be called "weaknesses," but we've evolved. To ensure maximum candor, feedback providers enjoy anonymity. Their responses are not identified with the rater's name in the final report. Otherwise you'd get some watered-down version on your areas for improvement—people know that not everyone takes feedback well—which would render the entire exercise pointless.

[handwritten margin note: Who Can give a 360° evaluation]

In a 360-degree evaluation, you are typically asked to rate yourself as well, which can provide valuable insight into where your self-perceptions match how others see you and where they diverge. In other words, you'll get a very good idea of the areas in which you lack self-awareness. Usually 360-degree feedback surveys consist of a series of questions. Our own proprietary online survey, developed by my colleague Dr. Laura Belsten, is focused on emotional and social intelligence and features 78 questions in 26 categories, such as stress management, innovation and creativity, organizational and situational awareness, and resilience, to name a few. Also included is a section of open-ended questions, such as "What are this person's greatest strengths?" and "What is the one recommendation you have for this individual's improvement?"

The resulting data help clients get a wide panorama of perspectives on their behavior, providing one or more potential areas for development. A 360-degree feedback report is usually what yields the most valuable insight on coaching needs and development opportunities, in addition to the developmental feedback we get directly from the client's bosses and their talent-development colleagues. For more senior executives we usually conduct interviews in lieu of an online survey, typically involving 7 to 10 colleagues, whom we ask about strengths and development opportunities to help determine how to make the person an even more effective leader and manager. This feedback is gathered verbatim and presented to the client in aggregate, again, to protect the innocent. It often furnishes the jolt that's needed to provide clients not only with better self-awareness, but with the type of self-awareness that will enhance success in their highly competitive work environments. In other words, strategic self-awareness.

Strategic Self-Awareness

Consider engineer Sylvia Acevedo, who, after graduating from Stanford and working for NASA, ended up at IBM. Once there, she noticed that a less distinguished colleague, who happened to be a former football player, was receiving a constant stream of feedback from multiple mentors about everything from his clothes to making presentations. "No one was doing that for me or the other women who were there. I began saying, 'I have to innovate.'" She paid careful attention to what was expected and rewarded in the workplace, then built her résumé—including booking trips to Hong Kong on her own dime in order to accumulate international experience. Her ultimate goal, of course, was to demonstrate that she had the skills and the ambition to excel in the workplace.

She also got a key bit of feedback from "one guy who was a good mentor," who noticed that a lot of people might not understand what she had to offer: "You have to start with how you're like them," he urged. "You need to tell them you're a Stanford engineer and you've done this and that. Because they're not listening to you for the first ten minutes. All they're thinking is, 'What is this Hispanic female doing in front of us?'"

In other words, the mentor was saying, it wasn't enough for Acevedo to do well on her own. She had to let her male colleagues know that she did, indeed, belong among them.

What Acevedo and her mentor were able to devise was an informal kind of what the aforementioned Robert Hogan calls "strategic self-awareness"—the kind of awareness necessary to compete and succeed in a specific environment. "For self-awareness to be truly strategic," Hogan explains, "strengths and weaknesses can only be fully understood when compared with those of others, particularly those who form a defined reference group."

Strategic self-awareness, then, is comparative: It's not enough to understand yourself or even how others see you. You have to know where you stand in relationship to your peers. Hogan offers the example of a soccer player who in high school might be judged the best; in college, average; and at the heights of the premier league, not good enough even to earn a tryout. If that player wants to succeed at the highest levels, then he needs to judge himself by the standards of that level.

Similarly, Acevedo was able to define her reference group and, with the help of her mentor, figure out how to make herself stand out. In fact, years later and after she had left IBM, she was working on a presentation to investors who "look at me and they can't even pronounce my name." Recalling the advice of that mentor, she paused her pitch and said, "I went to school down the street. You may have heard of it—Stanford? And I was a rocket scientist. So numbers don't faze me." Once that was out of the way, "They were like, *Okay*."

Acevedo's mentor gave her what Hogan calls "informational feedback," one of the most effective forms of feedback, along with suggestions on how to adjust her behavior. Another type of feedback is motivational feedback, where the coach may point out how far the client has come (positive) or how much further he or she needs to go (negative). Both can work, although Hogan notes that whether positive or negative feedback is more effective will vary from individual to individual. Regardless of what type is used, such feedback should "target improvement areas, and evaluate progress over time."

To satisfy these criteria, Hogan recommends both structured interviews and multirater assessments (like the aforementioned 360-degree assessment): "The multi-rater assessments indicate what a leader does and how a leader does it. The personality assessment indicates why a leader does something, or, more accurately, indicates what the natural tendencies are that underlie the behaviors demonstrated in the workplace."

Thus, while Hogan's focus is on strategic self-awareness, he also recognizes that for it to be most effective, it should build on the other forms of self-awareness.

Dynamic Self-Awareness for Executive Presence

Developing all the different kinds of self-awareness is required to master dynamic, or complete, self-awareness. This can seem exhausting, and yes, it is work: Taking psychometric tests, undergoing 360-degree assessments, and challenging yourself to absorb and truly make use of feedback all require an ongoing commitment, not to mention constant self-monitoring. But remember the purpose of all this work: to create and sustain an *authentic* executive presence that will equip you with the type of influence that goes beyond any positional authority you may have.

Authenticity is key. Your executive presence will wear thin if it's not authentic, not rooted in who you are, and if it takes no account of your values and your aspirations. You want a real, not Potemkin, presence.

Dynamic self-awareness will provide you with the clarity and foresight you need to understand how you're perceived by others, what impact your behaviors have on others, and what you need to work on to lead others effectively and gain their respect and admiration as you move through your career.

In the next chapter you'll learn various emotion-regulation strategies that will help you stay cool and poised under pressure, to maintain a strong and reassuring executive presence.

3

Mastering Your Mind

Emotion-Regulation Strategies That Work and One That You Should Never Use

IMAGINE YOURSELF AS a five-year-old. You're sitting in a small room with nothing but a piece of your favorite candy right in front of your nose. A friendly adult tells you that you can eat the candy right now, or you can wait 10 minutes and get two pieces of candy instead of just one. And then the adult leaves you alone.

You may recognize this "cruel" little experiment as the "marshmallow test" by Stanford University psychologist Walter Mischel, originally conducted in the 1960s and 1970s with preschoolers between three and five years old. The experiment aimed to measure the children's impulse control and ability to delay gratification. Some kids contorted themselves into pretzels trying to wait out the agonizing period before the adult reentered the room with the additional treat, while others barely waited for the door to click behind the departing researcher before wolfing down the temptation in front of them.

After the original experiment, Mischel and his researchers tracked the kids over several years to see how they did in terms of successes and failures and published their findings in 1990. The results: Kids who were able to control their impulses and hold out for the bigger treat went on to demonstrate higher intelligence and overall more productive behaviors later in life.

Only, this famous experiment was largely debunked when Mischel's results failed to replicate in a much larger study by researchers from New York University and the University of California–Irvine. That study, published in 2018 in *Psychological Science Journal,* and involving 10 times as many kids, found that once a child's family background, home environment, and early cognitive ability were taken into account, the differences between the delayers and the grabbers by age 15 were so minimal that they were statistically insignificant. In other words, it wasn't so much a child's ability to delay gratification that determined future success, but a variety of social and economic factors that failed to make it into Mischel's original research.

Of course, as working adults, we don't need a longitudinal study to tell us whether practicing impulse control makes us more successful or not. Take the manager who yells and routinely lashes out at others in frustration. He's unlikely to be on the radar for bigger leadership roles—at least not in more evolved organizational cultures. Or imagine the emerging leader who would rather blend into the safe background than face the scrutiny that comes with presenting new ideas to senior management. Both types would benefit greatly from learning to manage their worst impulses and regulate their emotions in order to improve their reputations. Leaders who easily get rattled can quickly lose credibility in the eyes of those they lead, not to mention their ever-watchful bosses.

Self-control, calmness, composure—those are some of the key characteristics that signal executive presence, according to a study published by the American Psychological Association.

Fortunately for those interested in developing executive presence, these qualities, also known as "emotion regulation," have been heavily researched by behavioral psychologists and neuroscientists. In the following pages I'll share several of the most effective strategies you can use to manage your mood and emotions overall, to prepare for emotionally tense situations, and to stay composed once you find yourself right in the middle of one of those situations. I will also share one commonly used emotion-regulation strategy that can actually harm your health and relationships and that you should avoid whenever possible.

Welcome to the Emotional Roller Coaster

Unless you're a real-life Mr. Spock—the fictional half-Vulcan science officer in the popular TV series *Star Trek*—then you're a regular passenger on the emotional roller coaster. You leave your house for work in the morning, still humming your favorite song, when you realize your Uber driver just canceled your scheduled pickup. You timed your departure just right, but now you're running late for your morning meeting. Your anxiety rising as you scramble to find alternative transportation, you get a text from your teammate that a proposal you'd worked on together was accepted by the client—*Yay!*—but the client wants to renegotiate the fee schedule. As you arrive at work a few minutes late, your boss's boss recognizes you by name in the lobby and stops to congratulate you on the inspiring sales forecast you presented last week. From the corner of your eye you notice your actual boss over at the coffee shop, sharing a laugh with your rival for a position you're both gunning for.

It's barely 8:10 a.m., and you've already completed several rides on the emotional roller coaster.

So what is emotion? Is it passion, feeling, mood? We often use those terms interchangeably, but it makes sense to distinguish them from one another. For example, lawyer and psychologist Delee Fromm defines emotion as a psychological state of "high intensity, short duration, and directed at an object, person, or event," while mood is a more stable state. For many of us, mood and emotions tend to align—more positive folks will generally experience more positive emotions—but most of us can experience a wide range of emotions on any given day. If you're generally positive and in a good mood, you may find yourself in the dumps when your favorite team gets a thrashing from a hated rival, while the curmudgeon next to you may experience a dopamine squirt and unbridled joy when *his* team wins. That is, until someone blocks his parking space and he's right back to curmudgeon-ness. You get the picture.

Scholars James Gross, Jane Richards, and Oliver John get a bit more technical, referring to emotion as a *process*, rather than a single *event*, one that "begins when an external or internal event signals to the individual that something important may be at stake." In other words, something happens that sets off a whole series of responses that "involve experiential, behavioral, and central and peripheral physiological systems." The important thing for us to understand is that these responses can be modified—regulated—in different ways, which in turn means you can change your behavior.

To elaborate: Gross and his colleagues distinguish between the *experience* of an emotion and its *expression*; so, for example, you might *feel* angry, but you don't necessarily *act* angry. This is a key aspect of our emotion-regulation strategies: Sometimes we're able to control that initial experience, while other times—say, in "count-to-10" moments—the feeling rushes in, but we're able to put a brake on its expression. This plays into their discussion of strategies that are "antecedent focused" (trying to regulate emotion prior to a moment) versus those that are "response focused" (in the moment). I'll talk about these two strategies later in this chapter.

There's another distinction that matters: that between "integral" and "incidental" emotions. Harvard professor and social psychologist Jennifer Lerner and her colleagues Ye Li, Piercarlo Valdesolo, and Karim Kassam note that "integral" emotions, or those "arising from the judgment or choice at hand," are directly related to a situation you're experiencing and affect your behavior in that moment. For example, you might be someone who usually avoids confrontation, but when you see someone mistreating your favorite server at the diner, your anger leads you to step up in defense.

"Incidental" emotions, on the other hand, are less about the moment than they are about the shadow of a different moment. As Lerner et al. put it, "Incidental emotions pervasively carry over from one situation to the next," stringing together unrelated events in one big emotion. The train is packed or the highways are jammed so that by the time you get to work you're tense and frustrated; someone steps into the elevator just as the doors are about to close and you seethe; then, at your desk, the file drawer jams and you go off, swearing at the "stupid @#!$ drawer!"

That bad traffic cast a long shadow.

So making sense of our emotions means we have to have a dual focus—from what's right at the surface of their expression down to the roots of the experience. Understanding this puts you in the driver's seat of that proverbial emotional roller coaster (I trust you'll forgive my tortured metaphor). Emotions are powerful, but so are the ways we can control them, as you'll learn shortly.

Why Emotion Matters

People often think of emotion as the opposite of reason—heart versus head, feeling versus fact—but the relationship between the two is actually one of interdependence. While we might think we ought to prize rationality over emotionality, especially in work settings, social science and neuroscience research clearly show that paying attention to both reason and emotion in negotiations or in decision making will lead to better outcomes than focusing on reason alone.

Consider the emotion-laden challenges that leaders regularly face:

- Presenting an idea or results to senior leadership or boards and staying composed when challenged or asked tough questions
- Showing appropriate enthusiasm when offering new ideas or sharing an exciting vision of the future
- Responding productively when facing angry shareholders or customers
- Managing conflict in meetings when discussions get heated
- Demonstrating assertiveness in defending an idea or course of action, without appearing aggressive
- Projecting confidence in situations where more senior leaders are present, rather than hiding for fear of appearing unprepared, inadequate, wrong, etc.
- Listening with empathy and without judgment when others present their point of view
- Accepting negative feedback or constructive criticism after a failure, without shutting down
- Demonstrating patience with members of your team who fall short of expectations and electing to mentor them instead of venting frustration

Rick, a VP of project management at a health insurance carrier that I have advised, furnishes a good example of the last point. He is generally well liked and balanced in his approach with people, but under stress he can come across as a perfectionist with impossibly high standards. He's been described as having little patience for people who "don't get it" and aren't performing to his expectations. Rick's coworkers note that he "wears his heart on his sleeve—both a strength and a weakness." They appreciate his drive and intelligence, but they also observe that "he holds things in and seems stressed out a lot" and that he's "had a few outbursts" that have resulted in high turnover among his team.

To improve his reputation Rick needed to better regulate his emotions, either before they emerge or when he's in the thrall of the moment. When he feels people are falling short of the standards he has set, rather than driving them away with emotional outbursts, he needs to provide them with opportunities to learn and improve.

Lacking impulse control under stress can lead to all kinds of undesirable consequences. Consider LeBron James, one of the best basketball players in NBA history. James is physically gifted, intelligent both on and off the court, and possessed of an incredible work ethic: This is an athlete who wants to win. Why, then, would he risk injury by punching a whiteboard following a close loss in Game 1 of the NBA finals against Golden State? "I was very emotional, for a lot of different reasons," he said after his team eventually lost the finals. A win in that first game would have buoyed the underdog Cleveland Cavaliers; instead, the loss deflated them. "I had emotions on how the game was taken away from us," he explained. "Emotions got the best of me, and I pretty much played the last three games with a broken hand."

"Emotions got the best of me": There it is, "emotion as flood," drowning out all sense.

We do know, of course, that emotions aren't inherently bad, even if we want to occasionally punch a whiteboard, literally or metaphorically. After all, passion is emotion, and passion is what got James to the NBA finals. It's usually not raw ability, technique, or skill that wins in overtime when everyone is tired and everything is on the line. It's the heat of passion. The trick is to control those passions, those powerful emotions, channeling them into only productive uses, and this is as true in the boardroom as on the basketball court.

How Emotions Affect the Body and the Brain

You've been there before. You walk into a room full of people, and before you know it, your body registers all kinds of emotions: You blush, your heart beats faster, your muscles tighten, and your jaw clenches in anticipation. In anticipation of what, though? Why did your body just switch to fight-flight-or-freeze mode? The answer: Because your body knows something's up, and those physiological changes, putting you on high alert, are precisely what kept our cave-dwelling ancestors alive in potentially dangerous situations. If they had remained calm and spent leisurely moments pondering whether that rustling grass signaled a curious lion or just a gentle breeze, they could easily have selected themselves right out of the gene pool. Instead, the hair on the back of their necks told them it was time to make a quick exit.

Consider it your hardwired personal alarm system—the body's reaction to perceived danger. Unfortunately, this ancient system kicks in just as efficiently in today's corporate jungle, during high-stakes presentations, say, or an important status update to the executive committee, or the introduction to your new boss. And if you tend to freeze, fight, or, God forbid, run, in those situations it's likely that you might get deselected from the high-potential pool, or worse.

Unfortunately, in our highly competitive work environments, the threats to our psychological safety just keep coming—and that can be bad for your physical health. Monash University senior lecturer Dr. Craig Hassad notes that there's a biological cascade effect when your body enters high alert. Your adrenaline surges, leading to an increased heart rate and blood pressure and faster breathing. You sweat more, as your body's biochemical processes are redirected toward instant readiness—the levels of your blood glucose, fats, white blood cells, and inflammatory hormones are all altered, and your gut shuts down. Finally, your blood itself becomes "stickier," as it anticipates the need for greater clotting power to stop bleeding.

This all sounds dire, but in the short term some of these physical changes can help you meet various modern threats. An increase in adrenaline, for example, can enable you to focus on a niggling problem at work, and a surge in energy can speed you up when you are facing a crucial deadline. As long as you wind down after the threat passes, there's little risk to your overall health.

Fail to decompress occasionally, however, and health problems can take root. Constant stress and anxiety, putting your body in nonstop flight-or-fight mode, can erode your overall health. It's like that old *Spinal Tap* joke: If everything is dialed up to 11, there's nowhere else to go. And a body dialed to 11 is vulnerable to inflammation, diabetes, atherosclerosis, and bone loss, which can lead to immune system dysfunction, depression, and poor work performance. Even your ability to manage your emotions can be undercut. If everything is an emergency, then you may overreact to small irritations and underreact to truly urgent situations. Yikes!

But health issues aside for a moment, as a leader you need your most sophisticated mental resources in the daily battle for increased market share, revenue, and profit—not to mention the Herculean task of getting people to cooperate and thrive in their jobs. And those mental resources—primarily the prefrontal cortex—can take a serious hit when you're under constant stress, unable to regulate your emotions.

That prefrontal cortex, located at the front of the brain, is generally agreed to be responsible for what are called the "executive functions": our ability to plan, reason, use logic, or form memories. Impair the prefrontal cortex, and those functions may be correspondingly impaired.

To give you a bit more insight into this topic, we turn to Harvard psychologist Daniel Goleman, who is famous for his research on emotional intelligence. Goleman has focused on how a small section of our midbrain that plays an outsized role in the processing of our emotions, an almond-shaped set of neurons known as the amygdala, can overwhelm the restraints that the frontal regions usually impose on our emotions. The amygdala, he explains, holds a "privileged" position in the brain that allows it to override the functions of other areas—a kind of supervisory dispatcher rerouting normal calls to emergency services.

Goleman calls this process the "amygdala hijack," which, in a real emergency, is exactly what you want: the aforementioned flight-or-fight response. The amygdala shuts down the more measured functions of the prefrontal cortex to focus all of the brain's resources to ensure one thing—survival. Goleman himself was building off the work of neuroscientist Joseph Ledoux, who discovered what he called the "neural back alley," which allows for the hijack. Incoming information that would usually be routed through the prefrontal cortex before being further processed elsewhere in the brain would—in case of a perceived threat—take that neural back-alley shortcut into the amygdala, which is then able to hijack the functions normally performed by the prefrontal cortex.

Again, in a real threat situation this shortcut could save your life, but with all the perceived social threats tickling our amygdala on a regular basis, the shortcut itself could lead to reputational disaster.

One such reputational disaster is "choking"—a phenomenon that you don't have to be a Wimbledon-ranked tennis pro or champion golfer to experience. One of my clients, Seth, a VP and corporate controller at a global software giant, is a talented executive who had been in consideration to succeed the company's CFO. But he suffered from this affliction in those crucial moments when he was giving quarterly updates to members of the board. He would lose his train of thought in mid-sentence, stammer his way through financial projections, and draw a blank when presented with a simple question about operating budgets. He'd choke even during the rehearsal of his presentations, while he would be perfectly fine sharing his updates with a colleague in a casual conversation. What was happening?

Sian Beilock, a University of Chicago psychologist and the author of *Choke*, who's become an expert on the topic by studying pro athletes, notes: "Choking isn't just poor performance. It is worse performance than you are capable of precisely because there is a lot on the line."

What happens is this: The more important the outcome or the bigger the reward, the more likely that some people, like my client Seth, are to scrutinize every aspect of what they're doing rather than relying on their finely honed skills and knowledge and trusting that they'll deliver like so many times before. Golfers who choke, according to Beilock, think too much about what they're doing, whereas those who don't have mastered the art of tuning out the prefrontal cortex while letting their subconscious take over. And this doesn't just apply to golfers.

Like the athletes Beilock studied, corporate managers and executives also can have much to lose if a performance goes badly. Just as the Olympic athlete may have just one shot to get into the annals of her sport, the corporate leader in a tough question-and-answer session may not get another chance to show his board that he's up to a bigger job.

And it isn't necessarily a hostile audience that causes you to short-circuit either. In the world of sports at least, the friendlier the audience, according to some studies, the more self-conscious some players get. Meanwhile, back at the cubicle farm, this would explain why some people have a harder time giving presentations to well-meaning colleagues than to emotionally distant audiences, such as customers or complete strangers at a conference.

Other insights from research have shown that smarter people, who tend to be able to retain and process more information in their short-term memory than the rest of us, are also more likely to choke under pressure. The theory behind this pattern is that their reliance on their above-average problem-solving abilities puts them off-guard when the amygdala shuts down part of those precious resources to attend to more pressing matters—like an incoming threat in the form of a pointed question or cold stare.

A heightened aversion to loss is another reason why we choke when the stakes are high. Winning is everything to some people, but for those who fear losing much more than they enjoy winning, the mental pressure they feel makes choking more likely.

How can you avoid the potentially career-limiting effects of choking? Beilock recommends distracting yourself by focusing on something mean-ingless—like the dimples on a golf ball if you're a golfer—or simply speed-ing things up to avoid deliberating too much while executing a critical task or performance. In the workplace you might focus on the pattern of someone's tie or quickly summarize a point you're making to avoid getting stuck in the minutiae, which could make choking more likely.

While golf ball dimples and the like are good as far as they go, the businessperson intent on burnishing an executive presence needs broader, more widely applicable strategies for emotion regulation, which I will present next.

General Emotion Regulation

It's often the big event—a job interview, a performance review, an import-ant presentation—that has us wishing we'd be better at managing our emotions and staying calm under pressure. But the fact is, keeping on an

even keel day-to-day can help us improve our mood and mindset overall,
as well as prepare us for when the big day arrives.

Craig Hassad, who noted the wear and tear of emotions on our bod-
ies and brains, suggests that making ourselves less reactive overall can make *interesting*
it easier for us to deal with intense emotions when they do arise. Various
forms of mindfulness, including meditation, may help to "remodel the
brain and thereby protect the body from the damaging effects of chronic
stress and depression." Some people might prefer meditation, others might
practice yoga, and still others might favor walks in which they pay attention to nothing other than what they see in front of them. Below I suggest
some specific exercises to increase mindfulness. The point of such mindfulness is to declutter your senses and give you more direct access to what is
happening around you, a process that may help to rewire the brain so that
when things get hot, you stay cool. *Do things that require no mental activity*

A few years ago, I was about to board a flight from Denver to
Milwaukee, to work with clients over the weekend. As I sat in the waiting
area, I became acutely aware of the constant low-level hum of anxiety that
I'd been feeling in my gut for months. My mind was constantly racing,
and I couldn't seem to get any reprieve from the onslaught of random
thoughts at all hours of the day. I had a few minutes before boarding, and
I headed over to a nearby bookstore. I'd heard about Eckhardt Tolle's *The
Power of Now* and figured I could use the flight to see if this mindfulness
thing would work for me. I found a copy, I boarded the plane, and by the
time I landed, I'd managed to get through a good chunk of the book. I
learned a few things. Most importantly, I learned how to quiet my mind.
The instructions in the book were simple, along the lines of "Try to empty
your mind of all thoughts. If they come, gently swat them away. Don't
follow them. Just be in the moment." The idea of *just being* resonated with
me. I found I could ignore any incoming thoughts quite easily. And while
I don't remember all the particulars from Tolle's book, I also took away
the concept of focusing on something I could feel in my body, like my
breath, or the pressure of a chair I was sitting in. This would reliably bring
me back to the moment whenever my mind was about to power-boost me
into the stratosphere.

To be sure, mindfulness takes practice. A wandering mind is a powerful thing. But the act of bringing it back to the moment when it wanders

is what actually builds the "muscle" of focus and concentration, ergo mindfulness. I entered my clients' office that Saturday morning in Milwaukee with a sense of calm and mental clarity I hadn't felt in a long time.

One easy way to practice everyday mindfulness is to focus on physical sensations. For instance, take a sip of water like you mean it. Feel the temperature of the liquid against your tongue. Notice it filling the cavity of your mouth. Explore the blunt edge of the glass with your lips. Inhale as you drink. See what scent you might notice. You can practice the same focus on the moment by eating a piece of candy or smelling a flower. These are simple actions you can take any time of the day. Caroline Webb, an economist and former McKinsey partner, suggests working "micro-mindfulness" into your schedule: You don't always have 20 minutes to focus on your breathing, but maybe you could take 10 or even fewer counted breaths while you're in the middle of a meeting. That pause, however brief, can help to reset your response and infuse your body and mind with a sense of calm.

Mindfulness as both a general practice and a specific tactic in dealing with stress can bring physiological and psychological benefits. It reduces blood pressure and improves memory, according to Hassad, and makes a person less emotionally reactive overall. Social psychologist Matthew Lieberman, who has studied the right ventrolateral prefrontal cortex, or what he calls the "brain's braking system," notes that regular meditation can increase the efficiency of this system, giving you more control over what you feel and how you express it.

Using your mind, then, can help you to keep your brain from short-circuiting—and you from blowing a fuse.

Emotion Regulation Before the Moment

There are times when you can predict, with some confidence, that you are going to lose your cool. You know it either because you've been there before or because you recognize emotional triggers that will likely set you off. This may include a dreaded public speaking engagement, a meeting with someone you loathe or fear, or a task you abhor—like doing your taxes or giving someone negative feedback. The common thread here is that while these scenarios may still be in the near or distant future for you, you can predict your emotional response to them. And that's where the opportunity lies.

James Gross is the go-to scholar for modulating your emotions: Almost every other thinker refers to his and his colleagues' discussion of "antecedent-focused" and "response-focused" strategies. The first strategy, antecedent-focused, requires you to game out how you'll manage yourself during a potentially charged situation and involves the following options:

- Situation selection
- Situation modification
- Attentional deployment
- Cognitive change

These options basically enable you to change the fate of your emotions before you actually experience them, or as Gross puts it, "the modification of future emotional responses." Here's what these strategies mean:

Situation selection involves choosing whether to accept or avoid a situation. Simply put, if a situation is likely to make you happy, you're more likely to opt in; if unhappy, you'll opt out. If you hate to fly, for example, you might choose to drive or take the train. On a more work-related note, if the thought of presenting the financials at the next board meeting makes you sick to your stomach, you could delegate the task to someone else and thereby remove yourself from the situation. However, and Gross echoes this in one of his papers, avoidance may not be an adaptive strategy if presenting the financials is part of your job. There's only so much sidestepping you can do before someone calls you out on it.

Situation modification is the emotion-regulation strategy you may use when you're unable to avoid a stressful situation. In such a case you seek to alter some aspect of the situation—the environment or the task itself—in order to make it more manageable.

For example, people often freeze up at the thought of a big project. One way to modify this daunting situation is to break the one big project down into multiple smaller projects. For example, writers don't write an entire book at one go; they work paragraph by paragraph, chapter by chapter, section by section. Similarly, you can split a complex presentation into its different components, such as introduction, closing, key points, charts, graphs, and videos, and tackle them one by one.

If, as in our earlier example of the financial presentation, your fear is public speaking, a possible modification would be to present the financials sitting down, as opposed to standing up in front of everyone. This would transform the presentation from a speech into a conversation.

Changing the environment is another way to modify a situation. If you've been dreading giving someone negative feedback in a performance review, take the meeting out of your office and into the coffee shop. The feedback is still there, but instead of feeling queasy about the power differential that is obvious in your office, and that may hamper a productive dialogue, you're blunting that feeling by relocating to a more power-neutral environment for this important conversation.

Attentional deployment refers to how we use our focus—what we *choose* to pay attention to. In the financials presentation example, you may focus not on the ever-frowning curmudgeon on the board, but on the more approachable members. Please note that I'm not recommending that you ignore your tougher audience—that wouldn't be wise—but rather to inhibit your limbic system from going haywire due to your outsized focus on the skeptics in your audience. You still must know your stuff and make your case to the critics, but by keeping your cool you preserve your most sophisticated mental resources for the pointed questions that come flying in your direction.

Cognitive change involves reinterpreting how you think about a situation. This can take the form of "reappraisal," or reframing a situation to change its emotional impact on you.

Writer and advertising professional Jenny Cooper offers one example of how reappraisal can lead to change. She wrote in *Slate* about her workplace anxiety and how it led her to frequently interrupt and correct her coworkers whenever they were giving presentations. She recognized that this behavior "was coming from a fear that my manager thought my new teammates were more knowledgeable than I am." Cooper subsequently challenged her assumption and considered whether this was true, decided there was no evidence to support this fear, and as a result "started pausing before each meeting to remind myself I had nothing to prove." She reframed the situation from one in which she was on trial to one that was more collaborative and where others' knowledge did not cancel out her own.

Other forms of cognitive change for emotion regulation include what Columbia University professor of psychology Kevin Ochsner calls the adoption of an "acceptance and allowance perspective" (recognizing that "this too shall pass"). There's also "distancing," a strategy in which you "imagine yourself experiencing an event not in the first person but in the third person." For instance, in anticipation of a difficult conversation, you might imagine the scene where you see yourself sitting across from your fellow interlocutor, as if you were the proverbial fly on the wall. And you'd want to observe what's happening in a dispassionate way, without judgment. This creating of emotional distance has been shown to lower the heat in people's emotional response. And if you took the acceptance perspective that Ochsner suggests, you would simply square your shoulders and say, "All right, I'm going to get this done and move on with life."

Researcher Natali Moytal and her colleagues Avishai Henik and Gideon Anholt suggest one refinement to Gross's model: They would add *emotion recognition* as another option to Gross's list. They note that "labeling," in which a person literally names an emotion as it arises, is a conscious process of emotion recognition for "dealing with highly intense emotional situations." Say, for instance, your boss is angry with you about a mistake, and you expect him to call you out in a team meeting for it, as is his habit with anyone in the doghouse. The emotion you expect to feel at that meeting is embarrassment and humiliation, especially with your peers looking on sympathetically. In this case it can help to consciously say to yourself beforehand, "Calling me out like that in front of my peers will make me feel embarrassed and angry." As simple as it sounds, this labeling of the emotion alone has been shown by research to weaken its intensity. And while I always tell my clients this labeling won't fully solve their problems, it does enable them to keep their wits and consider a more reasoned response than just to shoot an insult right back at their boss.

Labeling can also make cognitive change more effective. For instance, after regaining your self-composure, you might then reappraise your boss's emotional outburst not as evidence of his disdain for you (or incompetence on your part) but as a sign that he's under intense pressure himself to deliver on business objectives in light of a crucial deadline.

These various strategies for reining in your emotions can be combined in different ways. Danish sociologist Anette Prehn, for example, adapts the label-and-reappraisal strategy to her "Framestorm" method of emotional regulation, which I've used quite successfully with my own coaching clients. Prehn notes that our emotional experiences echo and reinforce one another in our brain, which, if those experiences are bad, can make new situations even worse—a negative neurological and emotional feedback loop.

Let's say, for example, that the last major presentation you gave was an unmitigated disaster. The PowerPoint projector kept switching off, the battery in the remote died, you stammered your way through the Q&A session, and to top it all off, you referred to your client by the wrong name. As a consequence, the idea of presenting anything ever again fills you with dread. Now, you do give smaller presentations here and there, and they go fine, but the higher the stakes, the more anxious you get.

In order to pull yourself out of this emotional feedback loop, you need first to recognize that you're in it. Once you realize this, Prehn recommends the Framestorm, which consists of three steps:

1. **Ask calibrating questions.** What is my current view of this situation? What emotional reaction is triggered because of it? Does my current framing get me closer to my goals? Do I want my current frame to become reality? Do I feel good about the current frame?

2. **Start the Framestorm.** Pepper your current negative frame with an exhaustive list of questions, from the substantive to the silly. These can range from asking yourself what benefits you could get from the current situation, what someone else might find positive about the situation, and how your mentor or a role model would view this situation, all the way to what your first grade teacher or your mom would think of this. Then, Prehn recommends that you come up with 15 to 30 alternative frames,

[handwritten margin note: ask questions to dissolve stress of the situation]

[handwritten note above "Pepper": seasoned]

however out-there they may seem, to break the hold that the anxiety-inducing frame has on you and to give yourself as many options as possible. The point of these questions and alternative frames is to "pause and disturb" the automatic connections our brains make by guiding our focus away from the worst-case scenario to perspectives that are either neutral or positive, and just as plausible as the negative conclusions we jumped to.

An example: Maria was a high-potential manager at a U.S.-based multinational IT company, with direct reports of different generations, from baby boomers to generation Z. Maria, herself a millennial, knew that an important part of her job was to provide regular performance feedback to her team members. But whenever the time came for a conversation where she'd have to deliver developmental feedback that she perceived as negative, she froze and would either delay the meeting for months or skip it altogether. This was especially the case with the older employees. The more she avoided the difficult conversations, the more anxious she got around her team. The automatic connection her brain made was that the more experienced members of her team wouldn't respect her if she criticized them and would end up resenting her for thinking she "was better than them." Maria became so uncomfortable around certain members of her team that her mood suffered and she felt like a failure as a manager.

So after deciding that her current frame about this situation was anything but helpful to her reputation, not to mention team morale and output, Maria tried framestorming. She developed a number of alternative perspectives that would dislodge her from the unproductive emotions attached to her current frame of "They will resent me." Some of the alternative perspectives that she came up included:

"My team will appreciate my honesty."
"No team members want to be in the dark about their performance."
"They are resilient adults who can handle constructive feedback when delivered tactfully."

"Delivering regular feedback will help me get more comfortable doing it."

"By not providing certain feedback, I am cheating my team out of the opportunity to grow."

"We can't win as a team if we're not aware of our strengths and weaknesses."

"I will ask them first so I can get their views on what they need to improve."

"I have their respect in general, so they will know that my feedback is coming from a good place."

"These conversations will help me build stronger relationships based on honesty and transparency."

Maria ended up with 20 to 30 different perspectives, and just by generating them she helped to calm her frayed nerves—nerves that were stressed simply by her original, negative perspective that she'd be resented for providing negative feedback.

3. **Choose your reframing.** This is the step in which you prune that mega-list down into something usable and something you feel good about embracing. Choose a couple of the options you generated that make sense to you and on which you can focus in place of your far less productive default frame. Maria decided that a respectful approach to feedback and the genuine intention to develop her team would make it easier to have these conversations as well as enable her to build her executive presence.

Again, the point of this process is to disrupt that negative feedback loop and reroute your response along more productive lines.

Each of the suggested antecedent-focused (before the moment) strategies is meant to change how we *experience* an emotion, and that, it seems, changes how our brain *processes* that emotion. So instead of the threatening information taking a shortcut via the neural back alley straight to the amygdala (which hijacks it for its own purposes), it takes the longer route through the frontal regions, which allows for a more modulated response to the situation.

Lieberman, for example, cites a number of studies demonstrating that the right ventrolateral prefrontal cortex is involved in a variety of forms of self-control, including emotional self-control. These studies, he explains, "suggest that each time we engage in self-control we are activating a system that might cause several kinds of self-control simultaneously." In fact, exercising any form of self-control can activate the brakes on the whole system, thus slowing down your emotional response.

A number of other scholars, looking at MRI studies, have noted that deployment and reappraisal strategies are particularly correlated with higher frontal lobe activation and lower amygdala activation—that is, with greater emotional regulation. In fact, in terms of tamping down on an overactive amygdala, the various forms of cognitive reappraisal appear to be quite effective in regulating emotion. As Gross and his colleagues note, "Our findings suggest that everyday use of reappraisal is related to greater experience of positive emotion and lesser experience of negative emotion." Those who make use of reappraisal "also have closer relationships with their friends and are better liked than individuals using reappraisal less frequently," are also less prone to depression, and are "more satisfied with their lives and more optimistic." Adding the labeling strategy to the process to increase emotion recognition appears to activate the brain's braking system, which can further boost the power of reappraisal.

In short, taking charge of your emotional response to a situation gives you some control over your brain—which in turn gives you control over the situation itself.

Emotion Regulation in the Moment

Regulating emotion in the moment, which Gross calls "response-focused" regulation, is often more difficult than the antecedent-focused methods, not least because you are attempting to manage both the experience and the expression of the emotion simultaneously. It's one thing to game out in your head how you're going to act in a situation; it's quite another to actually go through it. Unfortunately, angry customers don't always announce themselves before venting their frustrations at whoever will listen; nor do meetings with colleagues always go as planned. An offhand comment that inflames dormant feelings, an ambush accusation that rattles the nerves—it's situations like these when response-focused strategies can keep your emotions in.

Conveniently, the strategies that work for in-the-moment situations are mostly the same as the ones described for antecedent-focused situations, just with a little adaptation. One response-focused technique that works particularly well is *time delay*, or trying to outwait whatever emotion pops up. Social psychologist Lerner and her colleagues note that this is a remarkably effective strategy—even a 10-minute delay between experiencing an emotion and acting on it can change the emotion itself. I personally don't believe you need even 10 minutes, however. When you find yourself in the throes of a strong emotion but stay completely aware of what is happening and consciously observe the abating of the hormonal rush, you may find yourself in calmer waters much sooner. Try it the next time someone cuts you off in traffic. Try to follow the entire process, from the generation of your emotion to the moment you calm down. Be intensely curious about perceiving every sensation during every stage of the emotional response—emotion recognition is part of the time-delay strategy. Instead of focusing on the other driver with grimaces and outraged gestures, notice the physiological effects that the mix of fear and anger have on your body and brain, and try to closely discern when the feeling subsides. You'll find that you can quickly regain the ability to think clearly, not to mention make better choices, than if you weren't consciously observing this process.

Harvard-trained brain scientist Dr. Jill Bolte Taylor talks about waiting out the rush of chemicals in her book *My Stroke of Insight: A Brain Scientist's Personal Journey*: "Once triggered, the chemical released by my brain surges through my body and I have a physiological experience. Within 90 seconds from the initial trigger, the chemical component of my anger has completely dissipated from my blood and my automatic response is over. If, however, I remain angry after those 90 seconds have passed, then it is because I have chosen to let that circuit continue to run."

And this too is an important point: Unless you are in a life-and-death situation where fight or flight makes sense—boardroom presentations don't count—wait until the physiological reaction has subsided, and realize that if you still feel the need to scratch that emotional itch, say, to slap back at someone who has insulted you, it is because you *want to*, not because your emotions carried you away. To help with this calming behavioral pause, you can use a variation of Webb's "micro-mindfulness" technique by taking a few deep breaths. (The breathing-out part is more important than the breathing-in part.)

Lieberman and Moytal highlight labeling—the "emotion-recognition" strategy described above as useful for antecedent-focused situations—as another way to switch your emotions to a lower gear, as in "I'm being challenged in front of my peers, and this is causing me to feel embarrassed." This emotion-recognition strategy can also help you to deal with the long shadow cast by incidental emotions, those unrelated joys and irritations that intrude on a current situation. Lerner and her colleagues note, for example, that people who can identify these emotional leftovers are less prone to be influenced by them.

The ability to detect these leftovers can be especially useful when it comes to *triggers*, because it is within the leftovers that these triggers—things you overreact to—often lie. Our earlier example involved the irritation you feel at the packed train or highway, the slow elevator, the sticky drawer, so that when the meeting doesn't start on time, you start huffing and snorting over the waste of time. These "leftover" triggers are like a series of small pokes that make you more and more sensitive to the next small poke.

But sometimes those small earlier pokes are not necessary. You may be in a good mood or neutral mood and be fully triggered by a comment or action that taps into something deeper in your past. Delee Fromm identifies a number of different types of triggers that can occur during negotiations; if the other side is being dismissive, and you are sensitive to that kind of attitude due to something in your past, it may be all the trigger you need. As a regulation technique, if you can identify what sets you off, then you can dial it back down—whether by taking a break, addressing your concerns directly with the other party, or adjusting your own negotiating stance.

In addition to recognizing triggers, NeuroLeadership Institute founder David Rock recommends both perspective-shifting and increased focus. Ochsner, too, includes perspective-shifting ("distancing") as part of the process of cognitive reappraisal, and Prehn uses this in the second step of her Framestorm. But Rock notes that this can be used in real time as a way to step out of the moment in order to grasp the big picture: "Practice seeing things from completely different points of view regularly so that you literally build your switch function." And like so many others, he suggests that you learn how to focus better through mindfulness.

Finally, let's look at a regulatory strategy that's been proved over and over *not* to work: *suppression*. Trying to put a lid on your boiling emotions can actually make them boil more, as well as make it more difficult to figure out why you got so upset in the first place. Kevin Ochsner cites a study in which one person's attempt at suppression during a conversation made him more distracted (the person was trying to control his expression while also keeping up with the conversation) and made his blood pressure go up—and his partner's, too. So trying to pave over your own feelings can make both you and those around you even more emotional. That's not something you want in an already heated debate at work. In evidence, Ochsner points to work by Gross et al., which shows that suppression can lead to an *increase* in amygdala activity—precisely that area of the brain that you want to keep firmly in check.

More ominously, suppression has long-term effects on your state of mind. Gross and his colleagues point to evidence that those who deny their emotions have fewer positive and more negative emotional experiences, higher rates of depressive symptoms, and lower levels of social and emotional support. Those who deny their emotions are effectively denying a part of themselves, which can lead to a downward spiral marked by increased feelings of inauthenticity, greater avoidance of others, and overall lower life satisfaction.

So the research is clear, and everyday life is our laboratory for practice. Whether we use before-the-moment strategies to keep us from experiencing unhelpful emotions in certain situations, or in the heat of battle we engage in impulse control and regulate our emotions up or down, the resulting perception that we are cool, calm, and collected under pressure can add greatly to our perceived executive presence.

In the next chapter you'll learn various strategies to improve your social intelligence in order to foster more fulfilling and productive relationships with everyone around you. This is another crucial way to boost your perceived executive presence.

4

Develop Your Social Intelligence
for Better People Management

MANY PEOPLE BELIEVE that success depends less on *what* you know than on *whom* you know. Although that belief continues to define the culture of professions such as consulting and moviemaking, the technocreep of the last three decades has proved the reverse to be equally true: You don't need ~~disagree~~ to know a soul if your idea is some combination of timely and hot. Since 1990 the Internet has spawned more millionaires, each with an evolved entrepreneurial digital sensibility, than Merrill Lynch and Amway combined did in their heyday. Often, thanks to the miracle of e-mail, not even a handshake has been involved.

Lately there's been a third element in this career-ascent mix, and it's getting some serious ink thanks to a bumper crop of utterly clueless corporate executives who seem to have insulated themselves in steel towers of their own making while losing touch with the very people they are supposed to lead. What they haven't realized is that yesterday's dog-eat-dog management sensibility went out of style with Jack Welch's office furniture. Today's generation of managers is realizing that nice guys don't necessarily finish last, that, in fact, being anything other than socially sensitive and evolved—whether it's a genuine or a strategic agenda—can get you a seat at a congressional hearing and a few heavy-handed punch lines from Stephen Colbert.

This mysterious requisite for managerial success and the attention of the C-suite is called *social intelligence*, and if you think it has any substantive connection to the analytical and reasoning skills that get a person a Mensa card, think again.

At a glance it might seem that social intelligence is synonymous with or at least a subset of *emotional* intelligence, itself a relatively recent take on the controversial belief that "intelligence" is only a global term that refers to the sum of various discrete human capabilities. However, the term "social intelligence" is much older than that 1980s' revolution of thought. It first was used by Columbia University psychologist Edward Thorndike in a 1920 article for *Harper's Monthly Magazine* in which he explained that "the best mechanic in a factory may fail as a foreman for lack of social intelligence." He further observed, "By social intelligence is meant the ability to understand and manage men and women, boys and girls—to act wisely in human relations." In the decades that followed, other scholars emphasized the ability to get along with others, but over time the term was used less, and by the 1970s it had pretty much been dropped by those studying intelligence.

Still the idea kept popping back up. Even if researchers didn't think much of it, their subjects would bring up the notion again and again, pointing to things like "admits mistakes," "is sensitive to others' needs and desires," and "is on time for appointments." The researchers might not have taken "social competence" seriously, but the regular people they interviewed did. Not until Howard Gardner's work on "multiple intelligences" appeared in the 1980s did "social intelligence" reemerge as a topic of study in its own right. Since then, others have looked at social intelligence, most famously Karl Albrecht and Daniel Goleman, who have done much to popularize the term: a quick Internet search yields over 430 million results.

Social Intelligence Versus Self-Awareness

Social intelligence is clearly linked to self-awareness. Knowing yourself, knowing how others view you, and having the ability to regulate your emotions in difficult situations are all foundational to managing your relationships with others—"to act wisely in human relations," in Thorndike's words. My client Jim, for example, whose emotional transparency was generally valued by his boss, was unaware of how his intensity and facial expressions could seem like aggression to his colleagues. The first step toward changing this perception he'd created was simply to become aware of how others saw him, and then to adjust how he expressed himself—that is, attain both internal and external self-awareness.

This is not the same as social intelligence, however, even if there is an overlap. Think of it this way: Self-awareness is about understanding yourself and how you behave around others. Social intelligence is primarily about understanding those others and using that information to optimize your interactions with them. Social intelligence, then, is very much about how you are perceived by others or, better put, the *management* of what will be perceived by others. It is the understanding—and when you get it right, the mastery—of what elicits a positive response from other people in both relationships and casual encounters and even in front of an audience full of strangers. Why is it that some managers get people to line up behind them with staunch to-the-death loyalty, whereas others remain the target of cruel water cooler banter? The answer is social intelligence. The first type of manager has it; the second doesn't. If the second one somehow has risen to the position of boss—though this is fortunately becoming more difficult without drawing senior management's concerned attention in today's business culture—everyone has a problem.

Clearly, social intelligence is not the sole defining element in success. There are, after all, many famously cantankerous yet charismatic CEOs that show that tough guys and even complete jerks can change the world. The half-full view of social intelligence, though, contends that the achievements of megalomaniacal, chronically demanding, and socially toxic leaders might have been even more astounding if they had been able to foster loyalty instead of keeping employees on edge with fear. Studies have shown that uncertainty and constant stress are far from optimally productive states in a neurological sense; yet even brilliant tyrants succeed with people, perhaps in spite of themselves.

How then did our long list of legendary corporate Napoleons succeed? Again, social intelligence is not the entire ballgame. There are multiple aspects of intelligence, or so the theory goes:

- Abstract and cognitive intelligence that leads to quick and accurate reasoning and deduction
- Practical intelligence that empowers people to accomplish goals
- Aesthetic intelligence that takes the form of artistic expression and appreciation
- Kinesthetic intelligence that explains why certain people can do things with a ball that you cannot and why some people are naturals at flying airplanes and doing brain surgery
- Emotional intelligence that empowers self-aware people
- Social intelligence, which can potentiate them all if it inspires others to perceive a person as a leader and as someone worthy of their attention and respect

Think of these various intelligences as cards in a deck; we are all dealt different hands, but what you are holding doesn't necessarily have to define you. You can change your lot by expanding your mind and forging your own path.

It is simply not enough to be intelligent in the cognitive sense. Minimum security penitentiaries—so-called country clubs for white-collar criminals—are full of intelligent people. Some brilliant people sleep under bridges. It is also not enough to be emotionally intelligent. A doctor being judged on bedside manner, a hostage negotiator, a trial lawyer, a field sales rep, an organization's leader, an executive coach—all are defined as much by their social intelligence as by any other type of intelligence, including the emotional kind. The book *The Smartest Guys in the Room* proved that its title was stupendously ironic; many of the Enron executives who starred in it ended up disgraced and behind bars.

Some define social intelligence as a matter of demonstrating good *people skills*. This is like saying that LeBron James knows his way around a basketball court or that Beyoncé can put on a show. It would be more accurate to say that social intelligence is a *sense* of the energy and image that one is putting out to others, coupled with an understanding of what works and what doesn't, what will cultivate loyalty and approval and what will come off as egotistical, insecure, and insensitive. Social intelligence is more than getting along—it's about getting ahead—with people. If your job is to lead, to convince, to appeal, to build a culture, to create a following, to sell yourself as an essential aspect of meeting your goals, social intelligence becomes the centerpiece of your skill set. The attainment of your goals depends on it no matter how well you know your stuff otherwise.

Another way to view social intelligence is to consider it the differentiator when everyone else is as talented and skilled as you are. If you are a surgeon, you are surrounded by brilliant peers, many of whom want the chief of surgery spot just as much as you do. Chances are that everyone on campus is possessed of high intelligence in terms of cognitive skills and the ability to get his or her head around the mechanics of the job; and if the job involves motor skills, everyone in the vicinity has the kinesthetic ability to get it done. General intelligence in this regard is simply the ante, and unless you use your social intelligence to set yourself apart and become a candidate for leadership because people are attracted to you and will line up behind you, you'll remain mired among those intelligent masses.

The late celebrity chef and author Anthony Bourdain became a beloved television personality and cultural ambassador not because of his cooking skills, but because of his ability to engage and empathize with ordinary people from cultures across the globe. He could share a meal and trade anecdotes with mountain dwellers in Colombia and fishermen in Tangiers, and be just as socially appropriate with them as he was with presidents and rock stars. He listened to them, laughed with them, complimented them, and asked the kinds of questions that showed them all that he really wanted to know them intimately.

Breaking Down Social Intelligence

Managers and executives looking to command the respect of their peers and superiors must remember that social intelligence involves a lot more than an infectious grin. Social intelligence can be seen as the confluence of a handful of distinct abilities, all of them driven by a keen understanding of what makes people respond positively. Even if you get along with everyone and are the first person that people think of when composing their invitation lists, you owe it more to the following five dimensions (as defined by Karl Albrecht) of social intelligence than to your razor-sharp wit.

1) Presence

What used to be called dressing for success has come out of the closet to include the totality of your presentation across all the senses, from your hair to your voice, your nonverbals, and the subtle ways in which you respond. Your presence communicates your self-worth and confidence as well as the level of respect you have for others and the occasion. Disrespect in the name of "just being who I am" gets you nowhere in the world of employers, peers, and clients.

2) Clarity

Anyone who has ever had a manager, no matter how nice, who couldn't communicate objectives, expectations, and other relevancies knows how hard it is to follow that kind of leader. The goal is to get others to appreciate you and follow you, and the clearer you are about what you want and expect, the sooner that will happen. (The ability to articulate messages in a clear and compelling way is also one of the key traits of executive presence as found in a study published by the American Psychological Association.)

3) Awareness

Awareness is the ability to read people and the moment and to respond with behaviors that fit the situation. This social radar is similar to external awareness, with the focus on your ability to "read the room." Upon meeting the First Lady, you don't say, "Hey, what's up?" though this might be exactly what you'd say when meeting the 16-year-old son of your CEO.

4) Authenticity

If awareness is your social radar, authenticity is appealing to the social radar of others by being genuine, honest, and respectful. Phoniness and bluster, no matter how proficiently conveyed, are easy to spot and consistently off-putting. This type of behavior conveys a sense of insecurity, which is not a quality others appreciate in a leader. The concept of honesty goes beyond telling the truth; it embraces conveying the truth about *yourself* as well.

5) Empathy

Dale Carnegie was onto something when he taught that the more we show a genuine interest in others, the more they'll be attracted to us. Social intelligence takes this a step further than showing interest; we also need to *empathize* with the experience and feelings of others, to *relate* to that experience and to them. When you communicate empathy, you are saying that we are on the same page, the same team, and that anything I ask you to do has taken your situation into consideration and I have confidence that you can accomplish the goal even though it's difficult.

All this may sound a lot like emotional intelligence until you recognize the context of expression as opposed to introspection. It is one thing to manage your emotions, control your temper, disassociate from unpleasant memories and biases, and quell the inner voices of insecurity when you are standing in the spotlight. Social intelligence, in contrast, is the way you manage those things to optimize the perception of others with the only element of that perception you can control: the raw input of what people sense about you. From there they will filter that incoming information in ways over which you have little control. They may cling to preferences and biases that make no sense to you, and they will pursue their own agendas and be swayed by their own memories. But you at least can provide the raw material that they will process.

How to Boost Your Social Intelligence Quotient in Only Seven Days

There's an old Steve Martin joke: "How do you avoid paying taxes on a million dollars? Well, first you get a million dollars." In other words, knowing how social intelligence breaks down into its component parts is only the first step in raising your social IQ above where it is today. Actually changing behaviors, especially one's own, is a monumental undertaking; that is why many professionals embarking on that process decide to use executive coaching to help them get there. Whatever you do, you can get a head start by taking matters into your own hands. It isn't hyperbole when I say that you can make serious progress in seven days by engaging in a systematic process where you practice self-awareness and engage in some key behaviors that define social intelligence.

You can develop your social intelligence, but it requires a keen sense of self, a concept we've covered in detail in Chapter 2 when we discussed self-awareness. To develop this sense, you must, of course, obtain the unvarnished feedback of others, both to assess your starting point and to identify the areas in which you most need to improve.

One way to obtain quality feedback is to conduct a *360-degree assessment* of the way you are perceived by others. If a formal 360-degree review process at your organization is not available to you, solicit this input on your own. Whichever way you come by the feedback of your colleagues and business partners, make sure to use the results productively to define what you need to improve about your social intelligence and what is already working well that you can build on.

What follows is not dissimilar to a diet that delivers basic biochemical science instead of fads and marketing agendas. Can you lose weight in seven days? Certainly. Can you change your life and keep the weight off after those seven days? Only if what you've learned during those days becomes a lifestyle. The same thing holds true here. If you can get your head around these concepts in the first seven days, chances are that you'll notice a change in the way people react to you and, more important, a change in the way you react to other people and the way that makes you feel.

Day 1: Start Using Your Senses More Deliberately

Begin the practice of using your senses instead of relying on autopilot when you are moving through the day. For instance, when you drive to work, you may not notice the sights along the way; you just arrive at work without having given much thought to the environment, the people, the architecture along the way. If asked, chances are that you couldn't describe any one of them in much detail. Try to pay close attention next time, whether you're heading to work in a car or the subway. Simply take a good look around you. Take notice of people's moods. Try to read their faces, check out their clothing, and note any peculiarities, and then assign meaning to what you see. Notice the businessman who eats an egg salad sandwich on the way to work in the morning on the subway, impeccably dressed but with mayonnaise landing on his tie. Notice the old lady cradling a toddler in her arms. Is it her granddaughter? Is she a nanny? If you're driving, notice the workers at any construction sites: Are they young? Older? Try to guess their ethnicity. Open the window and consciously perceive the fleeting smells in the air. What are they? Gasoline? Freshly cut grass? Pastries from a nearby bakery?

After a while you'll find that you're no longer guessing, that your perceptions are informed with subtle bits of information that lead to quality perceptions and deductions. Do this with deliberation for the next seven days and notice how it changes your experience. Notice how *present* you are and the way that makes the time richer. For the first five of these days, concentrate on one sense each day: sound, smell, touch, taste, or sight. Start over again on day 6. Become highly attuned to the stimuli entering your field of perception and pay attention to the narratives (explanations) you are assigning to what you see. Notice the emotions associated with the experience of your senses. Feel them.

The more you consciously use your senses, the more situational awareness you will gain. Soon you'll start noticing things that previously escaped you. Bring this skill with you when you arrive at work and you'll already have improved your social intelligence simply by being more aware of the different vibes in your office. As a result you should experience an improved ability to respond and communicate appropriately and effectively in professional and social situations, both in the workplace and outside of it.

Does all this sound familiar? It should: These are the same kinds of techniques you use in mindfulness training. Mindfulness, remember, is useful in developing your self-awareness and especially in learning how to regulate your emotions. The techniques that I recommend build on one another, broadening and deepening your abilities to map both your internal and external environments.

Day 2: Critically Assess Your Strengths and Weaknesses

Whether you have Tom Brady's looks, Michelle Obama's intelligence and grace, Warren Buffett's legendary knack for choosing smart investments, Elon Musk's visionary outlook—regardless of the controversies—or whether you fall short in all these areas, now is the time to take stock of the good, the bad, and the ugly in yourself. Why? Because to raise your social IQ and thereby strengthen your executive presence, you have to know how you stack up against everyone else. Being aware of your strengths not only gives you confidence; it also gives you an opportunity to offer your strengths to others, instantly turning them into fans, if not friends. And what about your liabilities? That's the stuff you'll want to limit—such as, for example, your tendency to overshare at the office water cooler, making your peers roll their eyes. Or for another example, your habitual tardiness to meetings, which you apologetically attribute to "being swamped," although your equally busy peers all seem to make it on time just fine.

How do you get this knowledge of your social assets and liabilities? Use the 360-degree feedback process we covered—formal or informal. You've created a reputation that's based on the sum of your behaviors, and the clearer you are about what draws others to you and what might push them away, the more informed your choices will be as you start on the path to improvement.

Day 3: Practice Being Authentic

Most of us hide behind various masks that we have designed to put forth our best image. Unfortunately, what gets lost behind the mask is our true self and genuine personality, which, let's be honest, is the most interesting part of us to other people. For others to feel a connection and trust us, we must strive be more authentic. Today you will start by giving people a more honest look at who you really are—the real person behind the mask.

How to Be Real: A Checklist

1. Have honest conversations with others about issues that matter to you deeply.
2. Build real relationships and practice empathy by having honest and heartfelt conversations with others about issues that matter deeply to them.
3. Admit when you're wrong and apologize when you should.
4. Forgive others and move on for the sake of the relationship.
5. Ask for help and offer it to others who may be reluctant to ask.
6. Take risks by showing your strengths—and weaknesses—in a public forum. Demonstrating vulnerability can prompt others to respect you.
7. Show your unique sides to others and watch them become curious about you.

Start by having more real conversations with the people around you today. See how they respond to the real you. Observe how much of your true self people feel comfortable with and adjust the amount you want to share. Pick the right time to open yourself up, since too much too soon or at an inappropriate moment will lead to the wrong perception. Observe whether people respond with self-disclosures of their own and whether they too become more *real* around you. Take the cue from them and ease into a more profound interaction with those with whom you want to connect.

Day 4: Start Communicating Simply

Communicate with clarity by using simple English everyone can understand. If it's more natural for you to say "It is not efficacious to indoctrinate a superannuated canine with innovative maneuvers" instead of "You can't teach an old dog new tricks," you've got work to do. Make your messages clear and to the point, devoid of clutter and jargon. If you find yourself using complex language and giving unnecessary details for the purpose of masking your perceived insecurities, stop yourself short and recognize that your new, evolved social intelligence is kicking in. You may be surprised at how often you do this, and when you stop doing it, you may be surprised at how much better the response will be.

Day 5: Practice Empathy: Look at Everything from Someone Else's Perspective

Do more than just comprehend another person's point of view. Really put yourself into that person's shoes and imagine what it—whatever "it" is—*feels* like for him or her.

We humans see and experience the world from our own perspective: We filter information through our own unique set of values, beliefs, and biases, and that determines what we conclude and how we respond. Seeing the world through eyes other than our own will give us a better idea of what's important to others and what moves them, as well as what they might resist. When we can see things from their perspective we can start communicating in a way that appeals to their unique manner of filtering. Doing this puts people at ease and breaks down barriers to trust and cooperation. In trying to get us to understand them, people often say, "Look at it from my point of view" or "Here's where I'm coming from." These statements simply ask us to do things that would make for better relationships and increased understanding, and it's more effective if they don't have to ask.

Day 6: Practice Listening with Empathy

When we communicate with others, we're often more focused on what we're going to say next than we are on what message someone is trying to convey. Our mind wanders, we tune the person out, and, contrary to what we may perceive, the person notices it and assigns meaning to it.

As a result, we miss important cues, nuance, and meaning, not to mention coming off as aloof and disinterested. We fail to establish a real connection when we are not listening because we're not fully attuned to the other person's message, rendering our responses as slightly *off*, consisting of ritualistic grunts, head movements, and hollow nodding. If feedback you've received tells you that this is you, your social intelligence needs a booster shot.

Moreover, as you listen to others, consciously put your own values, biases, and preferences aside and try to sense empathically what your partner thinks, feels, needs, and perceives, right there in that very moment. Do this without judgment. When appropriate, periodically acknowledge the other person's communication; that acknowledgment can be verbal, vocal, or nonverbal, and should be done with genuine interest. Be fully *present*. Observe what your conversation partner does, and how the two of you are engaged in a way that connects you. Observe in yourself how it feels to perceive fully all of a person's communication signals, many of which reside between and behind the actual words.

Day 7: Make a Plan and Implement the Steps

Since you're reading this book, you've most likely made the decision to construct or improve your executive presence. Gaining the respect of your bosses, peers, and other colleagues is a marathon, not a sprint. Although these seven days are just the beginning of a long stretch, you'll have a much clearer idea at the end of what it means to have a vastly improved social IQ. Now it's time to create a plan for you to practice and implement these steps. Chances are you'll have plenty of opportunities to engage in these techniques, all of which can move you upward in your career and strengthen your personal relationships, by, as Edward Thorndike said, "acting wisely in human relations."

In the next chapter we'll explore how you can convey executive presence by succeeding in getting buy-in for your ideas and motivating people toward common goals.

5

Keys to Gaining Buy-in and Motivating People to Action

THE MILITARY HAS been onto something since the days of muskets and keelhauling. It goes like this: The brass says "Jump," and the troops ask "How high?" Not only do the enlisted masses not have to like it, but the folks with the embroidered hats couldn't care less whether they do. In fact, if you're a drill instructor with a bit of a Napoleon complex, the less the grunts like what you say, the better.

The reason this works is obvious: There is no alternative. A soldier can't resign. Resistance gets the soldier some quality time in the brig. Request a rationale, and you're cleaning the latrine with a toothbrush—yours—for the next month. The only other situation in modern civilized culture in which this organizational dynamic works is revealed in a memory most of us hold dear: When asked to justify an instruction we found illogical, which was often the case, our parents said, "Because I said so."

Hence our generational problems with authority figures.

There was a time when corporate managers who wanted to assert their presence and advance through the hierarchy thought that this was the way of the world. And for a time it was, at least until three tough women named Parton, Tomlin, and Fonda rewrote workplace dynamics in the 1980 movie *Nine to Five*, in which the company head, played by Dabney Coleman, discovers that a title and too much insensitive swagger can get you tied up, literally, in misguided office politics that have significant consequences.

Although the megalomaniacal styles of middle and upper managers continue to pervade the workplace, there's a new cultural sheriff roaming the corporate campus these days—one who's been to all the postgraduate leadership seminars that postulate that people, along with the results they deliver, are best optimized from a specific psychological understanding of what makes them tick. This is a strategy designed for long-term success rather than the short-term benefits of carrying a metaphorical big stick and having an impressive title. When it comes to achieving organizational outcomes through others, nothing succeeds more reliably than creating psychological safety, understanding what motivates people, communicating with them clearly and frequently, and spelling out the purpose—the why—of the task. The goal of all this? Aiming for *buy-in* by the troops.

There are many ways—hundreds, in fact—to get *compliance*. However, we now know that it's the time and effort we invest in generating buy-in that makes long-term sustained organizational success possible. The mastery of that concept can help foster respect and honest effort from the members of your greater team—bosses included—while contributing to the executive presence you are learning to build.

 ## Buy-in Beats Compliance

Abraham Lincoln said, "Public sentiment is everything. With it, nothing can fail; without it, nothing can succeed." Perhaps this observation originated in the Civil War, in which it's hard to imagine Confederate soldiers shooting up their northern neighbors without buying into the racially biased belief system that was the crux of the dispute. A belief system is a form of buy-in; if you don't believe, you aren't buying in. Imagine giving your all to a company that touts its environmental stewardship and expects employees to give "110 percent" to meet organizational goals, then only to learn that the company has been illegally dumping toxic waste. In that case, you might suddenly find yourself less willing to put in those extra hours to ensure the company's success. Buy-in, in other words, comprises both the *belief* in something and the *willingness* to work in service of those beliefs. If people stop believing, they'll stop working.

Compliance, on the other hand, doesn't require belief; it is simply about obedience. This can work in the short term, and might even have you convinced that leadership is primarily about using fear to keep people in line. But compliance never achieves fully sustained commitment and effort. People will bolt at the first glimpse of something better.

Autocratic leaders learn this sobering truth about compliance: When people are no longer afraid, they no longer obey. The protagonists of the corporate tragedy called Enron are a classic example of the breakdown of buy-in. It's hard to imagine the members of the senior executive team at Enron behaving as they did—and for a time succeeding—without buy-in from lower-ranking executives. And once those who questioned the company's unusual accounting practices were laid off, those in power, with the help of those whose buy-in they had, ran rampant in their greed.

But the buy-in was not complete, and it was the *lack* of buy-in from several individuals that helped bring down the corporate giant. They're called whistleblowers, and one Enron whistler—a vice president of corporate development by the name of Sherron Watkins—blew the whistle in CEO Ken Lay's ear in a seven-page letter in which she basically worried aloud about Enron's "funny" accounting practices, likening them to a giant Ponzi scheme. Although Watkins wasn't the only one who didn't buy in—other former Enron executives also claimed the title of whistleblower for themselves—she was named person of the week by *Time* for her significant role in "smelling a rat" at work and documenting it in writing. Watkins and other corporate whistleblowers may have looked the other way here and there—who knows?—but they lacked buy-in to a degree that they sought to remove themselves from the company's immoral and unethical, not to mention criminal, activities.

A major commitment simply cannot be mandated, even by those with a big title and wielding the hammer of a looming performance review. A major commitment over time requires buy-in, the kind that permeates all levels of the culture. Consider the Cinderella success story of the 1980 American Olympic hockey team. The squad, staffed with college students, beat a team of hard-core professional Soviet players. Coach Herb Brooks was a hard man, not known for backslapping or even smiling, but he knew how to mold his young men into a team that *believed* it could win it all. The night before the big match with the Russians, Brooks gathered the members of his team and told them, "It's meant to be. This is your moment and it's going to happen." And it did. Then they went out and beat Finland for the gold, believing even when they were down in the third period that, of course, they could win—because Brooks made them believe in themselves. Imagine the improbable victory of that team if it did not buy into Brooks's vision. Or similarly, imagine a political victory without the buy-in of staff and all the volunteers putting in endless hours knocking on doors and passing out campaign literature and cold-calling voters. Incumbents may not have to be inspiring (although some of them are), but every underdog must reach out to doubters and skeptics and turn them into believers if she or he has any chance of scoring an upset.

In business, too, it is turning employees into believers that makes the difference. The superstars of corporate success have this in common—an across-the-board buy-in to a set of values and values-driven missions from their staffs. The list of CEOs who have achieved this includes Rometty, Welch, Jobs, Winfrey, and Branson. As with the 1980 American Olympic hockey team, it is impossible to imagine these business leaders' success without full and complete corporate cultural buy-in.

Buy-in, which often is easier to define than to achieve, is at minimum an agreement to support a decision. Ideally, it is the total alignment of a person or group with your beliefs and goals. It is a process of working together with people—not dictating to them—in a manner that leads to their understanding of the goal and its strategic importance to achieve a win-win outcome, all within a common set of values. To secure buy-in means gaining people's personal commitment to a goal and their willingness to do what it takes to get it done. The more complex and significant the project or organizational objective, the more essential buy-in becomes.

This definition shifts the role of a manager from one of task definer and taskmaster to one of task *empowerer*. Your first line of managerial offense—indeed, your most powerful strategy—is to strive to create a level of buy-in that makes all stakeholders feel they are part of the process.

As noted above, there are three overlapping elements to creating and maintaining buy-in: psychological safety, clear communication, and motivation and purpose. How you establish and make use of these elements varies with the setting—what works best at the office level differs from what works at the company level—which means you have to exercise judgment in deciding which elements to emphasize. I'll review each of the elements in the next few pages.

Creating Psychological Safety

Getting the commitment and buy-in of employees (as well as peers and senior management) is never easy, especially when it involves some sort of change that requires a mental and behavioral shift. One way to accomplish such a feat, according to the principles of evolved people management, is to make sure that people feel psychologically safe.

Organizational leaders ignorant of this basic concept are easily identified: They keep information close to their chest; they make careless offhand comments; they behave inconsistently; they play favorites; they blame others for failures but are quick to take credit for successes; they micromanage and humiliate; they pit people against each other; they stoke conflict rather than resolve it and otherwise threaten people implicitly and explicitly.

In contrast, enlightened leaders, seeking to make it easy for people to buy into a leader's vision of a better future, recognize them for their accomplishments, give them direction and feedback, help them understand the *why* of the work they do, treat them fairly, and bestow on them at least some autonomy over how they meet their goals.

These various efforts all rest on one basic tenet of human behavior: People need a safe and trusting environment to perform at their best. Deep in our DNA there is a voice whispering that if we feel unsafe, we must minimize risk, lest we end up with our head on a platter. If employees are fearful, they will put their energy into avoiding risk rather than engaging in analytic thinking, problem solving, and the spirited creative process necessary to pursue important goals. Remember my client Jim from Chapter 2, whose tendency to intimidate his team truncated discussions and stifled communication, not to mention limited his ability to exert influence with a positive executive presence. Only when there is an air of trust flowing through the organization's HVAC system will employees buy into the kind of risk taking that fosters innovation and growth, not to mention their own personal development.

When the people at Google investigated what made a team successful, they found that psychological safety was "far and away the most important" factor. Julia Rozovsky, a Google analyst, noted that "the safer team members feel with one another, the more likely they are to admit mistakes, to partner, and to take on new roles." Only when colleagues felt that they could take risks without being punished did they really push themselves.

The smart idea then is to create a culture in which people feel safe to speak up, to make mistakes and learn from them, and to have a chance to be part of the decision-making process, if only to be asked for their input. This is especially critical in small-group settings in which you have regular contact with your colleagues and peers. It is through their interactions with you that they will learn that you can be trusted to encourage them, to give them honest feedback, and to keep your word.

Here are some ideas that can help you foster a climate of psychological safety:

- **Respect others.** The most basic way to get people to follow you is to respect them. Tell them that you rely on their skills and that you appreciate their efforts, and they'll step up for you. Even more importantly, *show* that you trust them by letting them actually do the work. Don't micromanage; instead, have a conversation with them about your expectations, answer their questions, and let them get on with their work. If you trust them, chances are they'll trust you back.
- **Find out what they expect from you.** If you've moved from one culture to another, be it across international boundaries or just from one corporate style to another, find out what your colleagues and employees expect from you. Do they expect to be consulted when making decisions? Do they expect decisions and deadlines to be firm or flexible? Do they expect you to tell them exactly how you'd like something done, or are they used to accomplishing goals in their own way? Learning what others

expect may prompt you to adjust your style, as well as give you the opportunity to explain to them just what your style is.

- **Be clear about what you expect from them.** Few things are more frustrating to employees than being forced to guess what managers want. Tell them what you expect from them and then evaluate them by the standards that you set. If you want to see more risk taking, don't punish them when they extend themselves and fail; instead, work with them to make the risk pay off. If you call a meeting to brainstorm, encourage them to think big; but if the aim of the meeting is how to make something work, keep the focus on the practicalities.

- **Set the direction and stay the course if possible.** Just as guesswork wastes time, constantly changing the purpose of a project can be demoralizing. People crave certainty and are more likely to invest themselves in their work when they know that investment will pay off. Even if they're used to having flexible deadlines and revisiting decisions, wholesale and abrupt course changes can throw everyone off. If the direction does change, give your employees as much advance notice as possible. Keep them looped in, and they'll adjust their sails with minimal fuss.

- **Reduce uncertainty.** Setting direction and being clear about expectations will substantially reduce uncertainty. However, sometimes those general tactics are not enough to allay anxiety, and you have to investigate the particular triggers driving those concerns. Will the mission result in time pressures and too much evening and weekend work? Will it place the employees in a role in which they feel unprepared or uncomfortable? Will they feel supported in their role or alone with their sense of inadequacy? Are there enough rewards—do they understand what's in it for them? Do the stakes have implications for their careers or their immediate sense of wellness? Sometimes it is impossible to remove uncertainty from a mission, but you can strive to make them feel assured of their psychological safety and the availability of support. By keeping everyone in the loop and communicating frequently, you become the light your employees follow in the dark, which empowers them to buy into and support your decisions.

- **Be human.** We've discussed the need for social intelligence at length in Chapter 4. Demonstrating empathy and vulnerability with a request for buy-in helps others *feel* your recommendations rather than just hear them. Make your pitch personal: Research shows that people are more likely to help an individual in need than they are to contribute to a generic charity. Asking others for help signals anything but weakness, even if that seems counterintuitive. People have a natural instinct to help others. Tap into it.
- **Be the real deal.** Your credibility is the pivotal variable in how people respond to your requests. Make sure you're on solid ground, and if not, bring the data and the reinforcements necessary to qualify you as their leader. People value expertise and experience in their leaders, and it takes more than a title and a few boxes of pizza to get people on board with your ideas. Don't be afraid to showcase your competence, delivered with genuine warmth, and you're likely to bring even the skeptics around.

Communicating to the Core

No matter what the setting, to get buy-in clear communication always matters. Whether in one-on-one sessions or at large town hall–style meetings, whether with subordinates or with superiors, if you can't clearly and simply convey your point, people will tune out. But if you can, you'll find their ears—and minds—wide open.

Some strategies and tactics for communicating in a compelling way follow.

Know the Members of Your Audience and What's Foremost on Their Mind

What are their beliefs and values? What are their expectations? What barriers and distractions do you have to address before you can direct their attention to your message? In other words, "read the room." If your team or company has been through the wringer, you can't ignore that as you rally people to meet the next production target. Similarly, if you know rumors are flying about mergers or layoffs or other organizational change, address those rumors. Otherwise, people will fill in gaps in information with ideas spun from their biases and beliefs. You may not have all the answers they seek, but by acknowledging their concerns and the issues swirling in the organizational ether, you display your organizational awareness as well as your empathy for them.

At the senior level, you'll secure buy-in more easily if you've taken the time to meet the stakeholders individually and clearly communicate the risks and opportunities in a way that addresses their personal values and interests. The level of detail you go into in these meetings reflects your understanding of your audience. An instructive example comes from one of my clients, a recently hired technology leader at a global consumer products giant, who frequently interacted with the company CFO. In one of their first one-on-ones, the tech executive avoided detailed tech talk and instead focused on her understanding of the business needs and her recommendations on how to achieve several key business objectives. This was language the CFO understood very well, and he was grateful to her. At one point he said, "Hey, I want to thank you for really just talking about the business challenge that you see and not bringing in there a technology decision with me."

In fact, this CFO had long been frustrated with new people in the organization coming into his office and starting with a technology discussion instead of a business problem he was trying to solve. As the CFO himself put it: "They're coming in and they're telling me I need these data hubs, Microsoft Azure, da, da, da, when all they needed to say is, 'I think we need better consumer insights.' They would've had me sold. I wouldn't have needed to have a six-page deck on these boxes that look like there's clouds around them, but we didn't get the conversation about consumer insights. So I let them go for 30 minutes. Then I said, 'Guys, none of this makes any sense to me; what would've made sense, if you brought into me my challenges of getting consumer insights today, and that you guys have a plan to solve it. Do you need to show me the plan in this level of detail? Probably not.'"

The CFO's candor confirmed for my client the wisdom of her approach. "I definitely don't go in with that level of detail with a finance guy or a marketing guy," she said. "I know those guys, I'm not going to get buy-in—I'll lose them the minute I mention *the cloud*."

Tell Them Why They Should Care on a Human Level

When you're presenting facts, numbers, stats, and other findings, don't forget to tell your audience why the information matters—why *this* audience should care about the information, how it relates to *them*, and what it all means in terms of human outcomes. The people in your audience may be smart, but as we've seen with our tech-averse CFO, they can't necessarily connect the dots from the specs and technical data. So make it easy and spell out the "so what"?

[handwritten margin note: How info affects the partner]

For instance, if you're proposing to your local library that it purchase several new computers, don't build your pitch to the tech-unaware decision-making committee around contrasting the tech features of the library's old models with those of the more powerful new ones. Instead, point out to the committee that kids from the community's low-income families rely on the library's computers to do their homework, and that has grown increasingly difficult because the equipment is outdated. If you do that, you've tapped into more than just people's rational brains with a straightforward cost-benefit analysis. You've put a human face on the issue.

Ground Your Facts in Real-World Context

Imagine you're a lawyer representing a family whose child died because of a product defect. The company on trial had been aware of the faulty product for some time but decided against a recall because it would cost $3 million. And that is the amount you're requesting in compensatory damages. You know how difficult it is to put a price on a child's life, but you figure a jury would see the logic of compensating the bereaved parents at least the amount that the defendant company tried to save by keeping its flawed product on the market. The company's attorney argues that $3 million is too much, at which point you address the jury with a rhetorical question: "What is a child's life worth in our community?" And that's when you put it all into a real-life context.

You may point out, for example, that the annual compensation of the defendant's CEO exceeds $7 million and that you have no doubt he's worth every penny. You may show the jury a government spending report that NASA provided $15 million in grant money to a golfing equipment manufacturer so it could see how its golf clubs perform in space. You may also show the jury a story about an auction at which a Picasso sold for $179 million, and another about the *loser* of a recent heavyweight prizefight getting a guaranteed payout of $100 million. "All these amounts were fairly valued, I'm sure," you tell the jury. And then you ask again, "So what is a child's life worth in our community?" after which you add, "That's *your* call to make."

This strategy may or may not work, but by putting your request into a real-life context, you're doing two things: (1) giving your listeners the *good for service* opportunity to mentally step outside the situation at hand and see the proverbial forest instead of the trees, while also (2) tapping into their personal value system, where decisions are mapped onto principles that are deeply important to them. If buy-in is about alignment with one's beliefs and values, then it is people's core values that you need to evoke with context in order to get it.

Deliver a Gut Punch They Won't Forget

We never run out of problems to solve and challenges to overcome—often the only question is which ones to prioritize. So when you're looking to get buy-in, it's not always enough to make a business case and tug at the heartstrings. Sometimes you have to deliver a metaphorical punch to the gut to make people *feel* the issue you want them to move to the top of the agenda. One of my clients, the chief information security officer at a U.S.-based global consumer products company, did just that to help the company's leaders understand the importance of cybersecurity and the threat posed by the least likely of suspects—the company's own employees.

At an information security networking workshop, my client decided to do a demo—a phishing exercise in real time—with 45 of the company's directors from Europe, Asia, and Africa. Pretending to be the organizer of the event, my client's team sent spoof e-mails to the participants just five minutes before the session was to start. The intent was to show the directors the threat a simple e-mail can pose, while walking them through the exercise. However, before the session even got started, five people had already opened the e-mail and went looking for the organizer, telling him, "Hey, you had attached the wrong agenda—this appears to be dated." The organizer sat there thinking, "I know I didn't send this out . . . what's going on?" A couple of minutes later the session began, and my client started walking everyone through the exercise. The spoofed e-mails contained an attachment that, when clicked on, activated the computer's camera and took a picture of the computer user. It also took a snapshot of whatever was open on the desktop at the time and put it up on the server.

No fewer than 24 people had clicked on the attachment in the minutes leading up to the session, and the reactions were, in my client's words, "amazing." Speaking of the workshop participants, he said, "They hear about the dangers; they do phishing exercises; we tell them what they can and cannot click on, and they can't really contextualize it, but when you show them a picture of *them* opening up the attachment and whatever is open on their desktop, their jaws hit the floor. And they start getting it."

Sometimes, the best way to get buy-in is to let people *experience* the problem before you offer the solution. That's when actions truly speak louder than words.

Motivation and Purpose

There's no avoiding the fact that managers are dealing with the human animal when they marshal their troops for a mission. The emphasis here is on the word "animal," which indicates that despite our best intentions and evolved approach, we are dealing with very basic human needs and emotions. But when we understand these instinctive drives and default reactions, we are empowered to play to them in a way that can propel people toward buy-in.

Visionary leaders have long understood the need to emotionally connect with people in order to enlist them in a common goal. One of the most famous examples was developed over 400 years ago by Shakespeare, when he immortalized King Henry V's pep talk to a handful of English troops as they prepared to wage battle at Agincourt against 10,000 French soldiers. I analyzed Henry's St. Crispin's Day speech in detail in my book *Breakthrough Communication*, and the science appears to still hold true. Experienced veterans that Henry's soldiers were, they needed no instruction on how to wage war against a vastly larger enemy, but they *did* need meaning and purpose to keep them from turning on their heels. And the king delivered on that front in spades. Here's an excerpt from *Breakthrough Communication*:

> *It is midfall in the year 1415. Morning. King Henry looks out over his ragtag army, and even he is not sure if he and his soldiers can pull this one off. The mighty bluster of the French army can be heard not far off. Many of Henry's soldiers taste cold fear in their throats. Henry's own cousin, and one of his commanders, Westmoreland, remarks, "O that we now had here But one ten thousand of those men in England That do no work today!" It's a logical wish. A few more guys. Just to even the odds. And here is King Henry's brilliance, the moment when he takes just that fear, just that quite plausible wish, and turns it around into the fiery meaning that will ultimately steel his troops and make them follow him gloriously and unflinchingly into battle against the kingdom of France. No, says Henry, no more men. We have enough. "If we are marked to die, we are enough to do our country loss; and if to live, The fewer men, the greater share of honor."*
>
> *That's the meaning that Henry has injected into his current action: he is not asking his troops merely to pick a fight with a much bigger enemy. No. He is offering all present the chance to become legends, to leave the day, dead or alive, sheathed in honor. "I am not covetous for gold," Henry tells his assembled army, "But if it be a sin to covet honor, I am the most offending soul alive." No, he tells Westmoreland (and all else who may be similarly inclined), "wish not a man from England." In fact, the inspiring young king goes on to say, if anyone wants to leave, despite the numerical odds, he'll gladly let him go. In fact, he'll pay for the trip, "crowns for convoy put*

into his purse"! Because what remains will be a feast of honor, all the more honor to go around for those who stay and fight.

The St. Crispin's Day speech is justly celebrated and studied not just by actors and scholars, but by leaders in every field who want to create that spirit of bonhomie, the sense that "we're all in this together." But the speech does more than that. Shakespeare's Henry V exhorts his men to look beyond the battle to the fellowship they will share in glory: "Then shall our names, . . . Be in their flowing cups freshly remembered." Why do they fight, and to what end? Henry repeats that "But we in it shall be remembered—We few, we happy few, we band of brothers; For he today that sheds his blood with me Shall be my brother; . . ." The noble king, in tying his fate to those of his men, reminds them all that in binding themselves to one another, they bind themselves to the glory of England, now and forever.

Few of us will have the need or opportunity to deliver a St. Crispin's Day–type speech, but the good old-fashioned pep talk still has its place in the twenty-first century.

Laying out a vision and encouraging people to embrace it as their own is not confined to battlefields and packed auditoriums. Even a small office can benefit from a rousing speech by its leader. The content and delivery of such a speech will, of course, vary with the audience, but there are common elements to all effective motivational talks. Professors Jacqueline Mayfield and Milton Mayfield, who study "motivating language theory," have identified three key traits of an effective motivational speech. Such a speech is "uncertainty reducing," it is "empathic," and it is "meaning making." Each of these qualities, you'll note, addresses issues of psychological safety and purpose, and all require appeals to both reason and emotion.

As the Mayfields observe, "A good pep talk—whether delivered to one person or many—should include all three elements, but the right mix will depend on the context and the audience." Thus, *uncertainty-reducing language*, which includes direction, instructions, and performance standards, is the kind of nuts-and-bolts talk that you would emphasize if you're managing college interns or people new to a role. That kind of audience needs practical information on how to accomplish the stated goals.

Empathic language centers on concern for the employees—they need to feel you care about them. If you're staring down a hard deadline, for example, and need your employees to devote extra time to meet it, acknowledging the toll of long hours can assure them that their concerns are not being taken for granted. *Meaning-making language* links an individual's efforts to the larger organizational purpose—what Shakespeare's King Henry V was so expert at delivering on St. Crispin's Day. He didn't need to tell his soldiers *how* to fight, but *why* they fight. Therefore, if you're leading an experienced team into (metaphorical) battle, focus less on the practical and more on the purpose.

Motivating people is not just about delivering speeches, of course, but also about understanding what drives them. This is especially important in creating buy-in one by one. Do the individuals most desire status? Money? Creative control? Opportunities for personal and professional growth? Do they want to move up in the organization, or are they satisfied with their current position? Do they want to make an impact on the lives of others, or are they more concerned about their own happiness at work? Not all people have the same approach to their careers; your job as a manager is to figure out how to make those differences work for both you and them.

In considering those different approaches, psychologists Heidi Grant and E. Tory Higgins highlight the importance of *motivational focus*, or the primary driver of a person's behavior and goals. They identify two distinct types of motivational drives: "promotion focused" and "prevention focused." Those with a promotion focus "see their goals as creating a path to gain or advancement and concentrate on the rewards that will accrue when they achieve them. They are eager and they play to win." They are more likely to take chances and swing for the bleachers. They're fast workers and optimistic—which is great—but not always best at working through the details or coming up with alternative plans if their big idea doesn't pan out.

Prevention-focused workers, on the other hand, "worry about what may go wrong if they don't work hard enough or aren't careful enough. They are vigilant and play not to lose, to hang onto what they have, to maintain the status quo." These employees are meticulous and thus usually slower than their more high-flying colleagues and are less likely to dream up that big idea—but they are good at analyzing that big idea and figuring out how to make things work.

Few people are purely promotion or prevention focused, but most of us do lean one way or the other. For managers, knowing just which buttons to push to help others move toward shared goals can make a difference in how willing they are to do so.

Motivating people to adopt a shared goal or greater purpose is, in short, a tricky business. You can move a thousand people to cheers or tears with a great speech, but in order for it to take hold, there must be follow-through. For Henry V, the follow-through was the actual Battle of Agincourt; in the corporate world, follow-through means continuously working with teams and individuals and understanding how to motivate them to connect to a larger purpose.

Mind the Cultural Differences

The success of any effort to create buy-in depends in no small measure on the corporate culture and the drives of the people who work there. It also hinges on local culture and, specifically, on varying interpretations of *authority* and *decision making*. What works in the United States, the United Kingdom, and the Netherlands, for instance, may not work in China, Mexico, and Brazil.

INSEAD Professor Erin Meyer, who has worked with companies around the world, states that ignorance about a culture's approach to authority and decision making can easily damage international business relationships, presenting unique challenges to managers in charge of a globally dispersed workforce. Americans, for example, prefer an egalitarian approach to leadership, where employees at all levels are encouraged to contribute ideas and challenge one another's conclusions. In contrast, workers in China, Mexico, and Brazil are generally accustomed to a hierarchical structure in which leaders provide specific directions, with little interest in the perspectives of the rank and file.

Managers who are new to a global role and unaware of these not-so-subtle differences run the risk of diminishing their executive presence, not to mention causing frustration on both sides. As an example, Meyer points to a Chinese-American joint venture in which the American managers saw the Chinese workers as unwilling to think creatively and provide input, *Cultural difference* while the Chinese viewed the Americans as lazy and arrogant for not preparing proper directions in advance of work assignments. Counterintuitive as it may be, in certain cultures, trying to get buy-in from employees by soliciting their input may backfire and hurt your reputation.

It isn't just attitudes toward authority that differ. While you might expect that hierarchical cultures would also favor top-down decision making, Meyer notes that "on a worldwide scale, we find that hierarchies and decision-making methods are not always correlated." In the egalitarian United States, for example, decisions are made at the top but may be altered or adjusted as new information comes in. By contrast, in hierarchical Japan, decision making is consensual rather than top-down, meaning that the group comes to an agreement on an issue first, before a proposal is passed on for the same process to a more senior level. And while it may take time to reach that shared decision in a consensus-driven culture, once a decision has been made, it is virtually impossible to influence it afterward. The same applies to other consensual decision-making cultures that are hierarchical in terms of leadership, such as those of Germany and Belgium. In these cultures, a U.S. leader who is used to calling the shots may be in contravention of the norms of a workforce that very much expects to be an integral part of the decision-making process, and thereby may lose the respect of the workers.

These intercultural land mines are relatively easy to sidestep, provided one does a bit of preliminary research. Is everyone looking to the boss to make a final decision, or is the consensus of the team the deciding factor? The same sensitivity is required around attitudes toward leadership. In the hierarchical cultures of Germany and Japan, an employee would rarely question the boss's conclusions in a meeting, whereas in the egalitarian cultures of the United States and Australia, "speaking truth to power" is considered an important trait of executive presence.

For example, a U.S.-based automotive manufacturer I've worked with asked me to help develop the executive presence of one of its divisions' VP of engineering, who was Chinese. Specifically, his boss said, "I want him to challenge me more in meetings. I need his perspective on things." The American manager had sought to engage in productive debates with his

Chinese direct report because he valued his intelligence and expertise. But for the Chinese VP, who'd just recently been transferred from one of the company's factories in Beijing, this was a cultural barrier he had a hard time crossing. "In China you don't challenge your boss in meetings," he protested when I shared the boss's feedback with him.

To help the Chinese VP adjust his communication style, we practiced several ways he could tactfully challenge his boss's assumptions to make for more productive dialogue and brainstorming. Not only did the Chinese executive learn this new behavior, but as a corollary he also learned how to engage with *his* subordinates in the United States, speaking with individual stakeholders to get their input and seeking their buy-in before making any major decisions.

A concluding caveat: Although global cultural differences can be sizable and can sharply affect what approaches are the wisest in seeking to motivate people and secure their buy-in, it is also true that it generally works in our favor when employees feel their input is valued and the organization has a firm foundation of mutual trust.

Buy-in and Executive Presence

There are all kinds of articles available in all kinds of media on how to create buy-in. Some focus on getting others to go along with organizational change, or to choose a specific product, or to embrace a new idea, and they all emphasize, to a greater or lesser degree, how to sell that change, product, or idea. It's all about the pitch and the sale and the transaction—and these articles are not wrong to focus on how to get others to buy what you're selling.

What they don't say much about, however, is how to create buy-in in *you*.

This isn't an either-or proposition. One of the best ways to get others to believe in you and be willing to put themselves out there for you is to prove you can deliver results. But demonstrating that you're competent at your job is only one side of the buy-in coin; the other side is forging relationships with others so they trust you to lead them through whatever comes next. By engineering buy-in rather than banging people over the head with your ideas and expecting them to jump on board, you show a level of judgment, maturity, and confidence that one would expect from a leader.

In Chapter 6 we'll explore the power of strategic storytelling to help you establish your presence and to influence others at a deeper level as you move them toward your shared vision and objectives.

6

Mastering the Art of Storytelling for Personal and Professional Success

DEMONSTRATING VISION FOR the future—or describing the future with a story—is inarguably a trait no senior leader can do without. *Vision* is almost synonymous with leadership. After all, where do you want people to follow you, if not to a more promising tomorrow? And yet in my coaching work, I come across plenty of leaders who emphasize the technical aspects of their job over the need to tell a compelling story that conveys meaning, moves people to action, and keeps them engaged through the tough times. Convinced that storytelling is something best done in a place that has a happy hour and among a few friends, they arm themselves with steely analysis, technical minutiae, and data-packed slide decks they'll unleash in presentations that cause even the most left-brained engineers to scratch their heads—if they can stay awake long enough.

But it's also true that from the shop floor to the boardroom and many places in between, strategic storytelling to achieve an organizational goal is continuing to wedge its way into mainstream business practices. Why? Because a story can go where analysis is denied admission: the imagination. Cold hard facts can't inspire people to take part in a mission of change;

straightforward analysis won't get people excited about a goal unless you express it in a vision that fires the imagination and stirs the soul.

This is not new, of course; great leaders have always understood that the stories they tell are what spur people to launch themselves into battle for a greater cause and make the doldrums of daily life not just bearable, but an important part of the journey toward the vision.

Role models for this principle abound. One only has to watch video clips of IBM CEO Virginia Rometty or Cisco chief John Chambers in action—both leaders of technology companies who shun jargon and instead rally audiences with stories and down-to-earth substance and style.

Enticing followers with a more appealing future is only one of the many practical applications for storytelling, the utility of which can be traced back to the days when humans first started huddling together in small groups. As our fur- and leather-clad ancestors formed increasingly complex social orders and human bonds, they learned to track and make sense of interpersonal relationships by exchanging information with others through the narrative. Evolution thus has made storytelling part of our DNA. To support this point, consider an experiment in which Smith College psychologists F. Heider and M. Simmel demonstrated people's tendency to make up characters and narratives from almost anything they see around them. Showing the participants an animation of two triangles and a circle moving around a square, Heider and Simmel asked the observers what they saw. "The circle is chasing the triangles," people said, recounting the movements of the shapes as if they were part of a narrative with characters that had motives and intentions.

Subsequent research has confirmed the human tendency to think and make sense of the world in terms of stories.

A 2007 study by Jennifer Edson Escalas, a marketing researcher at Vanderbilt University, found that people had more positive reactions to advertisements that were presented in story form than to ads that were factually straightforward about the wares they were promoting.

The results of a different study, conducted a year earlier, can help astute managers frame information in such a way that it opens people's minds rather than closes them shut. In that study, researchers found that when information is labeled as fact, it is subjected to critical analysis and the apparent human tendency to want to make it wrong; but when the information is labeled as fiction, or as a story, people accept it more easily. Organizational leaders who are always pitching one audience or another are therefore encouraged to position their audience in story-receiving mode— as in "Let me give you an example" or "Imagine the following scenario"— before presenting new ideas. This approach should help lift listeners out of an analysis frame of mind that just makes them itch to prove you wrong.

Putting It in Context

Marketing guru Seth Godin makes the point for storytelling when he writes in his book *Meatball Sundae*: "People just aren't that good at remembering facts. When people do remember facts, it's almost always in context." And context *is* story. Context is about the people that are involved; it's about the background information that provides meaning; it's about the personal relevance we feel to the facts—whatever they may be. Often the more emotionally relevant the context, the better the recall. That's why we often clearly remember where we were and what we were doing during events of historic significance, such as 9/11 or certain presidential elections.

Let's say you want people to know that your organization prides itself on excellent customer service. Simply sharing this fact with the world would likely fall on deaf ears. That's because just about everyone makes this claim, and people have become cynical. It's probably one of the more brazen boasts companies make that often flies in the face of everyday reality. If you've ever been on hold with a company's customer service department for what seemed like an eternity while listening to an obnoxiously repeating message that goes something like, "Your call is important to us," then you know whereof I speak.

But even if a company in truth has great customer service, just stating that fact is not enough. Tony Hsieh, CEO of online retailer Zappos, says its customer service is great (which it is), but he also puts it in a *context* that stays with you. In one instance, speaking from a stage, Hsieh tells the story of a woman who'd ordered a pair of boots for her husband, only to contact Zappos shortly after, to arrange for the boots to be returned and to get a refund. Her husband, it turned out, had been killed in a car crash. As Hsieh tells it, after the refund was processed, the customer service rep sent a big bouquet to the woman and charged it to the company, without prior authorization. That's because—and this is the point—she didn't need one. Zappos's culture is such that employees have the autonomy to do "what's right" for the customer. While Zappos lost money on that transaction, the affection that rolled in from others who'd heard the story, including the widow's friends, helped reinforce Zappos's reputation as a company with a truly customer-oriented culture. What's more, this story has been discussed everywhere, from online forums to business school auditoriums. Context provides meaning and background that engages people in a way that facts and transactional details rarely can.

You can harness the power of context yourself, by painting a relatable picture that creates real meaning around your bullet points, by providing background that changes someone's perspective, and by making sure that there is an emotional element to it all.

People Love Drama

James does amazing at story-telling

An important aspect of executive presence is the ability to command attention, to draw in an audience, and to avoid the predictable snooze-fest that people have come to expect from business presentations. Aaron Sorkin, the famous screenwriter and producer who's behind such TV shows as *The West Wing* and such films as *A Few Good Men,* has a tip for his screenwriting students that I find applies just as much to storytelling executives. And that is to think about *intention* and *obstacle* as the driveshaft for a compelling story: "Somebody wants something; something's standing in their way of getting it." In Sorkin's words: "They want the money; they want the girl; they want to get to Philadelphia. . . . It doesn't matter." That is, it doesn't matter as long as they want it badly and the obstacle in their way is formidable.

Story telling on perseverance

Would you enjoy a movie where a few friends drive from New York to LA with the goal of making it there by Tuesday, and they do, with no trouble and with plenty of time to spare? Maybe that's how we want our real vacations to unfold, but not the ones we watch as entertainment. What we want from such a flick is for all kinds of things to go terribly wrong—from getting flat tires, to becoming lost, to being kidnapped, to being chased by bad guys, to getting the sense of "There's no way we're gonna make it in time" for the wedding, the funeral, or whatever. In other words, we want *formidable* obstacles, as Sorkin put it. Also, for the story to work, making it there by Tuesday can't be an option; it must be an imperative! Not making it by Tuesday—the *intention*—must have huge repercussions, or the obstacles on the way are just a laundry list of things to get through.

Robert McKee, a story consultant for television production companies, refers to this magic formula as the clash between a protagonist's subjective expectations and an uncooperative objective reality. And this is not unlike what business leaders face in the daily battle with competitors and other market forces that stand in the way of accomplishing organizational goals. This fact means that CEOs should have plenty of raw material from which to fashion compelling stories.

Why do well-crafted stories engage us so much? The answer is in our brain chemistry. By measuring the brain activity of people watching a gripping movie, neuroeconomist Paul Zak discovered that the tension created during a narrative (via intention and obstacle) results in increased attention and focus, whereby adrenaline and dopamine are released into the bloodstream. This explains the increased heartbeat and sweaty palms we experience when Tom Cruise is dangling off the landing gear of a descending aircraft with one hand while frantically dialing a number on his mobile with the other. Zak's lab has also found that character-driven narratives with a strong emotional element cause the brain to create oxytocin, the chemical responsible for feelings of trust and empathy. If you've ever walked out of the theater feeling you *are* James Bond, that is the oxytocin talking. From an experiential standpoint, a good story is really the next best thing to being there.

Matching Your Story to Business Purpose

The fact that people are wired to react so strongly to stories should motivate business leaders to develop their storytelling skills. But what business situations call for a story?

You might have guessed the answer—it *depends*. It depends on both the situation and what you'd like to accomplish in the situation. The situation might be a staff meeting where you're introduced to the people

Connect story to business

on your new team, for example. As their new boss, your objective might be to get them to like and respect you and to start dismantling the barriers of mistrust and uncertainty. Another situation might be that members of your team have lost enthusiasm for their work, and your objective is to restore their engagement and give them purpose, so they understand the "why" of what they're spending most of their waking hours doing. Or maybe valuable members of your team feel unappreciated or don't get the credit they deserve. In that situation, your objective may be to reinforce or highlight certain norms and behaviors with your stories and to draw positive attention to them.

Below are three *types* of stories that every leader should master. My hope is that they inspire readers to dig deeper into this topic and to identify and cultivate potential stories that can help you accomplish important objectives.

1. Stories We Tell Ourselves

We constantly assemble bits and pieces of information of what we observe around us and automatically turn them into stories that tend to reinforce our long-developed beliefs. If those stories are positive ones—you admire a colleague and tend particularly to notice the admirable things she does, you pride yourself on your own punctuality and pat yourself on the back whenever you find yourself (again!) to be the first person to show up at a meeting—these perspectives are often uplifting and empowering.

The problem comes when we tell ourselves negative stories. For instance, if I feel that the people around me are lazy and incompetent, the stories I create will be based on morsels of data that "confirm" that belief. Or if I feel that I don't measure up to others' expectations, the stories I create will reinforce this self-assessment, prominently featuring my mistakes, my failures, and others' expressions of disappointment in me. And so a vicious loop is created where negative perceptions—including of the self—determine the stories we tell ourselves, which in turn play out in full color to reinforce these perceptions.

Clearly these aren't productive narratives, nor do they serve the people and organizations we lead. And while I'm aware that years of cognitive behavioral therapy may sometimes be the most effective solution to modify such beliefs-and-values–powered narratives, I'd like to suggest that we have the option to intervene any time we recognize (self-awareness!) the unproductive nature of the stories we tell ourselves.

One young client I had came from a highly ambitious family where academic achievement was highly valued. During his undergraduate years at an Ivy League university, grades lower than an A+ were typically subject to stern rebuke by both parents and other credentialed members of his extended family. "He didn't apply himself enough" and "He'll bring shame to the family" were the kind of accusations lobbed at him during those "tough love" sessions. Little surprise then that over time he developed impossibly high standards for himself, suffering blow after blow to his confidence whenever he fell short of his, not to mention others', expectations. He felt like a loser who just didn't measure up. When he got accepted to a top-rated MBA program, the story he told himself was not one of accomplishment and optimism. Instead, he worried himself sick about failing and letting everyone down. He became a client right around that time, and one of the first things we did was to restructure the negative narratives he told himself about his academic future. We replaced his micro-stories of "I'll never be able to manage the workload" and "I'm going to fail" with more positive narratives like "This education will be a major asset for my future" and "I don't have to get As to succeed."

Remember the framestorming exercise in Chapter 3 on emotion-regulation strategies? That's how we developed my client's more productive narratives. In fact, we created 30 positive stories to replace the negative ones, and from those reframings I had him select the three stories that would motivate him the most. The challenge for him was keeping his focus on these aspirational stories; his old "wiring," which had been strengthened over many years, was thick and strong. But as we know from neuroscience research, that to which we attend becomes stronger in our brain. So while it was natural for his long-acquired belief system to serve up the self-flagellating stories whenever he thought about school, his relentless focus on the more productive narratives eventually changed his brain's neural network. Over time, this new circuitry, accentuating the positive, became the default option.

To get to that critical point, the moment the old negative stories started to play, my client knew to "change the channel" and tune in to one of the more productive ones. Eventually, these new stories increased his confidence to the point where he was able to build strong and rewarding relationships with his colleagues.

A different example illustrates how the stories we tell ourselves can impact an entire organization—especially when the storyteller is the boss. Responding to a question about his leadership style, Pedro Pizarro, CEO of utility giant Edison International, told the *New York Times* that he's not the type of leader who sees himself as the hub of the metaphorical wheel, with employees as the spokes, waiting to receive information from him. Instead, he sees himself as the rim, *not* the center, of the wheel. He explained, "My job is to keep the spokes together, keep the team together and really help that team perform because they, collectively, are going to have a lot more insights than I will. It also means that when you have to go through mud, the rim goes in first. But that's the way it should be."

It's clear that the stories we tell ourselves have an impact not just on our own behavior, but also on our engagement with others and in turn on their perceptions of us as leaders, colleagues, and partners. By carefully examining our dominant narratives and making sure they contribute positive value to our and others' lives, we're one step closer to wielding real influence with the power of storytelling.

2. Stories We Tell Others About Ourselves

Whether you are a leader joining a new team, or a job candidate in the first round of interviews, or someone meeting a potential new client for the first time, the stories you tell about yourself often set the tone for how the relationship will unfold, *if* it does, that is. Which are the *right* stories in such scenarios? It's hard to go wrong with stories that illustrate your humility, good judgment, integrity, and expertise and experience. As for what to emphasize, putting yourself firmly into the shoes of your audience should provide clues. The needs and expectations of the people in your audience will, of course, vary, depending on the context of the meeting and their future goals as they involve you. In Chapter 1, I laid out my suggestions for making powerful first impressions by communicating warmth, strength, and value.

I would suggest you also focus on stories that illustrate the values you know are important to your audience.

For instance, if you are the new boss meeting the members of your team for the first time, you know they'll wonder about your leadership style and how you'll treat them. Acknowledge this and share a personal story or two that show you empathize—maybe from when you met *your* boss for the first time. Mention the lessons you've learned in managing others and make sure to highlight any mistakes from which you've grown. Share examples of how you've navigated new cultures in the past—organizational or regional—and what you're hoping to learn in this next stage with their help. This shows humility, humanizes you, and reduces the power distance that can hamper the open and honest dialogue that builds trust.

If your audience—whether a group or an individual—is looking to engage you for your expertise, share stories that illustrate how you've delivered results or solved similar problems for others. Mention the challenges you encountered along the way and how you met them successfully—even if it took a few attempts to get it right. This is also an elegant way to share your strengths without bragging about your accomplishments.

When others want to get to know us, they aren't just looking for the content on our LinkedIn profile. They want to know the *real* us to determine whether we're trustworthy and whether associating with us will be of positive or negative value to them. That's why recruiters and hiring managers no longer have qualms about digging into our social media profiles and online musings to evaluate our reputation and our judgment.

And judgment is key whenever we share personal information. Faulty judgment can result in some awkward moments if not lasting reputational harm.

One of the several executives I've coached at a global insurance firm had recently joined its headquarters. Over coffee, this executive, an HR leader, casually shared with me how he typically introduces himself to colleagues at the beginning of a new assignment. From years of travel to exotic places with his partner, he had assembled the mother of all PowerPoint presentations: In one slide the couple might be riding elephants in Bali, in another picnicking in the middle of the Moroccan desert, and in another lounging on top of a parked Land Rover as they surveyed the Kenyan wilderness with their binoculars. He'd present these slide decks after a quick introduction to the team, presumably with the idea that "a picture is worth a thousand words." I saw one of these presentations myself, and what makes this a cautionary tale is three specific elements that struck me as reputational kryptonite:

1. In each picture (there were hundreds), the couple wore matching tuxedos, sported aviator sunglasses, and always had fully filled champagne flutes in hand—even on the back of the elephants in Bali. Aside from hitting your colleagues over the head with how cool you are and all the amazing vacations you can afford, you're also sending the message that you are way, *way* better than they are. Strike one!

2. Also in the pictures, native guides and locals in their dusty everyday garb were positioned around the tux-wearing gents like extras in a movie—sans smiles, which gave the whole thing an awkward colonial feel. Especially in an egalitarian society like the United States, this blatant juxtaposition of Western privilege with local poverty is sure to elicit groans and eye rolls under the cover of a darkened conference room. Strike two!

3. The show was 20 minutes long. I don't think—no, I *know*—that I wouldn't sit through anyone's vacation slides for more than 5 minutes, let alone a relative stranger's. Plus, a lengthy presentation devoted to your wealth, good taste, and all-around fabulousness is sure to irritate even the most congenial souls. Strike three!

So this storytelling strategy had all the makings of a reputational disaster. The HR manager hoped this glimpse into his life would present him as interesting and someone that people would enjoy being around, but it didn't. When I asked him what reactions he'd typically get to these introductions, he shrugged and said, "Mixed, surprisingly. Some really seem to like it, while others seem to tune out." I later learned that his introductions had led many of his colleagues to find him pompous, arrogant, out of touch, and quirky. Only after a sobering 360-degree multirater feedback assessment did he understand that his intentions were not at all what came across, which eventually allowed him to radically adjust his presentation.

Faulty judgment in personal stories isn't always this glaring. But if you are unsure of how your stories might land, run them first by people you trust. In the end, with personal stories less is more and humility is better.

3. Stories We Tell Our Teams or Organizations

I opened this chapter by pointing out the type of storytelling that is intrinsic to successful leadership—the ability to tell compelling stories of the future, to articulate a vison, to both internal and external audiences. Leaders need to master another kind of story too—this kind is about *organizational values*.

Earlier, to illustrate the concept of context, I recounted Tony Hsieh's story about Zappos's outstanding customer service culture. This story is also an example of a multipurpose one—that is, a story that can furnish different takeaways to different audiences. Investors and potential customers, for instance, learn from this story who the company is, which may influence how they will engage with the company. But when told to employees, Hsieh's story conveys what the expected norms of corporate behavior are, and it does so without having to explicitly spell them out in an employee manual or post them in random sequence on a cafeteria wall. The former would actually be a monumental task, as the authors of such a manual would have to predict all kinds of circumstances in order to prescribe the proper rules of conduct: "If a customer's family member for whom a particular product was purchased passes away before being able to enjoy said product, it is permissible for a customer service agent to purchase and send flower arrangements to said customer in value up to USD 75.00 to be charged to the organization without the requirement of prior authorization from a manager." This type of manual would make *War and Peace* seem like a pamphlet. Instead, all that the company's leaders have to do is share the shoe-return story with their employees, who will know exactly what to do on a case-by-case basis: Do what's right for the customer.

Whatever the management goal, there are storytelling strategies that can help further it. A former Facebook director of engineering, Bobby Johnson, once saw the need for a cultural shift in the company's infrastructure team. Although many of his engineers were drawn to exciting new projects and innovations, Johnson knew that other Facebook engineers, the ones who worked behind the scenes to ensure that the existing systems ran faster and better than before, also did critical work. He wanted to highlight these "unsung heroes," both to honor them and to get more engineers interested in their less glamorous but nonetheless essential work. To accomplish this, he would take every opportunity—in one-on-ones, in meetings, and in group e-mails—to share stories of important fixes that these day-to-day engineers made and to publicly praise them.

Similarly, if you want people to speak up more in meetings and challenge each other, share a story of how a lone dissenting voice was able to change your mind about a decision you'd made, and how this wouldn't have happened if the person hadn't felt comfortable in challenging you. Or if you want to increase collaboration among teams, share a story about two teams who decided to join forces and whose combined creativity and brainpower led to important breakthroughs for the organization. And if it's courage and risk taking you want to promote, highlight stories of risk-taking colleagues—and include their failures, to make the point that learning from mistakes is just another way forward.

As you can see, the formula is simple. Decide which values you want to promote and which behaviors you want to encourage, and then make those traits the themes of your stories, and include characters who demonstrate the desired traits. Do these stories have to be true? It helps if they are, and it's even better if your audience knows the protagonists. However, hypothetical scenarios can pack just as big a punch, as we've learned from neuroscience research and our own experiences from the myriad of stories that surround us.

Four Storytelling Techniques to Convey Complex Ideas Simply and Persuasively

Not everyone is a natural raconteur. And that's fine, if you keep these three principles in mind: People need to *feel* something for your story to have an impact. The story must be easy to follow and stripped of unnecessary detail. And finally, because focus is a scarce resource in the brain and attention spans are dwindling, the quicker you get to the point the better.

Here are a few techniques to help you put these principles into practice.

Technique 1: Make It Personal

Trial lawyers are among the best storytellers, and the late Moe Levine of New York was one of the greatest. Levine was able to use emotion in the summation of a case to such devastating effect that the result was the award of one of the largest verdicts in the history of New York State. Levine represented a man who had lost both arms in an accident. When the trial was coming to a close, everyone present, from the defendants to the judge to the opposing counsel, anticipated a long speech from Levine about the travails of a life with no arms. However, he surprised everyone. His concluding argument lasted no longer than a minute or two. It wasn't its brevity that won the day for his client. Its real power lay in his making personal what everyone knew yet no one had thought about. Here's what he said, as reported by Texas trial lawyer Howard Nations:

> *Your Honor, eminent counsel for defense, ladies and gentlemen of the jury: as you know, about an hour ago we broke for lunch. And I saw the bailiff came and took you all as a group to have lunch in the jury-room. And then I saw the defense attorney, Mr. Horowitz, and his client decided to go to lunch together. And the judge and the court clerk went to lunch. So, I turned to my client, Harold, and said why don't you and I go to lunch together, and we went across the street to that little restaurant and had lunch.*

He then took a significant pause before resuming:

> *Ladies and gentlemen, I just had lunch with my client. He has no arms. He eats like a dog! Thank you very much.*

And then he sat down. The lesson: Any time you want to emphasize a particularly strong point, simply make the human connection in an understated way. Avoid weakening the drama of your story with long-winded verbiage. As in Levine's summation, let the audience's imagination deliver the biggest punch.

Technique 2: Keep It Short

A story attributed to Ernest Hemingway (however, there's no proof of a connection) goes something like this: Hemingway was sitting at lunch with a few fellow authors when he bet the group that he could write a story in as few as six words. "Impossible," his friends said, accepting the bet. After everyone's money was on the table, Hemingway scribbled six words on a napkin: "For Sale: Baby shoes; never worn."

The others promptly pushed their coins in Hemingway's direction.

For a story to work, it has to take you somewhere in your imagination. It has to make a clear point. But it doesn't have to be long, as this anecdote shows. In fact, stories told for strategic purposes in business and the professions should be as brief as possible while still meeting their objective. TED Talks are a good example. These presentations, on just about any topic, are by design no longer than 20 minutes, with many of them less than 15. And they typically include several stories within the allotted time frame that serve as context for the speaker's key message.

Here's a fail-safe way to make sure your stories are short and sweet: Prepare versions of varying lengths. Write out the longest version first and see how much time it would take you to tell it. (People speak at about a rate of 150 to 180 words per minute, though this doesn't include the beats necessary for dramatic pausing or speeding up.) Now start cutting detail from your story. Go from a 5-minute version to a 3-minute version and see what happens. Does the story still make sense? Ask others for their takeaway; does the leaner version work? Next, cut it down to 1 minute—then see if you can do a 30-second version of the story without sacrificing the overall message. You'll be surprised how often even very short versions still accomplish the job. Condensing stories in this way will also wean you from adding too much detail to your stories that adds zero meaning and may also distract listeners from your primary point.

Technique 3: Pick a Theme

We're all consumers of advertising, and effective advertisements communicate in themes. A clever theme frames a story in just the way you want it perceived. How about this successful theme from the Las Vegas Tourism

Board? "What Happens in Vegas Stays in Vegas." What type of stories come to mind when you hear this? That theme gives all of them an unmistakable meaning. How about this one: "The Truth Is Out There." That was the theme for the ultra-successful TV series *The X-Files*, and it guided our understanding that each story in the series was about mysteries that needed to be solved.

Themes, in a sense, are simplifiers. Again, we can learn from the trial lawyers. In order to communicate a deluge of data as simply as possible to a jury—an audience of laypeople who are neither accustomed to legal jargon nor necessarily equal to the attorneys in their ability to grasp and process new information—trial lawyers often frame their case as one central theme. In so doing, these lawyers are simultaneously guiding the jury to think about the case in a certain way. "This case is clearly about corporate greed versus consumer safety" might be such a theme. Guess who the lawyer's client is? Not the corporation obviously—and every bit of evidence the lawyer introduces and every story line the lawyer presents will tie back to the theme of "corporate greed," making it the lens through which the jury will view all the evidence if the lawyer is successful.

A smart central theme transcends the story and gives it greater meaning. Think about what meaning you'd like your audience to take away from your stories—whether you're running a business meeting or a political campaign—and pick a theme that crystallizes that point. Some examples of business and political themes are:

- "David Versus Goliath"
- "Phoenix Rising from the Ashes"
- "The Customer Is King"
- "Our Secret Weapon"
- "The Turning Point"
- "Thriving in Chaos"
- "They Said It Couldn't Be Done"
- "From Underdog to Top Dog"
- "Our Employees Are Family"
- "Teamwork in Action"
- "Breaking New Ground"
- "Blazing the Trail"

- "No Risk, No Reward"
- "Better Together"
- "It's the Economy, Stupid" (James Carville's famous line from Bill Clinton's first presidential campaign)

The options are endless. There are virtually no new themes for stories, just fresh interpretations of countless classic themes that have stood the test of time. If you struggle with your own theme, bestselling book titles can provide powerful inspiration for fitting your stories with a powerful frame that makes your message "sticky."

Technique 4: Use Drama to Make It Stick

Whether you are still aspiring to leadership or you are already there, sharing knowledge with others is a key requirement at any level of responsibility. Stories are an effective tool to accomplish this sharing, but as we've learned by now, it takes the *right* kind of story to have the most impact.

Although it would make sense that a story highlighting how people made good decisions and solved problems can teach an audience how to do likewise, academic research says the opposite: In stories, we can increase the effectiveness of training and development by focusing on the errors and poor decision making. In one study, researchers found that firefighters who experienced mistake-riddled training scenarios not only paid more attention to the training and retained the information better, but vastly improved their judgment and displayed more adaptive thought processes than did those who got straight "how-to" training.

The key to success with such a story is not only to show how things went wrong but to discuss what actions could have been taken to avoid the negative consequences. In other words, a type of reverse engineering of how things unfolded with the pros and cons mulled over, analyzed, and advocated or rejected by your peers can have tremendous benefits.

In an article in the journal *Occupational Hazards*, Elaine Cullen, the chief of health communication at the National Institute for Occupational Safety and Health's Spokane Research Laboratory, says this about storytelling in various blue-collar professions: "You learn by working with someone who knows how to do your job. You are an apprentice. You are mentored." She goes on to say, "When an experienced miner sees a new hire doing something really stupid, he often steps in and says, 'Let me tell you a story. I had a new hand do something like that before . . .' and he goes on to detail some negative consequence ranging from injury to death."

This type of cautionary storytelling to share knowledge and teach effective behaviors can easily be transferred from the coal mines and the fire station to Wall Street. There, freshly minted MBAs learn from case studies what caused financial juggernauts like Bear Stearns and Lehman Brothers to go down in flames and their officers to be immortalized in Wall Street history as reckless, inept, and hopelessly greedy.

How Language Creates Reality

In his durable article "The Myth of the Rhetorical Situation," my longtime friend Towson University Distinguished Professor Richard Vatz explores the power of language and its ability to affect perception. This article was published in 1973 but is just as relevant and controversial today. Vatz wrote the article as a counterargument to another theoretician, Lloyd Bitzer, who argued that events and reality unambiguously dictate meaning, from which language and interpretations automatically follow. In other words, meaning is inherent in reality. Whatever is said about reality merely describes that meaning.

While this may seem obvious to many, Vatz argues that it's not so straightforward. According to Vatz, meaning is *not* inherent in events. Language does *not* reflect an objective "reality" accurately. Instead, language *creates* reality. The world is complex, bewildering, and largely abstract. Language takes these abstractions and turns them into concrete concepts. In a very real way, language leads to reality, not the other way around.

As Vatz points out, although we encounter certain events through personal observation—such as hunger, cold, and rain—for the most part "we learn of facts and events through someone's communicating them to us." Thus, the people who describe the events not only shape how we perceive those events; they decide whether we perceive them at all. This is significant, because, as Vatz says, "The world is a scene of inexhaustible events which all compete to impinge on . . . our sliver of reality." This is where spin comes into play.

Spin is the art of finding the context and the facts that support one's version of the story. Vatz states that every "communicator is involved in this sifting and choosing, whether it be the newspaper editor choosing front-page stories versus comic-page stories or the speaker highlighting facts about a person in a eulogy."

Consider a eulogy. We've all done good things as well as some things we're not proud of. We've had shining moments, embarrassing moments, and regrettable moments. A kind eulogizer usually interprets this mass of information in a way that is favorable to the deceased. But imagine how a hostile eulogizer might interpret the same life. Most of us certainly have made enough mistakes in our lives to fill up a 15-minute speech. Vatz's point is that the "reality" of a person is shaped by the words the speaker chooses.

In the next section you get to practice the art of spin yourself. You'll gain even more clarity on how perceptions of reality are created with the careful selection of the language with which you tell your stories.

Practicing the Art of Spinning Stories

For this part of the chapter, I'd like you to try one of my favorite exercises in persuasive language, an assignment I learned about from Vatz, who has been assigning this project to his students for over 30 years.

Interesting

First, choose an opinion article in the popular press, such as a book review, a movie review, a music review, a restaurant review, or something else along those lines. Then rewrite the article from a different perspective, reversing the essence of its position.

Here are the rules:

- **You may not change the facts of the article.** You may only reverse the subjective opinions of the article. For example, if the original negative review says a long-running movie "seemed to drag on forever," you cannot say that the movie was short. However, in your positive rewrite you can say, "Even at two and a half hours, the movie easily managed to hold my attention."

- **The changes must be relevant to the material of the review.** For example, in changing a positive restaurant review to a negative review, it would not be relevant to add that you were allergic to one of the dishes you tasted.
- **The changes must be plausible, reasonable, and substantial.** Don't just add the word "not" to make an affirmative sentence negative. The best revised articles will be the ones you easily can imagine picking up and reading, probably in the same place where you found the original article.
- **The viewpoint must be consistent.** If a negative original concedes a positive point, in your rewrite the same point must be made even more positive. For example, if the original movie review says, "The only bright spot was a workmanlike performance on the part of so-and-so," the revised review should take it up a notch with something like "One of the most inspiring parts of the film was so-and-so's masterful performance."
- **Quotations can be eliminated or truncated.** But you may not subvert the intended meaning or change the words. That is, if you choose an article that already has a positive or negative quotation in it, you cannot change the words of the speaker. However, as we saw earlier in this chapter, trimming the quotation may alter the speaker's intended meaning vastly. For example, if a speaker is quoted as saying that a particular restaurant "falls flat occasionally but overall offers an excellent dining experience," it would be acceptable to trim this quote down to its negative part—"falls flat."

Try this exercise on one or both of the two articles below, which were chosen by Vatz's students. Their "answers" are given below, but no peeking! Instead, practice these new skills by following the directions above.

Example 1: Roberta Smith, "Tate Modern's Rightness Versus MoMA's Wrongs," *New York Times*, November 1, 2006, p. E1.

But Tate Modern appears to have worked out many of its kinks. It is using its limitations to its advantage and evolving into a people's palace that the art world can also love.

The lessons of Tate Modern challenge a lot of conventional wisdom, at least that expressed in many American museums these days. Most important, Tate Modern's huge building proves that being big is not the same as being corporate: it is possible to have a large institution feel personal to its visitors.

Tate Modern is an enormously user-friendly place, physically comfortable and hospitable, with inexpensive places to eat and frequent opportunities to sit. Snack bars, restrooms, elevators, escalators and stairways are all conveniently grouped together in the core of the building.

Example 2: Bianca Sienra, "Catch the Wave," *Baltimore Magazine*, October 2006, p. 219.

It was probably a bad idea to have filled up so quickly on breads and accompaniments. The endless tapas menu is full of items we really wanted to try. So we bravely forged on and ordered our second round. An excellent version of tortilla Espanola—that wonderful omelet of potatoes and onions universal in Spanish tapas bars—was velvety and fluffy and rich with butter. Stuffed piquillo peppers were bursting with goat cheese and duxelle, and lay in a tomato sauce that gave an acid boost to the sweet, savory peppers.

When you've done one or both rewrites, compare your results with the rewrites below that were done by Vatz's students. Each of them received an A.

Example 1 Rewrite

But Tate Modern continues to be plagued by some of these kinks and has been forced to evolve into a largely pedestrian audience, with little support from the art community.

The failures of Tate Modern are ones that could have easily been avoided if the designers had investigated the conventions American museums hold dear. The titan feel of the building itself has eradicated all opportunity for a personal or intimate experience by museum-goers.

Tate Modern seems at times to have dumbed itself down for the rainy day museum visitors, emphasizing seating and inexpensive food over an awe-inspiring collection. Snack bars, elevators, and escalators are the main attractions, as they are prominently on display in the center of the facility.

Example 2 Rewrite

If one dares to go to this restaurant, it might be a good idea to fill up on the breads, because what comes after will quickly douse their appetite. While the tapas menu has a lot to offer, there were few items that seemed genuinely appealing. However, my guest and I bravely forged on and ordered the next course. The tortilla Espanola, a traditional omelet of potatoes and onions—a staple in Spanish tapas bars—was drowning in butter with such a creamy taste that it was hard to swallow. The stuffed piquillo peppers had way too much goat cheese and duxelle so that the tomato sauce it lay in tasted acidic, and the peppers gave way to a sweet taste that contradicted the theme of the platter.

If you want to flex your persuasive muscles a little more, try this exercise on a "hard news" article, rewriting it from a different perspective. This is a much more challenging task because these articles usually do not state an opinion; they're supposed to be as objective as possible. However, after close examination of a few news articles on the same topic, I think you'll begin to see how bias can operate even when no opinion is stated. Look for how the title is phrased, whose perspective the article seems to follow, which persons or entities are depicted as the subjects (conducting the major actions), and which persons or entities are depicted as the objects of those actions.

The power of storytelling has been with us since the dawn of time, and despite our reliance on all things digital—indeed, because of it—it will remain the heart and soul of an organization. Your executive presence is strengthened by the stories you tell, and your skill in strategic storytelling can help propel you and your organization to new heights, new markets, and new opportunities.

In Chapter 7 you'll learn more strategies and techniques to influence people's attitudes and behaviors so that you can create mutual success and gain the respect you need as a leader.

7

Influence

The Secrets to Changing Behaviors and Attitudes

WHETHER YOU ARE the CEO of a Fortune 500 company or the manager of a small group of direct reports, there are few skills more critical than being able to influence others' attitudes and behaviors.

We face the constant need to adjust to changing market conditions: innovation and disruption, new trends, consumer preferences, and government regulations, not to mention competition that never rests. Particularly for business leaders whose job it is to sell these changes to their teams, the ability to influence attitudes and behaviors in support of a new strategy or evolving critical objective is anchored in recognizing the difference between persuasion and manipulation. Confuse the latter with the former, and you may find yourself going it alone.

Persuasion Without Manipulation: Recognizing Attempts at Manipulation in Yourself and Others

From the moment we were born, we have been schooled in the art and science of manipulation, so much so that we hardly recognize it, whether we are its targets or its purveyors. It doesn't take a cynic to see that such ploys surround us at every turn, ranging from a daily onslaught of advertising to organizational politics.

Of course, manipulation is a form of persuasion in that the avoidance of negative consequences serves the needs of the target audience. "You get to keep your job" is a tried-and-true example of an effective manipulative strategy to anyone bothering to ask, "What's in it for me?" However, the key difference between manipulation and persuasion, one that differentiates successful cultures from toxic ones, is that manipulation is almost always a short-term strategy that is destined to self-destruct unless even stronger forms of manipulation are employed in the future. In the short term a manipulative strategy may yield results that justify the means, at least in the mind of the manipulator. But if that's your modus operandi, consider changing it in favor of ethical influencing methods that build respect for you instead of corroding it.

Manipulation is all about getting people to do something for you regardless of their interests. The magic pill of the art of persuasion, conversely, is to get others to take action that benefits them and also serves the needs of the persuader. In other words, while manipulation is inwardly focused, persuasion is a win-win proposition, an outward, connecting approach to exerting influence.

The fundamental element and criterion of effective and _ethical persuasion_ is _trust._ Manipulators are heard, but persuaders are believed because they are trusted. Without trust, an audience wonders, What are the consequences of compliance or resistance? With trust, however, they may open their minds and give your message every chance to resonate. Trust is the mortar that builds teamwork, whereas manipulation is the jackhammer that tears it down. Manipulation is destined to expose itself as such and quickly breeds contempt when the reality of it kicks in. People who are manipulated try to find ways to survive, sometimes to get even, and those goals rarely align with the goals of the team. In the short term, manipulation may work, but for the wrong reasons: People are seeking an escape from negative consequences rather than feeling engaged in contributing value to a common goal. They may react with fear rather than with passion. And if it isn't fear, there are plenty of other types of resistance that will eventually derail your best-laid plans, such as competing loyalties or naked self-interest. The win-win approach of persuasion, in contrast, will pay dividends long after the task or window of opportunity has passed.

When we understand the difference between manipulation and persuasion, we can recognize it in our own experience on both the receiving and the dispensing ends. So if your self-awareness tells you that the outcome only serves *one* of the parties, you know something's off.

There are several telltale markers of manipulation:

- Is the incoming information (outgoing if you are the sender of the data) based on solid reasoning or on the fact that the presenter is carrying a big metaphorical stick? Are emotions being appealed to, and is the specific emotion fear or positive anticipation?
- Are there alternatives on the table? To what degree is the recipient (perhaps you) being given latitude to choose a path, and is the path of least resistance the optimal choice in light of the consequences?
- What does the presenter gain from the logical choice? What does the other party gain? Who wins here, and at what cost?
- Do you trust the source of the information or choice being presented to you? If you are the presenter, why should you be trusted?

Once you make a conscious effort to keep others' interests in mind along with your own as you pursue your objectives, your leadership upside becomes unlimited. You'll never reach your potential alone, and in the end those who rely on manipulation often seem to find themselves in precisely that position.

What Makes People Change Their Behaviors, Attitudes, and Beliefs?

The answer to this $64,000 question can unlock doors, win contracts, and sell ideas to both the front lines and the highest levels. Because influencing attitudes and behaviors is at the core of what any manager or leader does, it pays to revisit a little Psychology 101.

Ex) Give a cookie... then ask for help

We casually use terms such as "attitude" in daily conversations with others, often without realizing that a clear understanding of the word might help us understand others a little better. We say, "Lisa has the worst attitude today" or "This attitude isn't going to get you anywhere." A common question we hear or ask is, "What's with the attitude?" We praise people directly and indirectly by saying, "Phil has shown a great attitude on this project." We use the word "attitude" interchangeably with concepts such as mood, behavior, and demeanor. It helps to know that attitudes are more than just fleeting moods or a range of behaviors people display on a whim. Attitudes, as psychology defines them, are the positive or negative evaluations people make about other people, ideas, events, objects, and messages.

Test yourself for a moment: What do you think about the new customer management software your chief information officer introduced? Do you like your office door closed, or do you prefer to work in an open environment where you can hear and see others around you? How do you feel about working overtime? What do you think about the new project you've been given to head up? What about the team you're in charge of? What do you think about conservatives, about progressives?

Whether any of this pertains specifically to you or not, you can see that you probably would have something to say about these or any other questions you could be asked. The sum of your responses constitutes your attitude, which psychologists sort into three conceptual baskets: cognitive (our thinking), emotional (how we feel about something), and behavioral (the actions we display).

Here's an example of a person's attitude that includes all three elements in the order listed above:

> *Paul believes that his lack of a postgraduate degree is holding him back in his career at his current company. He feels inferior whenever his MBA- and PhD-holding peers question his ideas and proposals. Whenever he can, he avoids presentations to this group and delegates the task to someone else.*

Before we can learn to influence or change a person's attitude and behavior, we need to understand one additional quality of attitudes: They have dimensions. Not all attitudes are equally strong, equally top of the mind, or strictly positive or negative. Here's an example:

> *Russell believes that outsourcing to offshore countries is bad for the U.S. economy and that it takes jobs away from Americans. Whenever he calls a customer service center and detects a foreign accent in the rep, he immediately feels anger, and his behavior toward that service rep shows it. Susan, like Russell, doesn't believe in outsourcing but understands why many manufacturers and service providers use lower-cost offshore companies for administrative tasks and customer service centers. In fact, her evaluations of the practice are ambivalent and equally negative and positive. When speaking to someone in India about upgrading her cable service, she barely notices the accent and doesn't feel strongly about it, and her behavior toward the service rep is not affected.*

By understanding the three components of attitude as well as its varying dimensions, we are much better equipped to influence someone's attitude in productive ways. In Paul's case, for instance, you might try to expand his beliefs, and show him how his highly specialized subject-matter knowledge more than compensates for his lack of credentials, empowering him to feel on more equal footing with his better-educated colleagues and thus to present his ideas with confidence.

The Delicate Mix of Science and Art in Changing Attitudes

To build our executive presence by flexing how we influence others, it pays to look to the social sciences for several useful theories and principles we can learn and apply immediately.

Learning Theory

Leaders who understand learning principles such as classical conditioning, operant conditioning, and observational learning can use their knowledge to influence others' behavior and create win-win situations. Here's how to use those three principles to have a positive impact on attitudes and behaviors:

- **Classical conditioning.** If you employ the classic conditioning method, you can affect the way a person feels and influence that person to form a positive attitude toward you. For instance, leaders who strive to appear approachable and engage people in a warm and respectful manner are, in effect, conditioning them to feel psychologically safe, trusting, and forthcoming with new ideas and feedback. In that sense, simply hearing the leader's name in conversation would prompt them to comment favorably without the leader needing to be present. Contrast that with a leader whose mere presence sends people running for an empty conference room for fear of being criticized, humiliated, or worse. The second leader has conditioned colleagues with communication and behaviors that negatively impact engagement and productivity, not to mention detract from the leader's influence and positive executive presence.

- **Operant conditioning.** Another powerful way to influence someone's attitude is by both being aware of and managing your response to that person's expressed attitude. Let's say Victoria, a direct report of yours, asks you to give her feedback on her recent presentation to the executive committee. Your comments, both positive in terms of what worked and constructive in terms of what would help her become even more effective next time, would reinforce her positive attitude toward growth and learning. However, if your response were focused strictly on the negative aspects of her presentation without offering any positive feedback and ideas for improvement, Victoria may choose to avoid giving these presentations in the future for fear of harming her reputation, at the same time limiting her opportunities to showcase her ideas and talents.

- **Observational learning.** Another way to influence others' attitudes is to make sure they witness your reinforcement of someone else's attitude. Say you want more active participation in your morning meetings with the other managers in the firm. By practicing active listening techniques and demonstrating sincere appreciation for everyone's ideas and concerns, you ensure that the more introverted and less vocal of the group will feel encouraged to actively participate. They have clearly observed and registered your desire to get open and honest feedback from all present.

Dissonance Theory

The social scientist Leon Festinger provided a gift to strategic persuaders everywhere when he introduced dissonance theory in 1957. Festinger's studies revealed that people perceive an unpleasant tension when they harbor attitudes that contradict one another. They often seek to reduce this internal conflict, also known as *cognitive dissonance*, by dismissing any new information that would conflict with their original attitude or by embracing the new information and changing their attitude to be more consistent with their new worldview.

Here's an example of how persuaders can use cognitive dissonance to influence people's attitudes:

Using the earlier example involving outsourcing, we know that Russell has a strongly held attitude that outsourcing is not patriotic, eliminates domestic jobs, and hurts the economy. You are charged with cutting costs and increasing productivity. You introduce the idea to Russell, a key manager, that if you outsource certain tasks in the company to an offshore provider, the company can free up funds that will make it possible for Russell to hire another designer. That would make Russell's division more efficient, provide better service to clients, and ease the workload of the others, a constant source of stress that has led to conflict and toxic behaviors in the department.

Ideally, Russell would see that an additional staff member would take pressure off him, and he would feel a sense of relief that outsourcing might indeed affect his division in a positive way through less overtime, less tension, and quicker output.

Russell, who is experiencing cognitive dissonance between his original attitude of "outsourcing steals jobs" and his new attitude of "new staff would help our company on a number of levels and affect me personally in a positive way," has to make a choice: reject the idea or embrace it and change his original attitude so that he believes outsourcing can sometimes be effective. What he won't do is hold on to both attitudes because that would cause an unpleasant cognitive tension.

Your job as the persuader is to tap into the values and attitudes in Russell that he subordinated or wasn't aware of until you introduced them as a possibility. By showing him the positive aspects (from his point of view) of a new attitude and getting him to verbalize them, you've created cognitive dissonance and set the stage for a potential attitude change.

Elaboration Likelihood Model

This model from the researchers Richard Petty and John Cacioppo posits that people change their attitudes and behaviors in more significant and lasting ways if they're exposed to persuasive messages that make them think and consider an issue in detail and depth. This is referred to as the *central route to persuasion.* It's important to note that people have to be motivated to hear your message, that is, find it relevant, as well as be able to process the message intellectually or physically. Distractions are a no-no if you want people to ruminate about something.

Persuasive messages that are lacking in substance but rich in peripheral cues such as the likability or the perceived authority of the persuader, or any other associations that give the receiver a shortcut to accepting a message, are thought to produce less stable changes in attitude or behavior than are substantive efforts to persuade. The former are called the *peripheral route to persuasion.* An example of this would be any number of 30-second commercials on TV that promise a better life via compelling images, music, and persuasive pitchperson.

Successful executives can use both routes to persuasion by presenting reasoned, relevant, clearly communicated messages to their target audience, at the same time making use of peripheral persuasion such as authority, likability, and the ability to make others feel at ease.

Political candidates often are chosen by voters on the basis of peripheral cues; assessing those cues is easier than wading through the issues and determining via deep thinking and elaboration which candidate may be more in line with one's personal goals and values.

In terms of maximizing peripheral cues, having lunch with your "crew" may be a good place to start. When the president visits the troops at the front lines, he sits in the mess hall in their midst, eating the same food, shirtsleeves rolled up, listening and responding to their stories. Even in corporate cultures that are more hierarchical than egalitarian—General Motors as opposed to Zappos, for example—it helps if leaders demonstrate the human touch and clearly signal that they care about their employees' well-being.

Ten Powerful Principles You Can Use to Get What You Want Without Violating Your Conscience

A leader's ability to influence others depends on the specific tools she has in her arsenal. Below you'll find a number of principles that can increase your ability to persuade ethically. Although the principles are clear—old-school manipulation is history; the empathetic win-win is in—the specifics of how to adopt and master a natural style of influence can be elusive without tactics that support the strategy. Here are 10 approaches that, when combined and implemented, will exceed the sum of their parts in making you a more persuasive rather than manipulative source of influence.

Approach 1: The Visibility Principle

Advertising professionals know that people gravitate toward the familiar. This is known as the *exposure effect*, in which familiarity breeds affection rather than contempt (that is perhaps more a domestic fact of life). This idea aligns with the concept of cultivating trust to become a better influencer: People trust what they know and understand, and they are skeptical of what they don't know and don't understand, even if on the surface it appears to be positive. Enlightened persuaders make sure to get plenty of face time and interactivity with those they need to influence on a regular basis.

Approach 2: The Supply-Control Principle

There are situations in which limiting the amount of time or supply of benefits can strengthen attraction. It's no accident that many advertisements have a "limited time only" tag; people become anxious and eager about that which is in limited supply. This is called the *law of scarcity*, and when it is used by enlightened communicators, it can translate into abundance in terms of a positive outcome. Be careful, though: By artificially limiting the supply of something others want and thus increasing demand, you are planting yourself on the manipulative side of persuasion. Creating demand by letting others know that what you're offering truly is in short supply keeps you in the ethical clear.

Approach 3: The Framing Principle

Words are powerful tools. They are so powerful that they become weapons of influence in the hands of professionals, and they become reputation busters in the hands of the uninitiated. The reason that words alone can influence people's thoughts and behaviors in a significant way has to do with what I call the *framing principle*, which refers to the creation of context and mental structures that evoke specific mental images and meanings for the person reading or hearing the words. A simple example: If you tell someone to "disregard the gaps in my employment history" when applying for a job, rest assured that's precisely what the person will think about. The frame you evoked—"gaps in employment history"—raises a flag with the interviewer because his frame for that term may summon up unfavorable concepts such as instability, restlessness, and lack of loyalty.

In this example, the attempt to negate a frame actually created the framework of the message itself. This is a situation familiar to former president Bill Clinton, a man known for his speaking ability. In an interview after his wife dropped out of the Democratic primary in 2008, against

I like framing

Senator Barack Obama, the former president said he still had regrets and insisted he was "not a racist" despite controversies surrounding his comments about Obama's win in the South Carolina Democratic primary. The reporter had asked, "Do you personally have any regrets about what you did while campaigning for your wife?" Clinton answered, "Yes, but not the ones you think. And it would be counterproductive for me to talk about." But then he did just that, saying, "There are things that I wish I'd urged her to do. Things I wish I'd said. Things I wish I hadn't said." As his coach, I would have advised him not to play into the reporter's hands by rambling on about any issues the reporter didn't specifically address, as this can lead one into dangerous territory known as *streams of consciousness*. "But I am not a racist," he continued. "I've never made a racist comment, and I never attacked him personally." That single explosive comment was all over the news the same evening, with pundits from every network asking, "Who said anything about being a racist?" and "Where did *that* come from?"

Clinton's disclaimer could have come straight from the *Richard Nixon Book of Rhetorical Blunders*, a thick volume no doubt, if it were to exist. In Nixon's 1972 resignation speech, which was televised, he famously protested, "I am not a crook." As with Clinton's "I am not a racist," social science researchers say that such disclaimers should be uttered only with the utmost caution. Whenever a disclaimer is issued, by defining something you say you are not, it actually directs attention to precisely the quality you are disavowing.

Why? The research shows that the unconscious mind cannot hear and does not process a negative sensibility; this means that the word "not" doesn't even register in the subconscious. This leaves the words "I *am* a racist" stuck in the mind. Although the conscious mind intellectually registers the word "not" in such a disclaimer, the unconscious mind, which records the entire experience on an emotional level, retains the memory of the word "racist."

Approach 4: The Authority Principle

People trust authority. Research has shown that people listen more carefully and trust more quickly when the information comes from a source they perceive as authoritative. Many people can recall meetings from early in their careers during which their contributions barely registered with others, whereas even offhand remarks by senior executives were scrutinized for meaning and often accepted without question. Expertise from a credible source fosters trust. This implicit trust also transfers to authority that is merely perceived, often in just split seconds.

To understand this phenomenon, consider a well-known social experiment that illustrates the power of the common business suit, one of the many icons of authority. A young man in his thirties, impeccably dressed in a pinstriped suit, shirt, and matching tie, deliberately breaks the law as he crosses the street against the traffic light. The result: Almost four times as many people followed suit (no pun intended) as did so when the man wore a casual shirt and slacks in the same experiment. This is the *authority principle* in full glory, and informed communicators know that they can leverage whatever authority they bring to a situation to gain trust. As we've just learned, trust is the key to quick and effective influence.

Approach 5: The Evidence Principle

The *evidence principle* holds that information that is corroborated by outside parties—eyewitnesses, research, past experiences, and, best of all, the firsthand knowledge of the listener—is accepted immediately by the listener. This creates a framework of credibility and trust that a well-versed speaker can use to influence a listener more effectively. When an auto advertisement quotes an endorsement from *Car and Driver* magazine, for example, everything else the ad offers is imbued with credibility. The more uncertain the listener is about an issue, the more powerful the effect of such third-party confirmations and endorsements is; and the more credible the outside source is, the less the trust depends on the nature of the information. The endorser is enough to win the trust of the listener, as in "If Warren Buffett thinks it's a good idea, that's where I'll put my money."

To get full value from this pattern, when you provide evidence in a presentation, make sure it's relevant and of specific value to key stakeholders in your audience. People are often—though not always—swayed by hard numbers and irrefutable data that support the points you're making. You may not easily change an entire belief system this way, but offering more than just your opinion makes good sense when you're looking to dislodge the barriers to acceptance of your ideas.

Approach 6: The Likability Principle

As we've discussed at length, trust is a major factor in influence. It is the key that unlocks the door to moving forward. Without it, listeners will be wary and open only to manipulation, which as we have seen is a short-term strategy that is bound to destroy trust and damage reputations in the long run.

Trust is gained through a combination of factors. Likability is one of them. People more easily trust those they like. Likability ties in directly with similarity. We trust those who are similar to us. To influence others with likability, you have to express genuine interest in them. You have to speak their language by using words they use and frames of reference they understand. Making people feel comfortable by subtly mirroring their nonverbal communication can also contribute to the feeling of similarity.

Research shows that people base decisions on emotions before they check them against the facts. Trial lawyers have long known that the degree to which they and their clients are liked by jurors can make a difference in the final verdict. A study that supports this thesis was reported in the now defunct *Trial Diplomacy Journal*. In that study, the 600 jurors surveyed about their motivation in deciding on a given verdict all mentioned "likability" as one of the reasons for their decision. Specifically, they liked the lawyer in whose favor they decided better than the other lawyer. The lesson is clear: Be genuinely likable and focus on communicating the similarities you have with others to gain their trust ethically.

Approach 7: The Reciprocity Principle

We learned this one as children: If you scratch my back, I'll scratch yours. For adults it becomes the landscape of political lobbying, the fuel that powers relationships, as well as a powerful social influencing method. The essence of the *reciprocity principle* is concerned not as much with the trading of favors and things as with the exchange of value. Whether someone offers to babysit your children so that you can run an important errand or you offer to give someone a ride home from the office, a sense of obligation is established for the beneficiary to return the favor. The when, what, and how of the repayment vary with the context and the relationship.

I'm not saying that you should do favors to get something in return, but by helping others when it is in your power and generally acting with generosity, you increase the potential for the types of relationships that make influence natural and easy.

Approach 8: The Experience Principle

This is the evidence principle taken to a personal level. Nothing says credibility quite like having been there, done that yourself. Confucius, a very enlightened communicator, said: "I hear and I know. I see and I believe. I do and I understand." This is something we, as influencers, can take to the bank.

We experience life in multiple ways, all of them sensory. A knowledgeable communicator knows how to bring this sensory, experiential realm into interpersonal encounters and presentations in a manner that adds credibility and trust. The more you can help others have a visceral experience either directly—a confident handshake, meaningful eye contact, and a genuine smile are a good start—or indirectly through the stories you tell, the questions you ask, and the insights you create in their minds, the more you will reach them at an emotional level, where much of decision making has its root.

Approach 9: The Salience Principle

When we're trying to get a message across and influence others, we naturally tend to focus on what supports our argument and play down what might be contrary to it. We all do this. Politicians, spouses, ministers, the media, and managers do it every day in the course of trying to influence others. The issue isn't whether such slanting is right or wrong but rather what's honest or overly biased, what's responsible or manipulative, and, more aptly here, what works to build credibility and establish trust and what doesn't.

We should amplify elements of information that conform to all the other principles presented here: those that build trust, those that create a win-win, and those that don't take advantage of others for one's own gain. As we highlight the points we consider important to our message, we ought to take care not to omit information that gives our listeners a different perspective that could also be of value to them. Although it can be counterintuitive to bring up information that's perhaps contrary to the message we're trying to get across, ethical persuaders present options—and work hard to show the validity and benefit of accepting their ideas.

When we exaggerate the truth—or turn up the volume on what we want the audience to believe—in a way that hides or alters the facts of any counterpoint, we're closer to manipulation than to a higher and longer-lasting form of persuasion. Strive to present a full and fair argument, using evidence and experience and all the other methods to influence. You can highlight, you can focus, but you can't exclude any portion of the truth without being manipulative.

Approach 10: The Passion Principle

Passion can't be explained. It is felt. Whenever you are looking to influence someone to accept your ideas and share your vision, you have to have a feeling that energizes your insides, that makes you become expressive and use language that stimulates the heart as well as the mind. If it doesn't come easily, think deeply about your relevant values and tie them to aspects of your idea so that you can feel it in your gut. Genuine emotion has the tendency to transfer to others. It is also what people expect from you when you're hoping to get their vote. After all, if you're not excited about what you offer, why should they be?

In Chapter 8 we'll look at the issue of interpersonal conflict and how we can manage relationships effectively to reduce negativity and build lasting rapport in our quest to create an executive presence that commands the respect of those around us.

Passion → a motivator

8

The Essentials of Managing Conflict and Improving Relationships

ONE FACTOR THAT weighs heavily in the evaluation of a leader's executive presence—at least from senior management's perspective—is how well the business units or departments perform. This shouldn't come as a surprise. After all, reliably delivering results and achieving key outcomes through others is the raison d'être for executives. What appears to be less obvious to managers and executives, however, is that the key to success in meeting organizational objectives and assuring outcomes lies in the engagement of their employees, and that many, many employees are not so engaged. One only has to look at Gallup research, which found in 2017 that an astounding 85 percent of employees worldwide are unengaged in their jobs. And these numbers don't budge very much from year to year, if you keep up with Gallup's findings.

The quantifiable results of such low engagement are, unsurprisingly, low productivity, low customer satisfaction, and low unit financial performance. In fact, Gallup attributed approximately $7 trillion in lost productivity, globally, to low engagement. Other research has shown that the better the quality of the relationship between leaders and followers, the more engaged employees are, whereas low-quality relationships lead to sagging performance and even retaliation by employees against their leaders. Citing his own research, Dr. Robert Hogan of Hogan Assessments quipped at an assessment conference in Prague: "70 percent of American employees would take a pay cut if someone would fire their boss." He continued, "People care more about how they're treated than how they're paid."

Clearly, this is a call to action for leaders. A focus on building strong relationships at work can have a noticeable positive impact on one's overall reputation as a manager and one's perceived executive presence.

Of course, if you've spent more than a day or two wandering the halls or filling a cubicle in a corporation or another type of organization—including schools and federally funded bureaucracies—you know that somewhere between the lobby and the backdoor exit lies the potential for interpersonal friction. In fact, even if the head count of your organization amounts to only single digits, you probably have the scars to prove it. Anywhere two or more people occupy the same space, professional or otherwise, in the context of a shared mission and under the looming shadow of personal goals and desires, the laws of human behavioral dynamics kick in. When they do, sooner or later, conflict will erupt. It's like weather to pilots and blood to surgeons: At the end of the day, success depends not on its avoidance (which is impossible), but on how well you land the airplane or sew up the patient. In other words, view these inevitable conflicts as opportunities to flex your executive presence, as chances to optimize the consequences of conflict. Conflict avoidance is a nonstarter strategy.

In one study on managerial effectiveness, the subordinates of 457 managers were asked to evaluate their bosses. The managers who were deemed most effective, as measured by the satisfaction and commitment of their subordinates and how well their organizational units performed, spent much more of their time motivating and developing people, and, most notably, managing conflict, than their less effective peers.

To be more effective in managing conflict, first learn about its more common causes.

Common Causes of Interpersonal Conflict

Most people don't require a definition of conflict any more than they need to know what *Webster's* says about hunger. However, in this case a definition can be helpful because conflict too often is written off as one party making another party angry by not giving the second party his or her way or by being obnoxious and unreasonable. Although this is a plausible definition, a better one is this: Conflict is a dynamic that occurs when one person does not receive the expected or desired response or behavior from another person.

This definition, of course, opens up a very expansive landscape of potential dust-ups. For rising executives whose organizational success depends on the support of various teams and other corporate stakeholders, the matrix of variables is deep and wide, resulting in a nearly infinite combination of combustible dynamics. Everything from personal values, to preferences and needs, to resentments and triangulated agendas, can furnish the spark that starts the fire. When conflict emerges from the frequent interactions of colleagues and peers or bosses and direct reports, it's sometimes less an issue of who is right and who is wrong and more a matter of a *stylistic* difference: a clash of perspectives, occasionally seasoned with a dash of insensitivity. And in a conflict, a tiny speck of emotion can detonate an otherwise reasonable disagreement.

In his 1992 book *The Eight Essential Steps to Conflict Resolution* (later in the chapter we too will explore conflict strategies), Dr. Dudley Weeks presents the following seven sources of interpersonal conflict.

1. Differing Worldviews and Cultures

Don't look now, but not everybody thinks the same way you do. You may have a fundamental difference of opinion with another person about a specific policy or situation, or the cause of the friction may be far broader: The two of you may view the world through vastly different lenses. Some corporate cultures value the giving and receiving of open and honest feedback; others prefer to "keep the peace" and avoid sensitive topics for fear of upsetting people. Some organizations value building consensus among the team for major decisions, whereas in others the boss makes the call and informs the team after the fact. Whatever the particular norms may be, if you didn't "grow up" in that culture, you may bring a contradictory perspective to work. And if you can't sign up for *their* way of doing things, the potential for interpersonal conflict is high. Fortunately, more and more organizations these days understand the need for diverse perspectives and welcome dissenting voices. But where cultures are deeply entrenched, the battle may be uphill.

2. Priorities

You're fine with ambiguity; someone else needs crystal clarity. You think before you speak; someone else speaks in order to think. You believe the company should invest in a new facility; someone else thinks that'd be a huge waste of money that's needed elsewhere. People differ in everything from decision making to communication styles to business strategy; in an eight-person department, in fact, you are likely to find eight different sets of needs and priorities. Each of them is a potential bomb when it collides with the needs and priorities of others.

3. Perception and Filters

As we've seen from Chapter 1, how we're perceived by others may not remotely be how we see ourselves or intend to come across. And yet it's the everyday reality we operate in. You may be challenging someone's ideas in order to arrive at a better solution, but to the other person you may be seen as cunning and competitive. Similarly, you may think you're adding value in a meeting, where others may see you as hogging the spotlight. While adjusting your style may smooth things over a bit, such misperceptions can lead to many conflicts that eat up precious time and detract from the real issues.

4. Power

Managers who rely on power to get compliance, without giving much thought to whether others buy in or are even engaged in the work, often bump up against an ugly reality. From active disengagement to outright sabotage, people find creative ways to rebel against dictators. Genuine influence, rather than raw power, is the better way to sidestep this type of conflict, no matter how hierarchical the organizational culture may be.

5. Values and Principles

If you work for a company whose values and norms you don't share and can't get on board with no matter how hard you try, you'll be miserable on a scale that hurts your soul. Maybe you value working autonomously, but you're being micromanaged to the nth degree. Maybe you want to do right by customers no matter what it takes, but your organization has strict rules that allow little flexibility in case of a dispute. Missed the deadline for a return? Sorry, customer; not our problem. If what you value doesn't match the commitments you signed up for, conflict is pretty much woven into the fabric of your daily routine.

6. Feelings and Emotions

Especially on big projects, ones with massive investments of time, money, effort, and ego, emotions can interfere with rational thinking, and heated discussions can quickly escalate into a raging firestorm. One of my coaching clients, the general counsel and chief compliance officer at a fast-growing health insurance agency, whose job it is to keep the company's stakeholders from running afoul of the law in a heavily regulated industry, often finds himself the bearer of bad news. In one instance he had to tell colleagues from business development that a project they'd been working on for months, an innovative marketing initiative to promote the company's offerings to their provider network, would violate anti-kickback laws and could get the company barred from profitable governmental programs. As my client was new to the company and hadn't yet established strong relationships, the business development team—emotionally invested in the initiative—said he didn't know what he was talking about. This highly emotional clash prompted the CEO to hire two outside law firms to provide a second opinion on the matter. Later, at $50,000 in consulting fees, the law firms confirmed my client's legal assessment. Although the resolution was expensive, this conflict was almost certainly unavoidable; heightened emotions had drowned out rational thinking and reasoned dialogue. In such cases, the more that awareness exists around individual hot buttons, emotional biases, or lingering feelings in a discussion, the more likely an efficient resolution to a conflict becomes.

7. Conflicts Within a Person

This catchall category could pertain to people who bring personal problems to work as well as those with neuroses, substance abuse problems, hidden resentments, and a host of other issues that, when not successfully managed, can easily lead to conflict and bring down entire teams.

Regardless of the source of the conflict, there are always stakes surrounding a successful resolution. When upwardly mobile managers and executives learn to recognize these and other originating sources as potential conflicts in the making, they can prepare for and minimize what seems to be an inevitable clash. From our discussions on *social intelligence*, you may already be equipped to read some initial warning signs. The following section provides additional tools.

How to Recognize and Prepare for Brewing Conflicts

The warning signs of impending interpersonal conflict in the workplace differ from person to person. Big red flags may be noticed, but someone who seems perfectly well adjusted may one day go off the deep end, up to and including the dark incidents that make the evening news. Given this wide range, it is better to look for behavioral and attitudinal *variance* in the people with whom one works. Someone who for years has been friendly and jovial but lately seems down and quiet may be a source of conflict in waiting. Changing patterns of attendance and tardiness can signal trouble, as can unexpected requests for time off or schedule or assignment changes—especially when motivated by a desire to get away from someone else. Increasing emotional outbursts and uncharacteristic moodiness are other warning signs.

Although it seems far-fetched to assume that any of these symptoms is signaling that an employee is ready to detonate, it's prudent to look closely and see if you can somehow help. Such circumstances also present an opportunity to assert your executive presence; after all, interpersonal integrity and compassion are recognized hallmarks of executive presence. For instance, if a colleague is timid about coming forward with personal issues but his workplace behavior has turned troubling, take him for a coffee. By taking notice of the altered behavior, you can intervene in a supportive manner rather than the critical or threatening one that is common after conflict has surfaced. That early move can sap the energy out of whatever potential conflict resides just below the surface. In addition, the respect you'll possibly gain from the interaction—or intervention—contributes to others' perception of your executive poise.

Preparation for conflict resolution comes in two flavors: creating a means of *prevention* and offering resources for *resolution*. The former may include having an employee grievance process in place as well as a safe way to discuss issues with supervisors or coworkers in a confidential manner. Some companies offer counseling to employees whose problems warrant that level of attention, and others train managers in spotting conflict before it happens and intervening accordingly. If neither practice applies to your workplace, you can assert your status as a rising executive and approach appropriate stakeholders in the company—human resources might be a good place to start—to discuss the possible adoption of such programs. This is not a bad initiative to have on your curriculum vitae when promotion time arrives.

Back in the trenches, once a conflict has ignited, the response becomes trickier, especially when the supervisor or leading manager is part of the square-off. Firm company policies can mitigate the problem, such as a no-physical-contact rule whose violation can result in immediate termination, a take-it-behind-closed-doors rule, the availability of immediate mediation, and a culture of peer involvement and enforcement to help employees resolve issues quickly among themselves. An overarching corporate culture that prizes peacefulness, respectful debate, and comradeship is also highly valuable.

Choose Your Ideal Conflict Management Approach

Conflict is not inherently bad. If everyone agrees all the time or if no one is ever challenged out of fear of reprisal—in other words, if employees have no voice—by definition a cultural ceiling has been placed on the company's potential. Conflict can be viewed as an opportunity to strengthen relationships and fortify cultures, though this can happen only when the ground rules and consequences line up with a process of healthy debate and open and honest conversations. Without a foundation of trust and the commitment to such rules of conduct (and in the presence of unfortunate consequences), relationships and cultures almost always take a hit when trouble arises.

In marriages and long-term relationships, for example, conflict is as opportune as it is inevitable. It presents a chance for the partners to clarify intentions, perceptions, needs, and feelings, to be heard and to hear. A committed relationship grows through conflict, or at least it should. In a perfect world, the result is an opportunity to make changes as part of the resolution process, to strengthen respect and solidify the process of meaningful communication. This principle works just as well in an organizational culture, corporate and otherwise, albeit with a wider range of personal issues and styles than in a marriage. When executed poorly, however, in either environment, the result is likely to be resentment, anger, and an ongoing agenda of revenge that can turn into a vicious circle of simmering conflict.

By understanding our own default conflict management style as well as that of others, we have the opportunity to make positive strategic and behavioral choices that reflect both a mature confidence and a desire to preserve valuable relationships—both qualities that can add to one's executive presence.

A tool I've often used with clients to help them gain awareness of their dominant conflict management style, as well as alternative styles available to them, was developed by two professors of management from the University of Pittsburgh—Ken Thomas and Ralph Kilmann. The Thomas-Kilmann Conflict Mode Instrument (TKI™) is a simple self-assessment tool that can develop more productive conflict resolution behaviors. One of its key ideas is that none of the identified conflict styles are either good or bad. They are simply options that may suit one conflict situation better than another.

We all have our go-to conflict management styles. Some people prefer to avoid conflict altogether, whereas others strive to accommodate, collaborate, compromise, or push back ("competing" is what the TKI calls this more assertive style). A corollary is that we may overly rely on one style.

You may recognize your dominant conflict management style below, as well as take note of others you rarely deploy. By understanding the utility of all the styles, however, you'll position yourself for quicker resolution of any conflict.

The Styles at a Glance

Thomas and Kilmann identify five conflict management styles. _Competing_, a power-oriented mode, pertains to someone who is primarily concerned with winning, with whatever power at his or her disposal and often at the other person's expense. It isn't as sinister as it sounds, and it can be a suitable choice at times, especially when it's important to stand up for one's rights, defend an idea, or win for the sake of the team. Other appropriate circumstances include crises and situations where rapid action is needed or unpopular measures—new rules, cost cutting—need to be implemented. Do you overuse the style? Maybe so, if people are loathe to disagree with you lest they get rebuked for speaking their mind, or if they commonly may put on a Potemkin-like facade of being more informed than they really are (which has obvious ramifications for a leader). Conversely, if you underemploy this style, you may fail to take charge or to exercise power when strong leadership is needed, or you may overly defer to others' concerns and feelings when decisive action is required.

A second style, _collaborating_, involves seeking a solution that meets the needs of both parties. This style can help preserve relationships by demonstrating that the other person's concerns are valid and that one is committed to finding creative solutions. It can also deepen one's understanding of a controversial issue by seeing it from the opponent's perspective. Overuse of collaborating can result in spinning your wheels and belaboring issues that don't warrant that level of attention, and can also result in holding off too long on making a decision because of an eagerness to seek consensus. On the flip side, if you underemploy this style, you may notice that others lack the motivation to buy into your ideas because you convey the impression that their concerns are none of yours.

Then there is *compromising*, a style that may work when both parties are interested in moving things along and don't mind giving something up in return. Both typically walk away satisfied to some degree, with a solution that may have come at a higher cost or lesser benefit if a different style had been used—say, competing or accommodating. If seeking compromise is your go-to resolution mode in any conflict, be aware that you may end up compromising some of your most important values in the process, all for the sake of a quick resolution that, in the end, may not serve your long-term goals. Conversely, if compromise is typically the *last* thing on your mind, you may sacrifice valuable opportunities to save a relationship or to get your fair share in a fierce competition for resources.

The conflict resolution style of *accommodating* is not the most assertive style but, like the others, may be the smart strategy to adopt in certain situations. Use it when it's important to keep the peace and prevent a conflict from escalating—especially if you have little stake in the outcome or it matters far more to the other person than to you. Accommodating may also be the best option when it's time to align with the boss or the team after a difficult decision's been made and you want to show you're a team player. Accommodate as a matter of routine, however, and you may come across as a pushover. If, on the contrary, to accommodate is anathema to you, you may be labeled "difficult to work with" and a person who is unreasonable and unwilling to take one for the team.

Finally, there is *avoiding*. While I mentioned earlier that it's virtually impossible to avoid conflict in an organizational environment, *avoiding* is a conflict management style that can be used when it makes sense to remove oneself from an emotionally charged situation, avoid giving oxygen to a trivial matter, or wait for a more opportune time to discuss a controversial issue. One sign that you may be too much of a conflict avoider, though, is that colleagues notice and talk about your lack of input on challenging topics. You appear to be missing in action when it comes to taking a stand on an issue, making tough decisions, or debating solutions to niggling problems. But if you use this style rarely, you may get embroiled in too many issues not worth your time or effort, sapping you of valuable mental energy. You may also come across as thin-skinned and quick to jump into an argument without first considering the stakes. This, in turn, can impact others' perception of your judgment, a key component of executive presence.

Diagnosing Style Conflicts

When the new CEO of a global food manufacturer asked me to work with Rob, a member of his senior leadership team and the CFO of the company, to help him develop his executive presence, I asked what he felt was missing. "I don't feel like I have a good business partner in him," the CEO responded, and "Rob seems disengaged in meetings and appears to constantly undermine my authority as CEO in front of others." When I interviewed Rob, he had a different take on this interpersonal conflict: "When I offer my perspective on an issue, in meetings or in private, all I get is a brush-off or silent treatment," he complained of his boss. "I don't feel like he respects me or even wants me in the position."

Both based their perceptions on certain behaviors of the other that they had observed over time. This made it so difficult for them to work together productively in a highly competitive environment that a member of the board was dispatched from European headquarters to the United States to mediate and bring the relationship back on track. Meanwhile, I had started to work with Rob, and I determined that it would be useful to conduct an assessment of both Rob's and the CEO's conflict management styles to see if a solution lay in that direction.

The results showed that Rob, the CFO, was off the charts high on the avoiding conflict management style, which would explain the CEO's perception that Rob was disengaged and unwilling to provide input or engage in debate. Rob's scores were almost equally high on accommodating—which meant that when he wasn't avoiding; he was simply acquiescing to whatever the CEO and the rest of the leadership had decided. On collaborating and competing, Rob's scores were as low as the other two were high, meaning he put little effort into working with the team to ferret out integrative solutions or vocally advocate for an idea he believed in (see Figure 8.1).

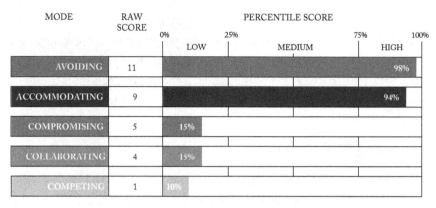

Figure 8.1 Profile of TKI scores

The CEO's conflict management styles? His competing score was exceptionally high, which, in light of Rob's extremely low competing score, could explain why Rob felt that whenever he did offer his opinion to the CEO, he was brushed off or made to feel wrong. In turn, this behavior of the CEO may have reinforced Rob's tendencies to conduct himself passively. Add the fact that, like Rob, the CEO had a relatively high score on avoiding, and it becomes clear why critical issues that needed resolving between them were simply left to fester.

A cautiously happy ending to this story was that both the CEO and Rob realized that each had contributed in his own way to their troubles, and both were willing—with my support as coach—to collaborate on holding each other accountable for more productive behaviors and conflict management styles.

Nine Powerful Ways to Resolve Conflict, Restore Harmony, and Strengthen Interpersonal Rapport

For business professionals who hope to positively impact their organizations while also building their executive presence, conflict can provide great opportunities to test their mettle and show enlightened leadership. The following list offers some additional tools and strategies to aid in that process.

1. **Use active listening.** Most of us understand the benefits of "being in the moment." In a conflict situation, this means listening carefully to all sides without an emotional filter, the way a judge listens to lawyers pitching their cases. If you're a manager arbitrating a conflict between two employees, this is a bit easier than if you are a party to the conflict. Nonetheless, being crystal clear on the reasoning of each side in a conflict is critical to helping create a mutually satisfying resolution. The term "listening" in this context applies to more than words; you should strive to perceive the multitude of signals—from vocal tonality to facial expressions and body language—all of which can speak volumes about the intent and motivation of the participants.

2. **Acknowledge and validate.** As an arbitrating manager, it is critical that you not only seek to understand both positions in a conflict but also *validate* each party's claim. You don't have to agree with the claim; just acknowledge each party's unique perspective. This alone can open the parties' minds with the assurance that they've been heard, even if the outcome doesn't exactly go their way. People need respect and consideration just as much as they want to get their way. In the game of conflict, sometimes emerging emotionally validated, with one's status intact, is enough.

3. **Empathize.** The power of empathy in conflict resolution cannot be overstated. Empathy happens when you put yourself, minus your biases and personal experiences, in the shoes (the circumstances) of both parties or, if you're one of the combatants, in the shoes of your opponent. Try more than to just see the situation from the other person's point of view; try to *feel* it, too. If you do, you may find that the picture takes on a slightly different hue.

4. **Implement boundaries and expectations.** Because you are a manager, people are looking to you to clarify boundaries and expectations for behavior and outcomes. If these things are muddy in the middle of a conflict, your job is to clarify them for the feuding parties. The idea here isn't to reprimand but to prevent escalating emotions from clouding the established

norms of conduct in a conflict and to reinforce the expectations for roles, behaviors, and outcomes. A good way to open this can of behavioral worms is to simply ask the parties to state what they believe the boundaries and expectations to be that pertain to debating the issue at hand, using their perspectives as a platform for your clarification and reinforcement. This approach enables open and honest communication and will keep the parties within acceptable boundaries as they (or you) work through the issues.

5. **Be tactful.** This may not be easy, as any one of the parties to a conflict may be way out of line from the outset. But don't get sucked into the brewing emotion, and don't convey even the slightest sense of disrespect for the parties or their views even if they originated on another planet. If you remain sensitive to their feelings, the chances that they'll remain open to your input increase—to everyone's benefit.

6. **Explore alternatives.** The parties to a conflict rarely are interested, at least at first, in looking at things differently. It's your job as the arbitrating manager to help them do this, and it happens when you begin exploring alternative views and solutions with them. Ask open-ended questions such as "How would you act differently if this policy were reversed?" that require thought and elaboration. If you can get them to talk about an alternative, you're a step closer to getting them to accept one.

7. **Use "I" statements.** When you are a party to a conflict, using a first-person context is much more productive than using other language. If you say, for example, "I was angry when you said that about me," you'll be greeted with more openness than you would be if you say, "What you said about me was wrong." People can't argue with how you felt, but they can certainly dispute the right or wrong of things. Speaking about how you feel avoids accusation, and accusations are fuel on the fire of conflict.

8. **Make use of the power of stroking.** It may sound manipulative, but if you can say something positive about the other person in the heat of a dispute, that person will be more open to hearing what you have to say about the issue at hand. Stroking the

interesting [handwritten margin note]

I can try [handwritten margin note]

other person says you aren't attacking her character and haven't lost respect for her, only that in this instance you disagree with something that was said or done. Conflict goes off the rails when it becomes personal, but ironically, injecting something personal in a positive manner is the best way to keep it from going there.

9. **Attack the issues, not the person.** Conflicts sometimes are smoke from another fire or the surfacing of past disagreements or personality conflicts. When you sense triangulation entering the argument—the use of an unrelated opinion or issue to create a negative context for the present one, such as "You always put yourself first in these situations"—you know that this is personal rather than issue-driven. As an arbitrating manager, listen for anything that is personal in nature and bring the conversation back to the issue as quickly as possible.

How to Nurse a Strained Relationship Back to Health

No matter how enlightened your conflict management approach is, when emotions run high and egos get bruised, relationships can suffer long-term damage. And particularly in a work environment where cooperation and teamwork reign supreme, this isn't something to shrug off. Fortunately, there are a few proactive ways to restore a relationship, or at least replace simmering resentment with mutual respect and collegiality

One key to healing a broken or strained relationship is to let go of any residual negative emotions that remain from the conflict. If you were one of the participants in the conflict, remember that holding a grudge certainly won't add luster to your executive presence or elevate your status with your colleagues. Being generous, however, might. Drop the grudge, and you may find yourself empowered by doing so. (For managers with a bird's-eye view of the conflict, it may be necessary to nudge the parties to repair the relationship if they are not sufficiently motivated on their own to do so.)

If you owe someone an apology, give it. If someone owes you an apology, make it easy for the person by extending an olive branch first. Show that you harbor no hard feelings and are willing to forgive (this is better shown than told). Asking for help or advice on something you're working on or inviting the person for a cup of coffee can do the trick. If you have trouble forgiving and letting go of resentment or continue to evaluate that person in a negative light, seek different perspectives from trusted coworkers. You might even consult a mentor, especially if you feel your attitude is compromising your other relationships. The bigger man and woman win points here. (But don't think of yourself as the "bigger" person. Instead, adopt humility as one of your new core leadership traits. It will serve you far beyond the context of conflict resolution and has shown to be a key predictor of business success among senior executives.)

One of the most powerful ways to heal a strained relationship is to go right at the problem. Be transparent, warm, and open-minded and find a place and time—again, lunch or a hot beverage can be a nice excuse for an occasion—to lay it all on the line, not with the intention to revisit the conflict in minutiae, but to mend the relationship. Looking forward, point out what you'll do differently from now on (this is not the same as admitting fault), given the lessons you've learned in the process. Ask your colleague what he or she thinks it will take from both of you to make the relationship whole again. And then listen with empathy.

When the intention is to heal and move forward rather than to revisit the past, you'll find the process easier than you expected.

In Chapter 9 we'll look at how we can assert and reinforce executive presence and gain respect by managing difficult conversations: the conversations we'd rather not have but need to have in various situations for personal and professional success.

9

How to Hold Conversations Nobody Wants to Have

A STRONG EXECUTIVE presence is an asset when you're a party to a difficult conversation. The confidence and professional poise you exude can imbue the situation with a healthy sense of respect. Also, successfully negotiating a difficult conversation can add another dimension to your executive presence, especially because a corporation is a challenging place to have such an exchange. The same is true for any organization in which a hierarchy is in place, especially when careers and paychecks depend on some semblance of order and responsibility. Because these things are delivered by human beings—not all of whom are enlightened in the art of commanding respect with warmth and strength—such conversations occur with wide variations in effectiveness and empathy.

But besides being challenging, these conversations are common. We've all been on the receiving end of difficult conversations, managers and rank-and-file alike. We've been challenged, reprimanded, reassigned, realigned, and, in some cases, fired. We've been called on the carpet, summoned to the boardroom, and put out to pasture. Unless it was done with tact and skill, chances are that we remember the conversation with zero fondness. On the other side of the table, most managers have faced the task of delivering feedback, discipline, and even the proverbial pink slip, and have found that role to be just as stressful. However, as with most managerial skills, aspiring leaders can learn to create the positive perceptions that will set them apart from their peers.

Specifically, the process of having difficult conversations can be made more effective and less stressful through an understanding of certain principles and the adoption of certain behaviors that minimize defensiveness and open the listener to the feedback, which is essential to meaningful change. In the process, you'll also build a compelling executive presence and command the respect of your peers, colleagues, and bosses.

The Anatomy of a Difficult Conversation

Difficult conversations are rarely simple. They may seem straightforward, but below the surface lurk issues that could fill an entire psychology textbook. Moreover, these exchanges often put the delivering party in a difficult position. As ambitious business professionals, we've learned our way around a spreadsheet, but tackling a tough conversation with a long-term employee is something we're just expected to *do*, without any sort of training. That's a shame, because doing it well or not certainly affects others' perceptions of our executive presence.

Below are the three major components of a difficult conversation, each of which can derail the exchange unless we've learned how to manage it:

1. **Body language matters.** Nonverbal communication adds critical nuance and emphasis to your words, often more than you know. I again point to my client Jim, from Chapter 2, whose facial expressions could shut down a meeting faster than a fire alarm.

    A boss who sits with an employee and leans forward while speaking softly and empathetically delivers a far different message than a boss who stands over a subordinate with hands on hips and speaks with a raised voice and a staccato delivery. Especially when there is a power gap, it behooves the higher-ranking interlocutor to lower his or her status and match the body language of the other to avoid creating unhelpful psychological barriers. And if the intent is for the conversation to shift from a sober tone of holding someone accountable to a more compassionate style of coaching on the issue at hand, let your nonverbals reflect the transition. Also, if the meeting is to end on an inspirational note, a sunny facial expression and increased vocal volume can inject enough energy to have both parties leaving the encounter feeling good and looking forward.

2. **Emotions will happen.** In the real world the term "difficult" often means "emotional." Emotions can arise on both sides and, as I discussed in Chapter 3, affect how we're able to process information. The person who delivers feedback or gets something off his chest experiences anxiety. The receiver experiences hurt feelings, wounded pride, and defensiveness. More often than not, both parties try to hide their true emotions, which is rarely effective in either the short or long term. In fact, the best way to keep the line of communication clear is to acknowledge both your and your interlocutor's feelings; try to manage those feelings rather than suppress them. This openness, however, has limits. If you're angry, you must manage your anger so that you do not cause unintended and irreversible damage to the relationship and, possibly, your position in the organization. Instead, as psychologist Delee Fromm has counseled, "Expressing yourself assertively (not aggressively) will prevent emotions from building momentum and allow you to deal with bothersome behavior or issues in a way that is both constructive and affirmative."

3. **Our identity is scanning for threats.** One of the reasons people feel threatened during a difficult conversation, and experience the associated emotions, is that their identity, or at least their perception of how they are viewed by others, is being challenged. Most people view themselves as competent; if negative feedback arrives, it collides with that self-image, which is deeply unsettling because our self-image tells us where we fit in the social order around us.

Research shows that our social status is always on our minds, informing us of whether we're doing better or worse than our friends and colleagues. If, in this constant comparison with others over intelligence, education, skills, looks, popularity, money, etc., we feel "less than" someone else, the resulting emotional pain (which our brains experience as profoundly as physical pain) can prevent us from thinking rationally. As Fromm notes, "Threats to our identity are profoundly disturbing" and can set off a cascade of fear-based emotions. Recognizing up front the centrality of status can enable you to conduct difficult conversations so as to lessen the threat to a person's identity.

Preparing for a Difficult Conversation

Preparing for a difficult conversation requires more than simply having an idea about what you'll say. If your emotions are driving your urge to meet—perhaps you are downright angry—you are unlikely to be as prepared as you should be. We know that raw emotions can cloud the issues and send people reeling. For this reason, your first job is to practice some of the emotion-regulation strategies we discussed in Chapter 3.

Once your emotions are in check, create an agenda for the impending conversation. Plot your opening—the first 30 seconds or so. A good way to start is to create the context for the meat of the discussion by summarizing the policies and cultural expectations that are already in place. These can be the wallpaper for the issues you are about to address. Then review those issues in order of priority, so that each issue creates the context for the next. For example, if the issue is a salesperson's habitual lateness for customer calls, plan to begin there and show her how this behavior creates a poor first impression and a negative context for the entire call. Also plan to ask quickly for the other person's point of view. How does she explain her behavior? What's interfering with her promptness? Are meetings scheduled too close together? Is it a preparation issue? Poor time management perhaps? Is there a way you can help? Professor Jean-Francois Manzoni, from the International Institute for Management Development in Lausanne, Switzerland, notes that this last point affords you the opportunity to see where your interests overlap and makes the conversation more collaborative than combative. More broadly, as you plan, be sure to position yourself as an ally and mentor rather than an outsider and a disciplinarian. If we know anything about human nature, it's that people are more open to the wisdom of allies and mentors than to that of critics.

As these are by definition conversations you'd rather not have, don't procrastinate and let issues and problems fester. Although you may need some time to cool off and get your emotions in check, be wary of delay for avoidance's sake. Avoidance means that the behavior or conditions that constitute the agenda of the conversation will continue unchecked, since the recipient has not heard your views. And so will the consequences of that unwanted behavior, whether it be poor performance, a disruptive environment, safety compromises, etc. Procrastination usually stems from anxiety and fear, but as Manzoni points out, difficult conversations "are not black swans"—they are not rare or unexpected in the business world. Given that reality, it might be better to reframe these difficult conversations as less dire and more routine. We learned earlier how effective cognitive reappraisal can be. Reframing "difficult conversation" more positively—as "a clearing of the air," or "a way to provide helpful feedback to help the person grow," or even "a chat"—can blunt your anticipatory anxiety and help you get on with it.

Finally, while planning the conversation can itself also help to minimize anxiety, don't overdo it and create an elaborate advance script. Neither one of you—certainly not the recipient—will stick to it. What's important is that you keep the agenda in mind, i.e., the topics you want to discuss. Having that as a compass and remaining flexible throughout the exchange ensures that you stay on message and fully present in the conversation.

Conducting the Difficult Conversation

Reasons to have a difficult conversation are as varied as the causes of conflict. One of the most challenging reasons is to hold people accountable for behaviors and results. This kind of tough conversation is so challenging that a global survey of 5,400 leaders revealed that 46 percent of them shirked the performance of this task.

An example from our coaching practice fits this statistic:

Rick is the cofounder and CEO of a highly successful social media and social networking company, and yet most days he hates going to the office. Despite stellar business results and the company's reputation as a darling of Wall Street, the office climate was nothing to brag about. Its rapid growth from R&D to full-on commercial operation had required Rick to hire a new senior management team very quickly, fostering a Wild West ethos where type A individuals arrived, headed up their function, and staked their claim. Rick soon gained a reputation as a pushover because he failed to hold the aggressive managers accountable for such toxic behavior as sniping at each other in meetings, undermining one another in public and private, and engaging in backstabbing and gossip. And when not engaged in those behaviors, they'd come to Rick to complain about each other, forcing him to spend precious time brokering various peace pacts instead of setting strategy and sharing the company's vision with the world.

When I talked to Rick in our coaching conversations about the importance of holding people accountable for their behaviors and not just for completing innovative projects or delivering business results, he countered, "It's tough to put teeth into accountability." He said that when he tried to talk to his team about abiding by certain behavioral guidelines, his CIO—also the chief antagonist in the executive leadership team—shot back, "Come on, we're not in high school." (The CIO likely missed the irony in that statement.)

So how can a difficult conversation about, say, toxic behaviors be conducted with as few bruises to the ego as possible and while keeping minds open instead of shutting down? Here's a simple map to guide you through this minefield.

Revisit Agreed-Upon Expectations

At some point you probably had a conversation with the recipient, or held a meeting that the recipient attended, about what your expectations are or what the cultural norms are in the team or the organization at large. If you haven't had that conversation or meeting, this might be a good place and time to start, but in the more likely event that you have, use this history as a factual jumping-off point to contrast the offending behaviors with the agreed-upon behavioral expectations and norms. By taking this factual approach, you're not blaming the other's personality, which might cause the person to batten down the hatches and focus more on self-defense than change and growth. Especially emphasize the *impact* that the person's behavior has on others in the organization and how a cascading effect can lead to more than ruffled feathers—maybe even a full cultural shift in the wrong direction.

Once all that's clear, move on to the next step.

Check In on Ability and Motivation

Expecting someone to deliver on a commitment he or she can't deliver on is futile. To avoid this, consult any psychological or professional assessments you have on the person to determine whether the behavior in question is part of the person's core personality—which means that without coaching or other intervention the behavior is unlikely to change. If it is not a core trait, i.e., the errant behavior is a one-off, it can probably be kept in check with increased self-awareness and disciplined self-monitoring. For instance, imagine a leader whose scores on a standard psychological assessment show that she's extremely diligent and has exceptionally high standards for herself and others, and that she tends to criticize others, often in public, whose work falls short of her potentially unrealistic standards. This leader isn't easily going to align with behavioral expectations that are outside these engrained traits without some help in the form of coaching, a solution you may suggest during your conversation. But if her offending behavior is more along the lines of frequent and rude interruptions of colleagues in meetings, simply urging her to self-monitor in meetings should result in a noticeable improvement (perhaps only after a few cold stares from you during such meetings to congeal the habit). Either way, simply by checking for whether the behavior is core or not, you signal that you care enough to help the person grow as opposed to just criticize and run.

Define What Success Looks Like

Once you're clear that both the clarity and ability to change are present, it's time to discuss what outcome you're looking for. Ask the other person to envision the impact of the changed behavior compared with the impact now. Our frequent interrupter, for instance, might offer such insights as, "Others will feel like they've been heard," "We get more diverse viewpoints," and "People will feel respected and more willing to collaborate with me." You might add that, without egos clashing, meetings will be less contentious and more productive. As for postconversation follow-up, you might suggest measuring success meeting by meeting, as explained in detail in our next step.

Agree On Timing and Frequency of Feedback

ike a pilot who relies on instruments and ground control to get where he's going, business leaders need others' perspectives on whether they are living *Scheduled* up to their agreements, or whether their darker behaviors have emerged *to debriefs* under pressure or exhaustion, or whether they have stopped self-monitoring. Annual performance reviews are hopelessly inadequate to provide useful, timely feedback, so find additional ways to deliver it.

In our example, the interrupter might receive her meeting-by-meeting feedback from you or another trusted stakeholder, right after each meeting, perhaps in a quick chat in the hallway or office or by phone. The more immediate the better, as nuances of the meeting will still be fresh in everyone's mind. "You did well in today's meeting hearing people out," you might say, while also adding, "However, make sure you extend the same courtesy to all of the team. I noticed you kept wanting to talk over Sylvia when she pushed back on your idea. In the end you agreed she had a good point. We may not have gotten there had you succeeded in interrupting her." This is specific, targeted feedback that enables a person to consider the context of the situation and prepare to adjust at the next opportunity. The more consistent you are with providing feedback, the less uncomfortable these conversations will become, and the more likely a behavioral change will manifest.

Enforce Your Red Line

Remember my client Rick's complaint that it's hard to put teeth into accountability? After numerous half-hearted attempts at getting his aggressive managers to change, Rick gave up and continued to tolerate their toxic behavior. In so doing, he lost credibility with the others, including the board of directors, which grew tired of the company's ballooning discord and infighting. Rick was losing his executive presence, too—and all because he was unwilling or unable to draw and enforce his red line, i.e., the consequences for bad behavior.

The red line may be the hardest part of a difficult conversation, but without the courage to say "Enough!" and follow through with action—whether reassignment, termination, or a performance improvement plan—there will just be more of the same behavior. When you draw your red line and it is crossed and you take decisive action, you eliminate the need for the same difficult conversation to occur over and over, all as you watch your leadership influence erode.

And if you do have to have the same conversation again, check the previous five steps to look for the snag.

Managing Negative Outbursts

Let's face it—no matter how evolved your approach to a difficult conversation is, there's always a good chance it may go off the rails. But striking the right balance between directness and sensitivity early in the conversation can help set the tone for the rest of it. Being too direct at the start can get you shut out as defenses go up, while soft-pedaling does you no good either, as the other fellow may not hear you as you intended. Manzoni recognizes that these kinds of conversations can be hard on relationships, and he says that being both straightforward and compassionate means that you can "deliver difficult news in a courageous, honest, fair way."

Still, none of this may work as planned. Sometimes you can engineer all the negativity and criticism out of the conversation, but the bad feelings are on standby, ready to erupt when a raw nerve is touched. At that point you have very little control over the other party's response. However, you do have total control over *your* reaction to that response, and if you manage it effectively with a clear focus on the overall outcome you seek, you can minimize damage to the relationship and return the dialogue to a productive realm.

One of the best ways to ratchet down the tension is to slow down the conversation. Manzoni notes that slowing down gives you a better chance to really hear what's being said, including between the lines. "If you listen to what the other person is saying, you're more likely to address the right issues and the conversation always ends up being better," Manzoni reasons. And as I discussed in Chapter 3, taking a break when things get heated is an effective way to restore some calm, both in yourself and in the other party.

One thing you shouldn't do, however, is to instruct someone to "calm down." This request, in effect, says that his response is unwarranted, which is another way of saying that he is wrong. And honestly, have you ever felt more at peace after someone told you to calm down? Another mistake is to match your own emotions with the person's. That is the quickest way to ignite a shouting match or, at a minimum, render the rest of the discussion dysfunctional. Instead, stay focused. Hear him out. Recognize his emotions—"I know you're upset; I would be too if my boss just said that to me"—and demonstrate the empathy required to convey what you really want, which is for the conversation to continue in a productive fashion. An emotional outburst is often a cry for attention, a signal of pain. He wants you to see how you've made him feel, so do just that. Empathize—recognize the emotion as it happens.

When an emotional outburst occurs, the best response is to allow it to run its course, as long as it doesn't endanger your safety or violate the corporate culture's norms. This requires a thick skin, but most of the time if you let people have their say, their energy will dissipate before your eyes. Also, the less defensive you are, the faster this dissipation will happen. Then, after an empathetic acknowledgment of the outburst, you can resume the discussion.

However, if you can't get the moment under control, avoid the temptation to plow through. Instead, either offer a short break or suggest picking up the conversation later—and follow through. Don't admonish or make the other feel guilty for this break. Simply suggest that a delay for a few hours might help each of you to gather your thoughts. People are often embarrassed by their own emotional reactions, which can in turn feed into their anxiety about resuming the discussion. When you do return to the conversation, acknowledge its difficulty without lingering on the outburst, and reinforce your intention to work with, not against, the person. Emotional outbursts are often par for the course in a highly charged and competitive organizational environment, and having the reputation of someone who remains calm—though not indifferent—during such sensitive encounters will amplify your executive presence to all the right people.

How to Ask Questions That Build Receptivity and Trust

There is a big difference between a conversation and a lecture. The former is a matter of give-and-take, but when the conversation is difficult, it can be hard to get the other person to do either one. The key to making sure the conversation doesn't degenerate in this way into a lecture is asking the right questions in the right way with a view to building trust and creating a positive, forward-looking context for the unfolding dialogue. Questions are a way to allow the other person to tell his side of things, and if they are posed strategically, they can get the other person to explore your side of things as well. "Why do you think we ask people to observe those safety rules?" is better than asking, "Don't you understand those safety rules?" It's a subtle shift that springs from a perspective of providing mentorship rather than criticism, even if the latter is also part of the agenda. An enlightened communicator knows how to impart criticism in a way that feels like supportive mentoring rather than punishment.

Whenever possible, questions should be open-ended. Any question that requires a yes-or-no answer is closed-ended and does little to impart learning. If it's an employee you're talking to, the more you can get her mind to process and explore what happened and what *should* have happened, the more the learning can stick. Yes-or-no questions spring from a lecturing-and-punishing approach, whereas open-ended questions involve the employee in the creation of a solution. The former makes you a bully who's in charge; the latter, a leader whose maturity and interpersonal savvy is acknowledged, appreciated, and respected by employees and bosses alike.

Asking open-ended questions—and responding appropriately to their answers—can also increase the trust a person has for the leader. The yes-or-no style of question can appear dismissive and unfair, making you seem biased and causing the person to shut out anything you have to say. As

David Rock notes, "The perception that an event has been unfair generates a strong response in the limbic system, stirring hostility and undermining trust." Similarly, Judith Glaser and Richard Glaser state that a perception of unfairness can also increase cortisol levels, which can decrease a person's ability to listen. If you demonstrate genuine curiosity and a willingness to learn by asking open-ended questions, people will generally respond in kind and open their hearts and minds to you.

There are limits to open-ended questions, however. If a person is likely to be evasive, for example, you might be better off asking for a specific response. Harvard Business School professors Alison Woods Brooks and Leslie John cite research that "people are less likely to lie if questioners make pessimistic assumptions . . . rather than optimistic ones." If someone has fallen behind in his work, for example, preface your question on the completion date with "It looks like you'll need more time" rather than "Everything's on schedule, yes?" By acknowledging the unhappy truth in advance, you make it easier for the person to tell the truth.

You should also pay attention to the sequence of your questions. Brooks and John suggest that in a conflict situation, leading with the most difficult questions can actually open up the conversation. "When a question asker begins with a highly sensitive question . . . subsequent questions . . . feel, by comparison, less intrusive, and thus we tend to be more forthcoming." You have to make sure not to push things so far with that first question, however, that you offend the person and cause her to shut down. This sequence should be reversed when you're trying to establish a relationship. In that case, you want to start with the more anodyne questions and build up to the more difficult ones. In these cases the gentler questions enable trust, which makes it easier for the person to respond honestly to the harder questions that follow.

What are the best kinds of questions to ask? Brooks divides questions into four types: introductory, mirror (asking the same question back), full switch (in which you switch topics), and follow-up. It is the last type, the follow-up, that can highlight your interpersonal integrity and build trust. As she and John observe, "They signal to your conversation partner that you are listening, care, and want to know more. People interacting with a partner who asks lots of follow-up questions tend to feel respected and heard." As I noted earlier about the sensitive role of "identity" in a conversation, people who feel respected tend to be less anxious and better able to hear what you have to say.

Asking smart questions in the right way can meet a number of objectives for the leader who is building a strong personal brand: High-caliber questions signal intelligence and an interest in personal growth; they show curiosity and a willingness to learn; they illustrate to others that you care and can be trusted; they teach by causing reflection and inspiring discussion; they convey knowledge and experience; and they enable the leader to frame even the most difficult conversation as an opportunity to learn from mistakes and move forward together.

Summarize Your Conversations for Maximum Impact and Positive Conclusions

It's true that people often tend to hear what they want to hear. And sometimes people misconstrue another's meaning. In highly charged, difficult conversations, these failures to communicate can be more frequent. For that reason, it is wise to always summarize what you've heard the other person say. Not simply to parrot the content, but to reflect what you understood the intention of the message to be. Ask the other person to do the same from her end. What did she hear? What meaning is she taking away from the conversation? What conclusions is she drawing? If important detail and nuance is misrepresented, this is the time to correct it and ensure you're both on the same page. Especially in difficult conversations, it benefits both interlocutors to be as clear about takeaways and outcomes as possible.

In Chapter 10 we'll discuss the dark side of executive presence and how the strengths inherent in a compelling presence can morph into weaknesses if not adequately monitored. In that regard I'll provide you with a number of coaching tips that can help keep your career on a winning track.

10

The Dark Side of Executive Presence

Coaching Tips That Can Save Your Career

Steve Jobs was a man who believed utterly in himself and his vision of not just his company, Apple, but of technology's place in the world. His resilience allowed him to power through devastating setbacks; after being fired by the company he founded, for example, he was hired back and led Apple to the top of the tech pyramid. Yet his incredibly high standards and demands for excellence, coupled with a famously volcanic temper, however much they spurred on acolytes, also led to such cringeworthy scenes as his blasting of an older employee at Whole Foods who didn't make a smoothie to his satisfaction.

Similarly, Elon Musk has cultivated the reputation of genius, going so far as to name his company after the brilliant scientist and inventor Nikola Tesla. Along the way he has inspired many with his ventures into space and fantastical promises of using tech to transform society. Yet while he has made good on some of those promises—the high-end Tesla models, the SpaceX rockets—he's also had some spectacular misses in his quest to shoot for the moon. Such setbacks are not unexpected for someone skating along the bleeding edge of tech, but Musk has also been unable to contain his very public frustrations with any criticisms of his work, which has, in turn, punctured the air of serenity and inevitability about his company's success.

Such at-the-limit visionaries have been a part of human society for as long as there have been humans. But over 2,000 years ago, a wise old Greek named Aristotle warned about the dangers of such recklessness and counseled instead that excellence was to be found in that sweet spot between too much and too little. In our modern world, however, we don't always pay attention to the shadows cast by always pushing to go farther and faster, We don't always realize that what can raise us up can bring us down.

Creating an executive presence is all about raising yourself up, but you have to be smart about it: Every trait, behavior, and skill that you cultivate to establish yourself as a respected leader can create problems if not monitored closely. Especially when we're under pressure, stressed, in the middle of a crisis, tired, or simply not self-aware, those same personality traits that constitute our strengths can take on a dark hue.

What Is the Dark Side of Personality?

There are a couple of different ways of understanding the dark side. One of the earliest comes from psychologists Delroy Paulhus and Kevin Williams, who delineate the "Dark Triad" of narcissism, Machiavellianism, and psychopathy, all traits that are almost wholly negative. More recently, Robert Hogan and Joyce Hogan developed the Hogan Development Survey (HDS), their 3-cluster/11-trait schema of the dark side of personality:

- **Distancing.** Excitable, skeptical, cautious, reserved, leisurely
- **Seductive.** Bold, mischievous, colorful, imaginative
- **Ingratiating.** Dutiful, diligent

Unlike the Dark Triad, the traits found in the HDS are not negative in and of themselves. They are dark because they are usually hidden, emerging only when people, usually due to stress, let down their guard.

This dark model can be contrasted to the "bright" model of the Big Five personality traits. The Big Five (also known as the five-factor model) are often referred to by the acronym OCEAN: openness to experience, conscientiousness, extroversion, agreeableness, and neuroticism/emotional stability. They can be understood as "bright" because they are apparent to others. Again, this doesn't mean that these bright qualities are wholly positive, just that they are visible.

Beyond that, however, there's not a lot of consensus about the dark side. Kaiser Leadership CEO Rob Kaiser observes that "dark-side traits can be seen as strengths in overdrive, with the potential to become weaknesses through overuse." There is a general sense that a dark side could be a trait that is excessively or, more rarely, too little expressed. Professors Seth Spain, Peter Harms, and James Lebreton make another distinction: that between "nature" and "effects." The traits in the Dark Triad, for example, may involve "malevolent intent" and thus be considered dark in nature, while others, such as those in the HDS, may not involve bad intent but may lead to bad or harmful outcomes—that is, have a "derailing" effect. "Harm of some kind," as they put it, "is almost a necessary consequence of the label *dark*."

In Figure 1.1 in Chapter 1, I introduced my own list of the traits and behaviors of executive presence, based on over 20 years of working with senior leaders and influenced by the Hogans' research as well as other social scientific research. For the sake of convenience, it is repeated here as Figure 10.1.

Communication: Mastering difficult conversations, engaging others, telling strategic stories, inspiring and persuading
Competence: Having intellect and expertise, delivering results, acting decisively
Personal brand: Having status and reputation, projecting calm under pressure, possessing a compelling physical appearance, projecting confidence, having interpersonal integrity
Courage: Holding people accountable, speaking truth to power
Political savvy: Networking and building alliances, managing up, generating buy-in and support

Figure 10.1 The Traits of Executive Presence

In this chapter, we'll look at the potential dark sides of these traits and behaviors, which are more about *effects* than intentions. Most of the people I work with have a sense of integrity that makes them want both to do well in their jobs and to become better people. In other words, it isn't that they're malicious, but that they lack the awareness to see when their strengths have become weaknesses that limit their executive presence. For instance, someone who is expressive and engaging and makes a strong first impression may end up dominating meetings and showboating in group situations. Similarly, someone whose executive presence includes self-confidence, competitiveness, and a willingness to take risks may start ignoring negative feedback and try to win at all costs. Research has shown that people with the ability to self-monitor and to regulate such dark turns of successful behaviors will advance in their careers faster and more consistently than those who lack these abilities.

Bringing Light to the Dark Side of Executive Presence

Below is an elaboration of the figure above, focusing both on how the various traits and behaviors within each cluster can positively influence others' perceptions of your executive presence and on how, if overdone, they can diminish that presence. To help you stay on the bright rather than the dark side of executive presence, I've included quick coaching tips for each trait.

Communication

That all aspects of communication are pivotal to one's leadership luster is hardly a surprise. Conversely, failure to monitor communication behavior closely can send matters off the rails and damage one's reputation in an instant.

Mastering difficult conversations, which I've discussed in some detail throughout this book, is an executive presence trait that can distinguish you from colleagues who avoid emotional encounters and thus leave critical issues unresolved. However, even as you proactively engage others in such conversations, there are minefields to avoid. When you strive to provide helpful feedback in these fraught exchanges, for instance, if you are overly sensitive to a colleague's feelings, you may end up not delivering the full meaning of the information he needs to improve. Or on the flip side, you might be so eager to give someone every bit of feedback that you drown her in a sea of information, rendering your efforts equally ineffectual.

There's also the possibility that trying to cushion the blow of bad news ends up leaving the other person feeling manipulated. One employee told *Ask a Manager* columnist Alison Green that putting the meat of criticism between two slices of compliments (otherwise known as a "crap sandwich") can be insulting, "like when you have to give a dog a pill and you hide it in a piece of cheese to trick them into swallowing. I always feel like there's some kind of mild deceit going on, and I'm put off by the feeling that the person didn't respect me enough to just talk to me instead of trying to 'handle' me."

COACHING TIP   Keep the desired outcome of a difficult conversation in mind, i.e., the reason why you're having the conversation in the first place. Not wanting to hurt people's feelings is a good intention, but rarely is it the objective that will move you closer to the conversation's goals.

Engaging others is a helpful executive presence trait in both short- and long-term interactions. Being outgoing, charming, and friendly can make you stand out and is especially useful when meeting people for the first time. One study observes, predictably, that those low on charisma are also low on perceived leadership ability. However, a less predictable observation from the study was that those who are highly charismatic are also seen as less effective. Those with low charisma "were seen as less effective because they were not sufficiently strategic, while high-charisma leaders were seen as less effective because they were weak on operational behavior," according to the study's coauthor Filip De Fruyt, PhD, of Ghent University. The sweet spot, as that old Greek man observed, is between too much and too little charisma.

If you are too engaging, you also could be deemed as too much of a politician or as someone who is overly ingratiating in order to gain favor with people, especially the influential. This perception can potentially put people on guard in encounters with you and close you off from developing authentic relationships.

[handwritten margin note: make people I engage with feel as if they are the only person in the room]

COACHING TIP   Be genuine in your interactions and make people you engage with feel as if they are the only person in the room. Observe their comfort level with your *[handwritten: energy]* attention and know when to move on, to leave them wanting more of you.

Telling strategic stories is another key executive presence trait, because stories are powerful ways to clarify, teach, inspire, motivate, and engage. Jack Welch, Tony Hsieh, and Sheryl Sandberg are examples of leaders who impart important lessons through stories. When overused, however, storytelling can look like a *shtick* and distract from your message. Not every situation requires a story, and responding with one when your boss wants a recommendation or an answer to a specific question can make you seem long-winded and unable to get to the point. There's also the danger of a good story gone trite—reciting the same anecdote so often that people roll their eyes when you begin, "Did I ever tell you about that time I was trapped in the elevator with a client . . . ?"

[handwritten margin note: Story telling w/ a purpose]

COACHING TIP   As discussed elsewhere in this book, storytelling to maximize your executive presence should have a strategic purpose—a specific objective for a specific audience. If you find yourself regularly regaling people with your tales around the water cooler, dial it back and save your best stories for when it matters.

Inspiring and persuading is what charismatic leaders do to drive engagement and motivate people to achieve a common goal. It can also degenerate into empty rhetoric and overpromising, not to mention burnout and backlash by followers. Both Jobs and Musk cultivated devoted followers, inspiring workers to throw themselves into their work and push themselves beyond what they thought possible. This devotion, however, often came at a price. Verinder Syal, a former Quaker Oats executive and one-time admirer of Jobs, was repelled by how absolute he was. As he admitted in a *Wired* retrospective of the man, "Jobs was like dynamite. Dynamite clears paths, but it also destroys everything around it."

Similarly, Musk has been called out for overpromising. He's missed deadline after deadline for the delivery of "car of the future" Tesla Model 3. The postponements led the *New York Post* (which is not known for its subtlety) to claim that "Elon Musk is a total fraud" and that his company is "best known for blowing deadlines and consistently falling short on production." And his recent declarations on underground hyperloops have led some to snark that what Musk was inventing was a less efficient subway.

While few people ever reach the stratospheric success of a Jobs or Musk, the risks of losing perspective in inspiring others play out regularly in meeting rooms and boardrooms worldwide. I've coached many senior leaders who failed to deliver on their lofty projections and whose inspiring visions failed to materialize. Helping them regain credibility and the trust of boards and employees after those colossal letdowns takes time and effort, but by learning to balance their ability to inspire with realistic optimism and humility, they can continue to play important leadership roles in innovative organizations.

COACHING TIP   When you paint an inspiring picture of the future, make sure that you caution about the risks as well. Also keep in mind that the more detailed and specific your vision, the more that people will hold your feet to the fire to deliver. So leave yourself some wiggle room: Temper your enthusiasm with a dose of reality, and underline the caveat that things *could* also go the other way. You'll preserve your credibility and lose none of the excitement your vision incites.

Competence

Without evidence of competence, executive presence can only be temporary. No matter where you are on the organizational chart, your colleagues expect you to contribute value and deliver results. How you deliver on those expectations, however, can determine whether you gain their respect or simply collect a paycheck.

Having intellect and expertise is necessary for gaining the respect of leaders and followers alike. In terms of your executive presence, intellect and expertise are foundational qualities that others will value long after the sheen of your positive first impressions has worn off. But these qualities don't always boost your leadership presence, especially when everyone else is just as smart as you are. One danger is relying on intellect and expertise to the exclusion of building genuine relationships. "My work should just speak for itself" is a complaint I've heard from many brilliant professionals who have been dropped from a short list of contenders for leadership positions. That complaint rings hollow. Because in a place where being smart is not a rare quality, but social intelligence is, it is the lack of that latter, in-demand quality that can diminish one's executive presence.

Another danger is wielding intellect and expertise as a weapon against people you perceive to be less experienced, credentialed, and, well, smart. Acting like a know-it-all or snob is unlikely to gain you friends, at least not genuine ones. Nonetheless, just like that brilliant surgeon whose arrogance leads others to whisper about his "God complex," many managers also have an off-putting belief in their own infallibility, even though they do not wear scrubs to work.

Finally, don't let your stellar expertise in a particular field prompt you to claim authority in all fields. Your specific talent may have a halo effect, spurring some of us to deem you an all-around expert, but the likelier effect is snickering behind your back. Take astrophysicist Neil DeGrasse Tyson, for instance. The widely beloved science commentator is regularly roasted in social media for his pedestrian remarks about the social sciences and humanities. For those of us who aren't famous astrophysicists, it is even more crucial to understand that our skills and talents in one area may not translate well into others.

COACHING TIP   Understand how your intellect and
expertise can help you project a credible executive presence,
but be sure to learn what other qualities are valued in your
environment. Smarts and credentials are often the ticket
that gets you into the game, but once you're in, you have to
develop other competencies that demonstrate your fitness for
leadership.

Delivering results is a metric by which most corporate citizens are
measured. And if you want to move up in an organization, being known
as someone who "gets stuff done" will go far toward raising your executive
presence.

deliver results

The dark side emerges when results become the *only* thing that matters. Arguing that "the end justifies the means," for instance, indicates not
only a lack of maturity and judgment, but a callous disregard for the people affected by those "means." When personal drive and a bias for action
morph into ruthless ambition, you have strayed from the productive side of
executive presence. Whether as a leader or individual contributor on your
way up, you'll need strong personal relationships to support you through
the challenges ahead. Most people have a strong intuitive sense of what's
ethical and fair, and alienating them in the name of delivering on objectives is shortsighted. As I've noted in Chapter 1, three questions always
on people's minds are *What's happening? What's going to happen next?* And
how am I being treated? The answer to that last question can make all the
difference in how you're perceived as a leader.

COACHING TIP   Leaders achieve great outcomes
through others—not on their own. Make sure you keep
your finger on the pulse of people's satisfaction, engagement,
and even happiness at work. By communicating frequently,
listening regularly, and satisfying both the basic and the
higher-level needs of those around you, you'll meet your

targets with the support of your team and with your executive presence intact.

Acting decisively is another cornerstone to success, just as it is to the perception of executive presence. One study published in *Harvard Business Review* noted that "high-performing CEOs do not necessarily stand out for making great decisions all the time; rather, they stand out for being more decisive. They make decisions earlier, faster, and with greater conviction." According to the research, even leaders who make decisions that turn out to be wrong but can later be corrected are viewed more favorably than leaders who hesitate or make no decision at all.

So when does acting decisively become a weakness rather than a strength? The study's authors note that successful leaders also know when *not* to decide. It is "too easy," in the words of former Arrow Electronics CEO Stephen Kaufman, to "get caught up in a volley of decision-making." In other words, you might end up prizing quick decision making over the quality of the decision itself, often in a situation that doesn't demand an immediate response. There's also the possibility that you become stubbornly resistant to new information after having made a decision. As Tony Stark, author and chief executive of The Energy Project, puts it, "Decisiveness overused eventually congeals into certainty."

It's also important—especially for leaders new to an organization—to recognize the culture's dominant decision-making style. "Move fast and break things" might work as a motto for a Silicon Valley start-up, but in a culture that expects "decision by consensus" and predictable outcomes, that motto can prompt a reputational crisis. In some corporate cultures, making decisions quickly and revising as needed is a valued trait, while in others, it might be seen as reckless and "shooting from the hip."

Finally, by being overly quick to decide, you may deprive others of the chance to practice their decision-making skills, especially if you're in a leadership role that involves coaching and mentoring. Delegating some decision making will also free you up to focus on other aspects of the job.

COACHING TIP Familiarize yourself with the decision-making styles that your organization values. While acting decisively is widely valued as a core leadership trait, strike a balance by knowing when more time for deliberation and information gathering makes sense and would improve the outcome. You can also use your skills to empower others to practice decisiveness by starting with low-stakes decisions and working their way up from there.

Personal Brand

A personal brand is your aspirational idea of how you'd like to be seen by others. It's something that you have some control over and that can help you convey the executive presence you need in order to influence those around you.

Having status and reputation is the root of executive presence, at least initially. A stellar educational background, significant professional and personal achievements, and a network of influential allies and mentors, as well as endorsements and testimonials from prestigious clients, can all open doors and inspire respect in those you meet on your career path. And while building your reputation is essential to maintaining your executive presence, the flip side is that you may be seen as spending too much time and effort on attending to how you are viewed by others. Are you always the first to volunteer for the most difficult assignments? Is your voice usually the loudest in meetings? Do you appear to have the answer to every question? Does it seem you're a card-carrying member of the in-crowd at work and that each anecdote you share prominently features your hallowed alma mater or internship at Google?

By being too invested in the image you've so carefully created, you may also, unconsciously perhaps, try to protect this image at all costs, loathe to admit mistakes and unwilling to accept constructive feedback when a course correction is required. Personal Branding

---

COACHING TIP   The higher your status and the loftier your accomplishments, the less you need to harp on them to promote your executive presence. It's a balancing act that kicks in once everyone is aware of your status and reputation, after which you should err on the side of humility and give others the chance to shine. Because humility is also a highly valued leadership trait, blending it with your achievements is a powerful booster of your executive presence.

Projecting calm under pressure is a quality that followers and bosses alike expect from a leader. During a crisis or in times of uncertainty, we look to our leaders to reassure us that all will be well and that someone is in control and has a plan. On a smaller scale, the daily occurrence of presentations in boardrooms, which exerts a more ordinary kind of pressure, often identifies those who have executive presence and those who don't. At a minimum, we expect our leaders to keep it together, sans the palpable fear that grips so many in such a setting. On more than one such occasion, I've witnessed leaders having a meltdown where clear thinking and succinct answers to questions were expected. Those are career-defining moments where emotion regulation is a major asset.

So when can this asset become a liability? When it is perceived as disengagement, for one. I've had clients whose detached affect made them seem uninterested or even incapable of creating genuine emotional connections with colleagues. For leaders this apparent indifference is particularly problematic, because followers must feel that a leader cares about them and is enthusiastic about the future into which they are to follow him or her. Absent that, the troops at the front lines may feel they are on their own. The same applies to meetings and presentations, where appropriate passion can work wonders in how your message is received. You can't convey urgency if you use the same voice you use when you drop off your dry cleaning. Whether you're sharing good news or bad, whether you're asking for something or selling something, your audience needs to feel that you care personally about the outcome, or the spark won't transfer.

And while cooler heads may prevail in times of crisis, they may also be underresponding to urgent situations. By focusing so much on keeping everyone calm and steady, you may gloss over or fail to recognize how dire a situation really is. One notorious example is that of Christine Todd Whitman, former head of the Environmental Protection Agency, who announced a week after the attacks on the World Trade Center that "I am glad to reassure the people of New York . . . that their air is safe to breathe and their water is safe to drink." This was, tragically, not true, and almost certainly led those in and around Ground Zero to forgo live-saving respirators. While Todd Whitman has apologized for her error, over 1,000 people have since died as a result of exposure to toxins in and around the site.

Fortunately, most of our workplace emergencies are less grim, involving the loss of time or productivity rather than lives. But automatically responding with "no problem" to real problems can frustrate your colleagues with your perceived ignorance or indifference.

COACHING TIP   Adjust your emotions to the needs of the situation. If you're generally calm under pressure, you're starting from a good place. Analyze each situation to see if, to effectively convey your message, people need your enthusiasm, compassion, reassurance, inspiration, or a hint of your frustration and even anger. Showing your colleagues that you are emotionally engaged can open the door to collaboration and the proactive sharing of information, which otherwise may be closed to you.

Possessing a compelling physical appearance is cited as an integral element of executive presence in every survey published on the subject. It's also a highly visible aspect of our personal brand. And while we have limited control over physical attributes such as height, size, and physiognomy, we do have significant influence over the rest of our appearance. In fact, by "looking the part" we often demonstrate good judgment and allow others to imagine us in a leadership position. Marian Wright Edelman,

Appearance

the civil rights activist and founder of the Children's Defense Fund, recalls her attendance at a meeting with rural Mississippians "who heard there was a Black lady lawyer in town . . . and who came to look for and at me." However, "When they saw me in blue jeans and an old sweatshirt, they were crestfallen," she said. "I never wore jeans in public again in Mississippi."

A caution when it comes to appearance: While you might like to express your personality, the organizational culture in which you operate would often prefer that you downplay it to show you fit in. This is a tricky area; my thoughts are based not only on my personal judgment and observations of countless corporate cultures over the past two decades, but also on comments I've received from leaders about the effect of appearance on their colleagues' prospects for advancement. Often, especially in more conservative environments, excessive grooming or over-the-top couture may put you on HR's short list of uncomfortable conversations to be had. For example, clothing that is too tight or revealing, no matter how attractive, is sure to put your executive presence, and cultural appropriateness, into question. One of my architectural clients wears a large amount of jewelry; that habit put her in the crosshairs of her ultraconservative boss, the 100-year-old company's first female president, whose unassuming style contrasted sharply with her "flashier" colleague's. Be wary of hairstyles and facial hair, too; one hirsute 30-something financial manager at a software firm where I conducted a leadership program asked me what I thought of beards. What surprised me wasn't his question, but the quick sideward glance and smirk he cast in the direction of his boss. The boss's eye roll and audible sigh left little doubt what *he* thought of this trend among millennials and gen Z men. In the same vein, I could spill some ink on the subject of tattoos, but I think you're onto my point. What's acceptable or even celebrated in one organizational culture is frowned upon in another. What's more, being seen as someone who appears to spend extraordinary effort and time on his or her appearance can, rightly or wrongly, lead others to believe your priorities are not aligned with organizational values.

COACHING TIP Learn what's valued and accepted in your organization and what would push the boundaries of the collective comfort zone. You then have a choice: authentic self-expression with the risk of an informal organizational narrative excluding you from certain opportunities; conformity, where you mostly fall in line and show your rebellion in the form of red socks; or some middle ground, where your brilliance allows you to push the envelope in a way that's not just tolerated, but seen as an integral part of your unique personal brand.

Projecting confidence is a critical component of executive presence. It's the driveshaft that makes all the other parts work. Without it, you wouldn't credibly project calm under pressure, you wouldn't be able to speak truth to power, you wouldn't be able to manage conflict or hold others accountable, *have confidence* and you wouldn't be able to engage and inspire people.

Too much confidence, however, or, more accurately, arrogance, reck- *↓ godly confidence* lessness, and overcertainty, can derail promising careers.

Professionals with highly specialized knowledge or an exalted status—certain types of lawyers, for example—have been particularly known to indulge in these delusions of grandeur. Not that other professions are immune, mind you. Accomplished business leaders at any level of management can fall prey to an inflated sense of self, especially those who surround themselves with sycophants who insulate the leaders from corrective feedback. The annals of leadership are packed with stories of highly intelligent people who bought their own press and subsequently failed, spectacularly, at their jobs. The signs are clear to everyone but them: They overestimate their abilities, competencies, and importance. They fail to acknowledge their limitations. They take risks without considering the consequences. They reject input and negative feedback, and they refuse to take responsibility for their mistakes, choosing instead to blame others. Harvey Weinstein, co-chairman of Weinstein Company, was so overconfident in his status as the linchpin of so many Hollywood careers that he behaved abhorrently for years, until the #MeToo movement toppled him.

COACHING TIP   Surround yourself with people whom you trust to be straightforward and honest and who aren't depending on you for income or support. Check with them regularly to learn about your perceived strengths and weaknesses and to get ideas on how to improve and grow. Practice showing humility and admit when you don't have all the answers. The higher you sit, the more that vulnerability makes you appear appealingly human, enhancing your status rather than detracting from it.

Having interpersonal integrity is a powerful trait that concerns your behaviors toward others. At its most basic, it involves your ability to remember who people are, what they do, and what conversations you may have had with them. One leader at a manufacturing plant who was in one of my workshops seemed to be having a rough day, and I asked if I could help with anything. Through tears she told me that her cat was in the hospital and might be suffering from kidney failure. I said I was sorry; having a 20-year-old cat myself, as well as two 17-year-old dachshunds, all of whom are like children to me, I added that I hoped the cat would recover quickly. Three months later I returned to the company for another workshop and ran into the leader with the cat. When I asked, she said her beloved pet had passed on. Two days later the firm's HR leader stopped me in the hallway to say how much it meant to her colleague that I remembered our conversation months earlier. Having interpersonal integrity means you care about the people you work with and show it in your interactions with them.

But you can lose your perspective on this quality by placing inordinate weight on maintaining harmony and protecting people's feelings, and doing so at the expense of holding people accountable and having the tough conversations in which leaders frequently need to engage. I've seen many leaders who let close relationships and personal feelings for someone interfere with doing what's right for the business. To be sure, I'm not advocating that you're *all business*, but rather that you maintain a balance between being an inclusive leader who acknowledges people's contributions and shows concern for their well-being and one who can spell out business expectations and hold people to them. This potent blend of leadership styles can earn you the respect and the engagement of employees and spare you from being labeled a "pushover."

COACHING TIP Practicing self-awareness will help you perceive if your interpersonal integrity at work is in balance. Some questions to ask yourself include: Do people seem to feel comfortable sharing their personal issues with me? Do these conversations dominate our individual interactions? Do people try to take advantage of my kindness and compassion? Do I have trouble getting results from people? Do I impose consequences when people don't follow through on their commitments, or do I seem to be having the same conversations over and over without getting results?

Courage

Holding people accountable is a trait every leader should master in order to do what a leader does—achieve important outcomes through others. It starts with creating clarity around expectations and capabilities and gaining agreement on milestones and definitions of success. It includes providing regular feedback so people know where they stand in terms of their performance. And it requires the courage to levy consequences when expectations aren't met and results are continually lacking. Leaders who follow through on holding people accountable—they are in the minority according to research—can count on the fact that their executive presence benefits from their resolve.

A drawback emerges, however, when leaders push too hard on any of the stages of "holding people accountable." Leaders and followers are well advised to partner in the process, rather than having the former simply imposing expectations, timelines, and success metrics on the latter. On the surface, such partnering may look like micromanaging and create the impression that the leader is "rigid," a "stickler for rules," or a "taskmaster," but enlightened leaders know the value of providing their teams with just the right mix of direction, autonomy, support, and appropriate check-ins.

COACHING TIP   When you're setting expectations, get input from your team. Are your goals realistic? Timelines reasonable? Success metrics fair? Does each team member have the capabilities and resources he or she needs to deliver? How often should you check in with each other to gauge progress? What should the feedback process look like? Discussing these issues up front ensures that everyone is on the same page and that unwelcome surprises are minimized.

Speaking truth to power is yet another quality that surveys on executive presence have found to be a key trait of successful managers. This characteristic requires a strong moral core and the courage to stand up for what you believe, especially when speaking to senior leaders.

That said, there is a dark side even to this quality. One version can emerge when you stray from doing what's right to being self-righteous. This may happen when you don't trust the moral compass of your colleagues or when you view those with perspectives different from yours as inferior or clueless. As a result, instead of engaging them, you end up ignoring or even punishing them, as well as jumping to conclusions and missing out on insights that can alter your understanding of the situation. In return, your colleagues may mistrust you. You might think you're being rigorous, but they just see you as rigid.

A simpler but no less harmful sign that you have taken a dark turn in speaking truth to power is that colleagues see you as belligerent and tactless. It's important to speak up to authority when you see wrongdoing or when you find your values being tested, but it is also prudent to do it diplomatically, so that your message gets through.

COACHING TIP   Practice taking perspectives different from your own. Engage your leaders in dialogue with genuine curiosity and the intention to learn. Choose your words carefully and explain your position by pointing to shared values that may be compromised by certain plans. After saying your piece, you always have a choice—fall in line with your boss's decision, no matter how much it goes against your grain, or pack your bags and move on, dignity and executive presence intact.

Political Savvy

If you understand who the influencers in an organization are and how to influence them, either directly or indirectly, to meet your various objectives, you are politically savvy. Rejecting organizational politics as "evil," "juvenile," or "so high school," on the other hand, is naïve and unlikely to serve you in the long run. That's because you really can't escape the relational dynamics that dominate the organizational beehive, no matter how "flat" the organization purports to be. Hierarchies are always in place—social or otherwise—and as Bob Hogan has correctly observed, it isn't necessarily the best leaders who occupy the top ranks in an organization, but rather the winners of intense political tournaments. To keep from being a perpetual loser in those contests, cultivate at least some degree of political savvy.

A Cornell business professor, Samuel Bacharach, defines such savvy as "the ability to understand what you can and cannot control, when to take action, who is going to resist your agenda, and whom you need on your side. It's about knowing how to map the political terrain and get others on your side, as well as lead coalitions."

Networking and building alliances is one strategy that can serve you well in your quest to become politically savvy. Networking furnishes you with critical information about who has power and who doesn't, whom to trust, whom to stay away from, and to whom you need to turn to get things done. You'll also need to network to create a strong set of allies, mentors, and sponsors, all of whom can keep you in the loop on important organizational developments, help you navigate obstacles, and help you accomplish goals when your competitors inevitably seek the same rewards and resources that you are after.

It may be easier to imagine this trait taking a dark turn than some of the others, considering that "politicking" often has a pejorative meaning. It certainly is possible to spend too much time on these relationships. An ambitious manager can become so fixated on expanding her network that she neglects to tend to the work itself. Instead of helping her team succeed, she's primarily focused on her personal success.

Another risk in overplaying the networking card is that you're seen as a "politician" in the sense of someone who attends to his base and sponsors while neglecting the needs of others who don't seem as important to his career progress. In the same vein, you may be asking too much of your network without providing enough in return, which could make it look like you are simply using people to get ahead.

COACHING TIP   Create a stakeholder map that allows you to see who is in your network and with whom you need to establish better relationships that benefit not just you, but also others inside and outside your organization. Connecting people with each other can go a long way in positioning your executive presence in the most positive light.

I'd like to exercise

Managing up is another element of political savvy that contributes to your executive presence. Depending on your vantage point, managing up can mean a number of things—from working around your boss's idiosyncrasies to get her support, to soothing the nerves of skeptical board members, to negotiating your way around those with more power than you. In the best-case scenario, as Alison Green notes, "It's about working with your boss in a way that will produce the best possible results for the organization, while at the same time decreasing your own stress level."

In managing up, however, you risk falling into a number of reputational traps. Being seen as a suck-up is one of them. Your colleagues will notice any excessive attempts at your ingratiating yourself with the boss and will likely punish you for it with derision and gossip. Your behavior won't be lost on your boss either, and while she may enjoy your obsequiousness, she won't respect you much for it. And if that weren't bad enough, a study from the Ross School of Business at the University of Michigan found that unrestrained flattery toward one's boss can cause the flatterer to feel resentment toward the higher-up, as the insincere act harms the flatterer's self-esteem. That's because most of us would feel better about getting ahead on our own merits and the value of our work, as opposed to gratuitous flattery. Further compounding the issue is the fact that this self-manufactured resentment causes the flatterer to potentially harm the boss's social influence by undermining her with others.

Another reputational trap arises when you are so invested in your superior's success that you set aside your own needs. In effect, you adopt your boss's priorities as your own, neglecting your own priorities and the solidifying of your own personal brand. While it can be a smart strategic move to hitch yourself to a rising star, the downside is that you become a part of the entourage, not the star yourself.

Another danger of managing up: becoming so adept at maneuvering around a superior's foibles that you end up manipulating him. Anyone who's ever worked for someone else has had the experience of massaging unpleasant information into something less distasteful or deploying strategic vagueness as a means of reassurance. Used with discretion, such tactics are generally harmless to your reputation, but if they become your go-to methods for dealing with superiors, you'll end up looking dodgy in your dealings. Even if your boss doesn't catch on, your colleagues will likely notice how comfortable you are manipulating him. And they may just end up wondering how honest you are in your relationships with *them*.

COACHING TIP   Check your moral compass as you manage up. Being supportive of your boss and even your boss's boss can benefit you as much as it does them; however, if it feels like you're compromising your values or you find that other colleagues perceive you in a way that puts your good reputation at risk, take a step back to evaluate your strategy. Get feedback from people you trust to pinpoint any issues and uncover potential blindspots. From there you can revise your managing up strategy for a more positive impact that simultaneously aligns with your values and aspirational career goals.

Generating buy-in and support, the topic to which I devoted Chapter 5, is essential to executive presence. You can't develop such presence without motivating people to follow your lead. In fact, this ability is the cornerstone of corporate success: What is a leader without a following? True, anyone with a title and some firepower can intimidate people into compliance, but to get the genuine support of stakeholders at all levels, you must be able to generate buy-in.

While that's easier said than done, *overdoing* it can lower your executive presence quotient by a few points. For instance, in your effort to get everyone on board with a change you're driving, you may not notice that you're browbeating people into acceptance "for their own good," rather than acknowledging and responding thoughtfully to explicit and implicit concerns.

You may also become so focused on pushing for change that you end up doing most of the heavy lifting yourself, rather than enlisting other influencers to support you in communicating key points to various stakeholder groups. The Lone Ranger may look good on TV, but in a corporate environment he just looks sad.

Finally, by pointing to shared values as leverage in your quest to bring people around to your way of thinking, you've got it only half right. It is *their* values to which you must appeal, the alignment of which with yours holds the real key to sustained support and real buy-in.

COACHING TIP Talk to many different individuals and listen more than you talk. The reasons for resistance to a new idea may seem straightforward but may, in fact, be a Frankenstein's monster of fears and concerns, stitched together by old alliances, conflicting interests, and a perceived loss of status. Uncovering them and responding to resistance with compassion and substance can open hearts and minds more easily than eloquent rhetoric and lofty promises.

Dealing with the Dark Side
and Developing Judgment

The mythical hero Ulysses wanted to hear the song of the Sirens, but he knew that all who heard it would dive into the sea to their deaths. Recognizing that he, too, was vulnerable, he asked his men to plug their own ears, then bind him to a mast to prevent him from going overboard as they sailed past that deadly chorus.

An avid adventurer and risk taker, Ulysses was accustomed to pushing beyond the horizons, but he also had the self-awareness to know that his great passion to experience what few other men had could lead to his doom.

So how do you avoid slipping over to the dark side of *your* executive presence?

You can start by acknowledging to yourself that no one is immune to the emergence of that dark side. We all have strengths and weaknesses, and sometimes our strengths *become* our weaknesses. Especially in times of pressure or stress, but also when we simply let our guard down and fail to self-monitor, we are more likely to exhibit behaviors that could damage our reputations and even derail our careers.

To avoid these dangers, increase your self-awareness and start self-monitoring. Keep track of your behavior during both good times and bad, and study the results. Keep a daily work log in which you jot down a few notes of what happened and how you handled it. If you know that your stress increases as a deadline looms or as the date approaches for a presentation, engage in the emotion-regulation strategies discussed in Chapter 3. And if you have a trusted colleague who'd agree to give you a heads-up when you appear to lose control, lean on your colleague for support.

To get a handle on your reputation and learn about potential blind spots that may weaken your executive presence, seek feedback from others. Chapter 2 explores the 360-degree feedback process; by asking bosses, peers, and people who work for you about their observations on your strengths and weaknesses, you can get a good panorama of perspectives. (Best to allow them to do this anonymously to get the unvarnished truth, rather than a sugar-coated version.)

The point of gathering all this feedback is to increase and maintain your self-awareness. But this gathering won't do much good for you if you don't change problematic behavior based on what you learn. This may seem obvious, but I've seen too many careers derailed where leaders simply sat on the feedback or took only nominal corrective action.

If the required changes seem overwhelming to achieve on your own or if you don't know where to start, check with the development professionals in your organization for guidance or engage an executive coach. When it comes to developing a positive executive presence, the worst you can do is nothing.

In Chapter 11 you'll learn to see yourself as a developing personal brand. You'll understand the foundational qualities that underlie strong brands and learn how to leverage this knowledge into an action plan for acquiring an executive presence that resonates.

Self-Branding Is No Longer a Choice

Strategies to Make Your Personal Brand Stand Out

WE LIVE IN a society that defines itself through branding. We rarely describe our favorite jeans by color or style; we identify them—and their place in the social pecking order—by their brand. We do the same thing with our preferred coffee shops, cars, bars, computers, ketchup, peanut butter, phones, golf balls, restaurants, and even hospitals. Our grandfathers divided themselves into "Ford men" and "Chevy men," which is nothing more than branding manifesting itself as a middle-class colloquialism. Such groups still exist: You're into Macs or PCs, and rarely will the twain meet.

This reliance on branding to fuel our self-image—and thus our buying decisions—is so pervasive that we cease to think of it as such. We don't use tissues; we wipe our noses with Kleenex. We move the earth with Caterpillars, and we Google new acquaintances. Despite the protests by marketing pros that using brand names generically is trademark infringement, the practice signals a status to which virtually all companies aspire. The brand name becomes synonymous with the product category, and thus, rightly or wrongly, those products define the standard. Any other product in that niche, no matter how well reviewed or how large its share of the market, is an also-ran.

Certain brands may not be quite at that level but nonetheless, rightly or wrongly, have an anointed status. Harvard, Stanford, and MIT are branded as institutions of unreproachable quality, even if other universities deliver the same level of education. Virtually every product niche has a branded front-runner in terms of prestige and reputation; beyond quality and value, a major contributor to that leading status is that the brand name has been nurtured and developed.

However, branding is no longer confined to just corporate names and product positioning. The phenomenon has now become personal. And because of the powerful technologies at our disposal, this trend presents a crucial opportunity for managers. Our Ford- or Chevy-loyal forebears would be mystified by this development, but there it is: Branding is now a potent tool for business professionals who are looking to create their own unique style of executive presence.

Brand Yourself Before Others Brand You *Very Good*

What exactly is a brand? People think of a brand as something that has a locked file cabinet full of design trademarks and copyrights and a suite of lawyers on call to protect and defend them. Brands appear to be something that takes hordes of specialists years to develop, and at a cost often in the hundreds of millions of dollars. That perception is not completely wrong: Brands don't just happen; they are the sum of everything that goes into the delivery of quality, the positioning and marketing of products and services, and over time the achieving of a tipping point in terms of word-of-mouth, on-the-street reputation.

Brands and reputation are often confused or used interchangeably. They are certainly linked—taking control and burnishing your brand will undoubtedly affect your reputation—but they aren't the same. Your personal brand is under your control: You decide what story you want to tell about yourself and how you go about telling it. Your words, your actions, what you emphasize, and the goals of the branding process are all in your hands. Reputation, though, is all about others and how they perceive and respond to you. The two concepts are linked, because through your brand you can influence that perception of you. Create a strong brand, and you get a jump on building a strong reputation.

The strength of your brand is especially important because it's durable. Deborah Maue, an administrator at Columbia College Chicago, argues: "A brand is enduring. Reputation is more temporary, yet it can bolster or diminish the brand over time." Even the best performers will suffer from down moments and dented reputations, but having a good foundation will give you the basis for staging a comeback. Your brand is like a house with "good bones": Even if bad weather damages the exterior, a sturdy structure will remain standing.

We're all familiar with the importance of brand in advertising. If you watch the Super Bowl, you will see the most expensive advertisements imaginable in terms of media buys (not necessarily in terms of production budget), and these costly spots strive not so much to pitch us product features and benefits as to increase our awareness of a brand. Famous musicians, top athletes, and television and movie stars say little in these ads about how a product stacks up, but they speak volumes about the essence of the brand.

Without a brand, a product must fend for itself, and research shows that that is usually not enough. Without a brand, good products, great ideas, and talented people sink usually into a crowded sea of mediocrity.

Although we don't tend to think of it this way, the phenomenon of branding has become pervasive for individuals. Celebrities and politicians are well known for employing professionals to mold, spin, and propel their brand into the marketplace, but they are now being joined by anyone who seeks to build a career, a social network, a business, or other entity. No matter how narrow a segment they are targeting, they want to show that they are worthy, talented, or downright cool.

For example, such famed business tycoons as Warren Buffett, Martha Stewart, Oprah Winfrey, Jeff Bezos, and Richard Branson owe their ascent to instant recognition as much to successful branding as to the viability of their products and the weight of their experience. These superstars of business and the media managed to make their names and likenesses inseparable in the public mind from the services and products their businesses provide. Each one's brand is unique, and their executive presence is palpable. They command respect globally not only because their products are superior but because they understand how to create a strong presence that connects emotionally and intellectually with their constituents. When you hear their names and see their faces, you instantly know what they stand for. This instant recognition of one's strengths and character should be your goal as you strive to create your own executive presence.

The notion that everyone already has constructed a personal brand may be surprising, but it is indisputable. People manifest and shape their personal brands in ways big and small, from the kind of car they leave in the office parking lot, to the type of suit they wear, to the way they carry themselves, to the manner in which they do their work. For better or worse, many people build their brand *randomly*, without the slightest awareness of its power. If you show up late for meetings, if your presentations lack substance, if you're generally unpleasant, then by default you're creating a personal brand. If you bring baked goods to the office to share, if you know the names of your coworkers' children and ask about them, you're also creating a personal brand—one that stays with you when the social niceties give way to doing business.

Personal brands often determine others' behavior. If it's you that everybody turns to when the computer goes down, you've created your own brand. Whether that particular bit of branding *serves* you, however, is another issue altogether. It's easy to create a random brand; in fact, as we've seen above, it's almost inevitable. However, to ensure that your brand earns the respect of your peers and bosses, and furthers your career and personal goals, you want to use a *controlled* approach to the art and craft of branding—one that can be every bit as effective and rewarding as the strategies employed on Madison Avenue.

Consider respected athletes who happen to play for less than stellar teams. Although attendance dwindles as their teams sink to the bottom of the standings, these athletes' personal brands are insulated by their standout performance. Here we're talking about not only on-the-field results but also their presence, character, integrity, and energy. Just ask Lance Armstrong or Tiger Woods what happens to a personal brand when a person's off-field comportment is not congruent with his or her athletic ability. The same is true for all of us: Job performance, as you'll learn in the next section, is only one component of a brand. Your brand is not just what you can do; it is a sum that includes how you do it and who you are in that process. It is the power of that sum total, its ability to influence choices and consequences, that can make you stand out. If you do it right, people will notice. You'll have developed a brand and a charismatic executive presence that will serve you going forward.

The Role of Status in Personal Branding

Critical to the success of your personal brand is your perceived status. Status is about your place in the social pecking order. It's about your social value in comparison with that of others. It's about the respect and deference others accord to you—or not. We've all known colleagues to whom others seem to swarm to seek advice, to socialize, to confide in, and to get approval. And we know others who are virtually invisible. No one seeks their advice. No one confides in them. No one is looking to bask in their dim light.

Needless to say, high status is better than low status. There's at least one exception, though. If you are a high-status individual, with all the interpersonal and reputational perks that status brings, you'd benefit from occasionally stepping down from Mount Olympus to empathize and gain the trust and favor of those who may respect you but find you distant and aloof. That quality of empathy that characterizes the lowering of one's status is also called *humility,* which, incidentally, further enhances your status rather than diminishes it.

But how can we elevate our status in the first place? Are we in the clear if we occupy a leadership role on the organizational flowchart? Not according to scientific research, which shows that status isn't always commensurate with one's position in the hierarchy. Rice University professor Rick Wilson studied low- and high-status leaders and observed, "In teams with high-status leaders, followers are more likely to go along with them, even though the leader does not necessarily set a good example." Low-status leaders, the researchers found, had more difficulty getting their teams to follow their direction, which in turn led them to punish team members more. Team members responded by punishing their leaders in return—creating something of a vicious circle.

Other studies have confirmed that low status combined with power can generate bad outcomes: University of Southern California professor Nathanael Fast and his colleagues found that executives with power but low status were more likely to assign demeaning tasks to subordinates, leading the researchers to conclude that "having power without status . . . may be a catalyst for producing demeaning behaviors that can destroy relationships and impede goodwill."

Studies of "status syndrome" demonstrate that the desire for status is universal among humans. "Everyone cares about status whether they're aware of it or not," argues Professor Cameron Anderson of Berkeley's Haas School of Business, noting further that "status differences can be demoralizing. Whenever you don't feel valued by others it hurts, and the lack of status hurts more people than we think."

In a study of farming villages in Bolivia, for example, UC Santa Barbara anthropology professor Michael Gurven concluded that differences in the villagers' social status "impacts their perceptions, their level of stress and their health." Interestingly, these villages had relatively egalitarian social structures—but that did not mean there was no variety in social status. "We're able to show that there are measurable differences in recognized social status even within the egalitarian context, and that these differences matter," Gurven reported. "They're all equal, and yet social status is important."

It isn't just humans with higher status who live longer and healthier lives; some similarly situated animals do, too. A zoology doctoral student, Nora Lewin of Michigan State University, has observed, "High-ranking members in hyena clans reproduce more, they live longer and appear to be in better overall health."

If it isn't power that automatically confers higher status in an organization, is it perhaps the value we contribute to others? Well, performance *does* matter—that study of Bolivian farmers showed that those who contributed more to the group were held in greater esteem—but as we've often witnessed, or even experienced ourselves, good performance in a complex and competitive business environment doesn't always translate to higher status. Plenty of managers who are subject-matter experts and highly capable individual contributors seem to get stuck in the middle rungs of the corporate ladder. Their abilities make them valued employees, but in letting their "performance speak for itself," they may end up being defined by their jobs rather than defining themselves.

What does consistently elevate one's status in the workplace is *speaking up*. Studies from the Haas School of Business discovered that people who speak up and appear confident are perceived to be more competent to lead.

The main findings of the studies were that assertive behavior can help people attain influence, at least in small groups. And while hundreds of previous studies had shown that dominant people take charge, what wasn't clear until now is why others so willingly followed them. The new research found that assertive people attained such influence because the rest of the group saw them as more *competent* than everybody else. They were seen as more creative, dedicated, and harder working than the others—even when they actually weren't. In the studies, small groups performed various tasks, and even when the dominant personalities didn't perform well in the group math and creativity tasks, they were still seen as the most competent, both by other group members and by the judges who viewed the recorded sessions afterward.

The big—and surprising—lesson, according to the Haas researchers, is that being assertive and dominant, not skill itself, is the strongest predictor of your reputation for being skilled. Assertiveness and dominance also induce others to follow your lead due to that perception.

When you understand how your status at work impacts your personal brand, you'll be able to make choices that contribute to favorable perceptions of your overall executive presence.

The Six Pillars of Branding

A successful commercial brand favorably influences the perceptions and behaviors of those who encounter it. A personal brand is no different; and by understanding some of the attributes that both types of branding share, you'll be better equipped to lay the foundation for your own personalized branding strategy. Below I share my "Six Pillars of Powerful Personal Branding"—essential strategies you can implement to build an executive presence that can't be ignored.

1. Appeals to Values

If a brand doesn't appeal to what's important to others and connect deeply to those values, it's not working. Think, for example, of Subaru and Volvo and their appeal to the value of safety. *Safety* is the first association that *interesting* people make when considering either brand. Nelson Mandela's personal brand appealed to values of *forgiveness*, *healing*, and *working together*. He put these values into action by forgiving his former jailers, even inviting several of them to highly visible events marking the changes in the new South Africa. He invited one of them, Christo Brand, to a dinner celebrating the anniversary of his release from prison, stating that his relationship with Brand "reinforced my belief in the essential humanity of even those who had kept me behind bars." He invited a second warder, Paul Gregory, to his inauguration, and he even had lunch with the man—State Prosecutor Percy Yutar—who had called for Mandela's execution following his 1963 conviction for sabotage. Most famously, Mandela sought to unite his country behind the Springbok rugby team, long a symbol of white supremacy and apartheid, during the 1995 World Cup final, even donning a Springbok jersey himself.

Think about the values that people care about. They are what guide virtually all their decisions. Decide which of those values you want to appeal to and how you can embody them so they resonate with others.

2. Conveys Authenticity

authentic
joy
&
energy
Do others see you as the real deal? A brand must feel genuine, showing that it *walks the walk*. Zappos, Harley-Davidson, and The Honest Company are examples of companies that are aligned in word and action on what they stand for and provide to consumers. And consumers trust them. Nobel Peace Prize laureate Malala Yousafzai, who was shot for her advocacy of educating girls in her native Pakistan, matches that description. She had been airlifted to the United Kingdom for lifesaving treatment, and as a victim, she could have chosen to withdraw and live in safety and relative comfort. But many months and surgeries later, it was clear that wasn't her path: "It was then I knew I had a choice: I could live a quiet life, or I could

make the most of this new life I had been given. I determined to continue my fight until every girl could go to school." She created the Malala Fund to push to educate girls around the world; in other words, at great risk to herself, she has continued to walk the walk.

Authenticity is a standout quality that becomes an even more powerful brand attribute when we consider the glaring lies and hollow promises we're subjected to daily by corrupt politicians, spokespersons, and others in whom many had placed their trust. Consider disgraced bicyclist Lance Armstrong, who repeatedly and forcefully denied that he had ever used performance-enhancing drugs during his long dominance of the sport—to the point of legally pursuing those who said otherwise.

Unlike Armstrong, tell the truth, keep your word, and follow through on promises and commitments. That is a good way to project authenticity.

3. Provides Benefits

A successful brand must deliver results. Apple delivers innovative products that make our lives easier with their constantly updated features, and the brand additionally confers a certain status on its customers. Tylenol is the most trusted brand in the headache relief category in 2018; if it didn't quickly and reliably alleviate headaches, it would lose that distinction. Jack Welch increased the value of GE by 4,000 percent during his two-decade tenure. Revenues grew from $25 billion to $130 billion, with profits increasing 10-fold, from $1.5 billion to $15 billion. Those impressive numbers explain why, even today, with Welch in his eighties, he is sought out for leadership advice. A contrary example is Tim Tebow, who was hailed as the second coming of Christ when he was drafted to the NFL but washed out when he couldn't land the ball in his receivers' hands. He's currently working out in the minor leagues, trying to rebrand himself as a baseball player.

If you consistently deliver on promises, meet people's expectations, and provide clear value, your personal brand will increase in value as a matter of course.

4. Inspires Others

Successful brands—through word and deed—set examples that others want to follow. Such a brand makes us *feel* something. Apple, again, according to annual surveys, is one of the top inspirational companies; it's become part of people's identity. People say it makes them feel more creative, more entrepreneurial. Nike just hired quarterback and activist Colin Kaepernick as a spokesman for its brand because he inspires people by speaking truth to power. Nike took a risk by associating itself with the controversial Kaepernick, but so far, in the campaign's first few months, the move has paid off with increased sales. Malala, too, is an inspirational figure, as is J. K. Rowling, whose modest background made her literary accomplishments and her influential advocacy of women's and girls' rights even more uplifting.

Finally, Elon Musk, despite his idiosyncrasies, has excited motorists with Tesla cars and space enthusiasts with SpaceX's rockets—and combined them with the launch of a Tesla into orbit between earth and Mars. As *Guardian* journalist Bonnie Malkin wrote of a photo of the audacious venture, "It takes a beat or two for the brain to compute. The image is startling, incongruous, barmy. A car floats in space. At the wheel is a spacesuit, seatbelt on. Earth hangs behind it. . . . The photograph was beamed down to Earth courtesy of Elon Musk's ego, bravado and taste for the absurd. It is human folly and genius rolled into one, a picture that sums up 2018 so far. Life on Earth feels precarious, so we look to the stars."

If you can get others to dream and reach for the stars, your personal brand and executive presence will inspire long after you've left the room.

5. Stays Consistent

FedEx built a reputation around delivering packages consistently on time. Starbucks—love it or hate it—consistently provides the same brew and its copious variations at over 28,000 locations worldwide. A Grande Hazelnut Frappuccino tastes the same in Singapore as it does in Seattle. A brand must be consistent to be trusted—and just like we've come to trust Google with our online searches, Google's leaders have found that consistency is also what makes for successful managers inside the company. Annual surveys of employees on their leaders' effectiveness have found that the quality that employees value most in their managers is predictability. In other words, if workers can count on their managers to provide the information they need, and then stay out of their way, they can do their best work without having to worry about managers meddling, criticizing, or taking over.

The secret to managing your personal brand is to monitor your words and actions to ensure they are what people have come to expect.

6. Manages Visibility

A brand that is tucked away on some out-of-view display or shoved onto a shelf several feet below eye level is a dud. The same goes for brands whose packaging is bland and forgettable. Billionaire entrepreneur Richard Branson personifies Virgin—speaks for it and creates attention for it with all kinds of stunts and appearances. As reputation strategist Leslie Gaines-Ross notes of a study her company conducted, "While it's important to be humble, a successful CEO can't be a wallflower." The vast majority of executives worldwide believe that their companies' reputations depend on a high-profile CEO. Furthermore, CEOs who are held in high esteem are far more likely to have created a profile so compelling that it draws the public to them. As Gaines-Ross summarizes, to rise above all the noise and competing narratives, the CEO herself has to "attend to the clarion call, standing up and standing out so as to tell the company's story."

To translate this for the rest of us whose executive presence is still under construction: You have to be proactive and speak up for your brand; i.e., let people see who you are, make some noise, share your discoveries and fresh ideas, show how you can contribute value. And do it in a socially intelligent way that attracts rather than repels people. As colorful as Richard Branson is, he's also an extremely warm and humble person who connects easily with people from all walks of life. Something to which we should all aspire.

You can't go wrong making these six pillars part of your effort to establish a strong personal brand and boost your executive presence. And if it all seems a bit overwhelming, start with one and work your way through the others. The next section provides some ideas on how to implement a step-by-step plan for your personal brand that you can easily apply to any of your development goals.

The Steps to Personal Branding

It's easy to perceive the process of personal branding as a theory, a set of social and psychological principles that quickly blur around the edges. It's sort of like dieting and fitness—we have a general concept of how it works, but to get anywhere with it, we have to break it down into actionable steps. By charting a sequence of steps and checklists onto the concepts of personal branding and executive presence, a road map emerges that will lead you to quicker results in your quest to reach those destinations.

To get started:

- Assess the nature and status of your existing personal brand, however randomly you may have created it. Do you have a concrete understanding of how you are perceived by your colleagues, peers, bosses, and other stakeholders in your organization? What is your current reputation? What behaviors, results, or energies have you manifested that have resulted in this perception of you? Get feedback from trusted sources and be open to hearing things you may not expect or like.
- Identify specific changes in attitude, behavior, character, and general energy that will strengthen your brand and reinforce your executive presence. Consider your role in the organizational system—what competencies should you develop to succeed in that role? What about future roles? What skills, behaviors, and attributes do you need to develop to prepare yourself for the next step in your career? Commit to a plan to get you there. Forgive yourself for missteps as you move forward one day at a time, always doing the best you can to live your new brand.

- Continue the feedback-gathering and self-assessment process by enlisting trusted colleagues, mentors, and sponsors to provide input on adjusting your development plan. Create your own scorecard and give yourself regular performance reviews, highlighting the areas in which you know you need to improve.

A personal branding exercise that I do in my workshops may help you form ideas for your aspirational brand and an action plan that gets you there:

I start by showing pictures of well-known personalities for a few seconds each. I ask people to write down the first five things that come to mind. For instance, when I show Steve Jobs, people write 'innovator," "genius," "tyrant," "impatient," "visionary," etc. They do this for each personality. Then I show them a silhouette with an indistinct face and say "That's you! What would you want people to say in just a few seconds about you if they saw your face up there or heard your name? *Not* what you think they'd say right now, which is your reputation, but what you'd *want* them to say in the future once you've had a chance to decide on and work on your most aspirational brand."

They usually write down things like "generous," "compassionate," "innovative leader," "intelligent," "problem solver," "strategic thinker," etc. I ask each person to pick one or two of those qualities, the ones the person would most want to be known for as a personal brand. One person might decide that she wants to be seen as someone who is "honest and has high integrity." Then I ask her to ask seven of her fellow workshop participants in the room to give her two ideas each in brief three-minute conversations on how she can accomplish this goal of being seen as "honest and a person of high integrity." The colleagues will then give (and get) two ideas each that the person can incorporate into an action plan. For the person seeking the attributes of honesty and integrity, the list might include:

- Follow through on commitments and keep promises.
- Don't betray anyone's trust.
- Be transparent in your communications and keep others in the loop.
- Be ethical even if it would be easier to cut corners and no one would know.

- Don't abuse your power.
- Be consistent in words and actions.
- Give credit where it's due.
- Be honest in all interactions.
- Give honest feedback when asked.
- Don't gossip about others or speak badly about them.
- Always tell the truth even if it's uncomfortable.
- Don't manipulate people.
- Don't cheat (fudge numbers, results, etc.).
- Don't let someone else take the blame for your mistake.
- Disclose conflicts of interest and remove yourself if necessary.

This is one example of how you can decide on and create an action plan to achieve your desired personal brand. You could also pick someone you admire and think about the qualities he espouses (such as honesty and high integrity), and then ask people you trust for their ideas on what observable actions you can take to get there.

You also need to network. Some people are naturals at this; others dread even hearing the word. But networking is about more than "glad-handing" and "backslapping"; it's about building the relationships that will sustain your career and help propel your brand. INSEAD professors Herminia Ibarra and Mark Lee Hunter observe that "networking is not a talent; nor does it require a gregarious, extroverted personality. It is a skill, one that takes practice." They define three types of networks: operational, personal, and strategic. The first, operational, is the most straightforward to cultivate, largely because this network consists of the people who are necessary for you to do your job. Mapping out and tending to work relationships can help you see who is integral to the work you do, as well as identify those outside your immediate area to whom you need to pay attention. The second type of networking—personal—may require a bit of legwork off the clock, as you cultivate relationships with others outside your workplace. As the professors put it, "Through professional associations, alumni groups, clubs, and personal-interest communities, managers gain new perspectives that allow them to advance in their careers." Personal networks also provide information, contacts, and opportunities for professional development. Finally, with strategic networking, you get "the ability to marshal information, support, and resources from one sector of a network to achieve results in another." Think of strategic networking as the kind of relationship building that benefits not only you, but your entire organization.

Broadly speaking, effective networking means you are building relationships with people inside and outside your company who can potentially help you to the next level in your career and become advocates for the personal brand you've created.

Finally, a word about branding for people who dislike putting themselves out there: namely, introverts. Introversion is often conflated with shyness, but they are distinct traits. Introverts aren't necessarily shy, but instead they have hard limits on how much social stimulation they can tolerate. Dorie Clark, professional speaker (and introvert), observes that many of the strategies suggested for building a brand require socializing of some form or another and are therefore daunting to those who can take only so much schmoozing. She recommends that these people rely heavily on social media to build a brand; it gives you time to think through what you want to present and allows you to reach a lot of people without being overwhelmed by them. Another strategy for the introverted is to go micro, reaching out to people one at a time in different areas of your organization. Make it a habit to take a new colleague for coffee, or suggest lunch. Introduce new colleagues to others. You can make a name for yourself by becoming a "connector," someone that others value based on your savvy in navigating both the social and bureaucratic barriers within the organization. By bringing others together, you elevate your personal brand without having to become the center of attention yourself. A third way to make yourself known is to simply display your credentials or awards as an indirect way to inform others about you. Just put your college diploma on the wall behind your desk and your Ironman medal on the bookshelf. People will take notice. These strategic ways of increasing your visibility can also be used by extroverts, of course, but are critical for those who dread the more socially forward path to branding.

What to Do When Your Personal Brand Takes a Hit

There is a big difference between rebuilding a personal brand and starting from scratch. The headlines are buzzing with familiar names who are taking hits to their personal brands, from a tech icon melting down on Twitter, to a popular comedian tossed off her television show, to a married member of Congress caught sexting minors. Whether such personal brands will be permanently affected by their protagonists' poor judgment depends on the nature of the offense and the fickleness of the public. Like the howling mob in a gladiator flick whose thumbs up or thumbs down decide the fate of the guy on the ground, people today love to sit in judgment—and will use *their* thumbs on Twitter and other social media to issue their verdict. For public figures, the go-to remedies for a damaged brand run the gamut, from teary-eyed apologies, to aggressive counterattacks, to acknowledgment of a personal problem—sex, drugs, and alcohol top the list—and the subsequent checking into some sort of rehab program.

For those of us without an army of PR flacks and crisis management consultants, however, the remedies are different. Consider the person who has cultivated the personal brand of "innovator" but who's no longer contributing smart, creative, successful solutions to problems. Or imagine an executive known as a "rainmaker" who suddenly stops attracting new clients for her firm. To fix their unraveling brands, both of these individuals need to swiftly figure out the cause of their faltering—or else watch their brands fade into oblivion. We often see this scenario play out in sports and entertainment, when a champion golfer no longer wins or an eminent director produces one flop after another. Unless you can fix whatever is keeping you from performing at your former best, your brand will no longer work for you.

Other challenges to your personal brand may focus on a loss of trust rather than a decline in performance. Maybe, for example, you are seen as a person whose integrity is beyond reproach, but you have now taken some ethical shortcuts in adverse situations. The only way to restore your reputation as a "paragon of virtue" is to take ownership of those ethical failings, explain your thinking, show contrition, and vow to return to the right track. Will you get the thumbs-up or thumbs-down? That depends on how egregious your errors were perceived to be and the context in which they were committed.

If you are a leader, though, personal ethical correctness is not enough. You are still on the hook if wrongdoing is rampant among the people you are supposed to lead. Wells Fargo leaders learned that lesson when thousands of their employees were found to have defrauded customers by charging them fees for fake accounts that they never knew were opened in their name. Only by "cleaning house"—being completely transparent about what happened, how you are going to fix it, and how you will prevent it from ever happening again—can you hope to regain your good name.

In the worst case, you may have damaged your personal brand so gravely that you've become "toxic" even to former supporters. People will not want to associate with you lest their own brand is tainted by yours. Examples of this abound in entertainment, where the #MeToo movement has sent high-flying stars and executives crashing down to earth. The highfliers' lunch calendars likely have been freed up as a result; few of their former friends and associates would take the risk of basking in their radioactive glow.

If damage you caused to your personal brand has similarly ostracized you from your peers, it's time to move on. You're not going to regain your former status in the same environment, or maybe even in the same industry. Take some time off to reinvent yourself and start afresh. And while a cloud may follow you to your other endeavors, by setting aspirational goals and consistently achieving them with the right skills and behaviors, and with lots of time and patience, you may find yourself once again the owner of a personal brand that others can trust.

In Chapter 12 we'll explore how you can expand your brand on the Internet as you continue to hone a compelling executive presence that tells others instantly who you are and what you stand for.

I 2

Virtual Branding

Using the Web to Bolster Your Personal Brand

I TRUST YOU'RE familiar with some of the more high-profile social media sites and how they've revolutionized and democratized communication on the web. There are now myriad opportunities to enhance one's reputation and personal brand online.

Before Facebook, YouTube, and other social media sites, brand management involved unleashing top marketing professionals onto a product or service (I include "branded" personalities in the product category here, such as *American Idol* winners, top athletes, authors, and business personalities like Sheryl Sandberg). The purpose, of course, was to furnish that product or service with a distinct identity, one designed to increase its perceived value and appeal to the end user.

Fortunately for those of us who don't command a marketing army, the rules of engagement have now changed. Social media has made it easier than ever before to connect with people who want to buy what you're selling. Here are the basics of this new, democratic opportunity to create an online brand.

Reach Through the Web

In the first edition of this book, I discussed the comedian Dane Cook, whose practice of engaging personally with his growing fan base served as a powerful example of how social media can be leveraged to build a successful personal brand. Since then, professionals from all walks of life have used LinkedIn, Facebook, Instagram, YouTube, and Twitter to build relationships with their audience and increase their reach. It's now become somewhat common practice for a growing number of CEOs to communicate directly with customers, for authors to engage with their readers, and for artists to have conversations with their fans. As a result, entire communities have sprung up around both people and products. Apple fans are among the most (in)famous for their brand loyalty, eagerly sharing rumors about the latest version of the iPhone, while controversial tech icon Elon Musk has drawn a loyal group of supporters to defend and promote both himself and his company, Tesla. And there's nothing better for a fan than to get a "like" or a retweet from a favorite celebrity.

The term that best describes this model of online brand management is "tribe management," a definition widely attributed to marketing guru and blogger Seth Godin, who wrote a book on the topic titled *Tribes*.

Think of Harley-Davidson and the tribes that have clustered around that powerful brand. It may be fun to ride a "Fat Boy" Softail around town by oneself, but it doesn't compare with the thrill of connecting with other riders and touring several states together or congregating by the thousand in Sturgis, South Dakota, every year. The true definition of a tribe, Harley-Davidson fans express themselves and show their tribal affiliation with their black leather gear, Harley-Davidson's orange logo, and their bandannas, sunglasses, and other markings. They are bartenders, accountants, pet-shop owners, financial analysts, truck drivers, and lawyers—people of all different backgrounds and socioeconomic levels, but all are members of this brand-created tribe.

It follows that such people love hearing from the company or the person—the brand—because it underlines that they are part of a community or tribe. They know that love of the brand binds them together, spurring them to chat, gossip, exchange stories, share ideas, and generally build lasting relationships that reward them with more than they could receive without being part of the tribe. What's true for Harley-Davidson's tribe is equally true of many other brands' tribes, such as those of the TV series *Game of Thrones*, billionaire entrepreneur Richard Branson, the TED conference, NASCAR, the Boston Red Sox, Oprah, Beyoncé, and many more.

Your challenge in creating a personal brand that grows through social media is to position yourself, and your wares, in a way that inspires and engages people and establishes an open line of communication. When it works, those people will be eager to share the experience with others, and with some added finesse, you'll develop a loyal following in the process. Give people real value and a visceral experience, and you'll keep their attention. Bore them, however, and your brand will have the life span of a Snapchat picture.

Online Generations: A Quick Overview

For those of us looking to expand our personal brand online, social media is both exciting and exasperating. There's always something new, but just as you get used to writing a regular blogpost on your site, you learn that posting your articles on LinkedIn would get you more exposure. The good news is that to keep track of who's paying attention, you just pull out your smartphone. Just as the Internet made information available with a few clicks of a keyboard, smartphones now bring all that information to your pocket or purse. In fact, cyberspace is now with us everywhere we go, not just with our smartphones but with our smart homes and Bluetooth-enabled cars, all of them accessible with just a few finger taps or simple voice commands. You can be as connected as you want to be—as long as you keep up with the changes.

The Pew Research Center has been tracking social media trends in the United States since 2012, and its latest 2018 studies estimate that a majority of Americans now use social media, with Facebook (68 percent) and YouTube (73 percent) in the lead. For those who are crafting a personal online brand targeted at certain demographic groups, the following data may be useful: Among 50- to 64-year-olds, 68 percent use social media, as opposed to 78 percent of those 30 to 49 and 88 percent of those 18 to 29. It is only among those 65 or older that social media use falls

facts on social media

below 50 percent. There are also wide demographic variations in what sites are popular. While those younger than 30, along with everyone else, favor Facebook (81 percent) and YouTube (91 percent), they are also more likely to visit sites such as Instagram and Snapchat. Breaking down the under-30 group even further, Pew notes that while a bare majority (54 percent) of those 25 to 29 use Instagram and Snapchat, roughly three-quarters of those 18 to 25 visit those sites—71 percent use Instagram, and almost as many use Snapchat (78 percent) as Facebook (80 percent).

Instagram + Facebook

These demographic data lead to valuable conclusions. If you'd like to reach generation Z, for instance, your efforts are best expended posting videos where gen Zers tend to hang out—YouTube.

Of course, it isn't just millennials and gen Z that use social media. While they are greater consumers than other age groups, gen X and boomers are major users, too. Nonetheless, those who grew up with social media, the so-called digital natives, are far more likely to experiment with new apps than those of us who grew up with landlines and newspaper delivery.

And while it's been reported that millennials and gen Z are abandoning social media in droves, I hardly think they'll return to smoke signals. While some millennials and other consumers say they could drop out of social media, these tools are such an integral part of the communications landscape that any such change is likely to be a long time coming.

What's more likely is that as millennials and gen Z age, the tools and apps they use will change. Some evidence exists that teenagers and the youngest adults are moving away from Facebook and hopping onto other sites. Another study, by the American Press Institute, notes, "Younger Millennials are even more likely to use a wider mix of social networks for news than older members of this generation. The average 18-to-21-year-old uses 3.7 social networks out of seven platforms asked about in the survey. For the average older Millennials age 30–34, that decreases to 2.9."

Even social media usage of the youngest users evolves. One participant in the API study, age 19, went so far as to delete his Facebook account, explaining that "I stopped using it because there are other things to use." Still, most young adults do use Facebook, relying on it to be entertained, to share content, and, especially, to stay on top of what's happening with their friends. And while Twitter use lags behind Facebook's, young adults turn to it more often to find out what's trending.

The upshot of all of this is that social media is massive, enduring, and evolving. Facebook both has become an institution and routinely introduces new features to keep users within its universe, adding Instagram and WhatsApp and even venturing into content production. Children whose lives were documented online have become adults comfortable with surfing across the cyberverse in search of the next new thing, and people of all ages have become increasingly adept at curating their online experiences. These stats make it very clear that a personal brand that isn't online is akin to the proverbial tree falling in a forest with no one around to hear it. Does your brand make a sound?

Ride the Social Media Wave

One constant in these turbulent tides is people's desire for connection. People want to connect to friends and family; they want to connect with their favorite thought leaders and artists; and they want to connect to the world to see what others are up to.

Even if you don't have a Facebook page, or a Twitter, Instagram, or YouTube account, you've almost certainly seen the tweets, posts, and videos and listened to the podcasts that others have created. You may be far from a pro with thousands of engaged followers, but you likely know your way around the basics of social media.

On the off chance that you don't, however, I strongly encourage you to dive in. Most sites make it easy to join, and once you've gotten the hang of posting your content or following a few favorites, you can quickly master more advanced features. For your questions, check out the FAQ pages, and if the answers aren't sufficient, a quick Google search will get you the information you need. Follow people you admire and see how they manage *their* brands, i.e., what type of content they post, how often they post, and how they engage their followers. Also pay attention to those who start popping up in your timeline, and gauge why everyone's suddenly talking about them. In other words, learn what gets you noticed, and notice what works.

The important thing is to stay true to the brand you've built offline. A Jekyll and Hyde strategy for offline-online branding can tarnish your reputation. For instance, if you've built a name as a thoughtful, soft-spoken sage, don't fill your Twitter account with biting sarcasm or ad hominem attacks. Similarly, if your reputation is that of the Zen master, posts in which you whine about slow service or the malfunctioning Wi-Fi on your flight will knock a few points off your brand quotient.

Be aware that the default setting of almost all social media is for content to be available to everyone 24/7. You have the option to change those settings and make your profile private or require that people ask for access before they can see your tweets or posts. Keep in mind, however, that building an online presence requires a certain amount of visibility and willingness to open up. You might have some longstanding accounts, such as Facebook, in which you interact primarily with friends and family and which may include some exchanges that you both cherish and don't want strangers to see. In that case, it might make sense to keep your personal account private and create a business "page" outside that account. However, it clearly makes little sense to lock down a professional networking account like LinkedIn if you're hoping to promote your brand across that platform.

How to Keep Your Brand Humming Online

Your brand lives by the attention it gets and the reputation it garners online. It's noisier than ever on the web—from advertisements for the latest fads, to a slew of pitches in annoying pop-ups, to news and blogs from thousands of channels. Add the hundreds of e-mails that people must plow through after a busy day of meetings away from the computer, and you'll appreciate how difficult it is to draw online attention to *your* personal brand.

To be heard above the cacophony, keep these basic principles in mind:

Present Well

Your website or portal or whatever the first stop is in your online home should be spectacular. I don't mean spectacular like your neighbor's Christmas display, which could power the Chrysler Building. It should be spectacular as in simple, elegant, and ultra-user-friendly: easy to navigate, easy to understand, and easy to find things. One very spectacular site under this definition is Apple.com. It's one of many examples of uncluttered, friendly sites that offer the online equivalent of a firm handshake and a smile. Unfortunately, however, there are thousands that are the cyber equivalent of a burp in the face and a grunted "Yeah?" In rare instances that reception is intentional, such as with a punk rock band. But if you've never heard of the Ramones and this description sounds like your site, remember this: Your brand lives online 24/7, and each visitor who comes to your site will walk away with an impression of whether the relationship has potential.

Innovation Matters

"Always be closing!" That's a famous line from the movie *Glengarry Glen Ross*, and it can be nicely adapted to your online brand like this: "Always be innovating!" Your competitors and rivals will always have new ideas, new articles, or new books popping up in others' timelines. If you think you've made your mark and proceed to settle into your recliner, be prepared to be unsettled—or "disrupted." For the stark reality is that the competition doesn't sleep. Steve Jobs understood this, and so should you. The Apple impresario kept the buzz going about new developments in the iPhone, the iPod, and those famous laptops that are thinner than a slice of cheese. He did this by consistently coming up with unexpected new product features and designs. The resulting chatter kept Jobs in the conversation, and even after his death, his successor Tim Cook has used these same techniques to keep Apple in the black.

Given modern society's fleeting attention spans and fickle tastes, we must do the same with our brands. Never rest; always think about ways to innovate and develop buzzworthy conversation starters. Participate in LinkedIn groups or online forums like Reddit or Quora to share your knowledge and demonstrate your expertise. Podcasts are also a great way to go deep. At the more topical level, keeping tabs on the latest hashtags can loop you into the latest topics. If your fans, customers, followers, and clients aren't excited about you anymore, they'll stop talking about you. Putting all your creative energy into improving what was hot about you yesterday—or five minutes ago, in Internet time—will pay off when you're the topic of discussion again today.

Accept the Invitation

Once you make it to the C-level, you have a head start because people want to hear from you. According to research conducted by Burson-Marsteller, a global public relations and communications firm that tracks participation in executive forums among C-level executives, CEOs are flooded with invitations to speak at conferences, receiving an average of 175 requests a year. Most of these high-profile events are covered by industry organs and often by national media, all of which can boost your online executive presence with their digital subscribers and visitors. So when the time comes, carefully sift through that pile of invitations on your desk and decide which ones give you the biggest return on investment. After all, you'll have a company to run.

Keep Talking

I think You want the world to talk about you, so you have got to talk a lot yourself. *Some people get nervous talking ab themselves but it can be a strength* It's called a conversation, and who better to tell your raving fans you want to hear from them than you, the brand? The Internet's hierarchy is flat, and people don't care that much to engage with marketing or customer service or some other hired gun who speaks for you. Get on the other side of the monitor, cut out the person in the middle, and start talking to your customers. It's time-consuming and fraught with risk—you may be asked some uncomfortable questions—but the fewer layers that people have to wade through to hear directly from the horse's mouth, the less BS and spin they feel they're getting. Entrepreneurs and CEOs who have gained the respect of their tribes and strengthened their executive presence by being chief communicators for their brands include Zappo.com's Tony Hsieh, LinkedIn cofounder Reid Hoffman, and Craigslist founder Craig Newmark. They tweet, they blog, they talk to their fans, and that's the way you keep the relationship fresh and your brand in the minds of your customers.

Put Your Name on Something

You may not have the spare change to put your name on a major sports center or arena, which can cost between $3 million and $10 million per year, with contracts up to 30 years. Having a law school named after you is not much cheaper, with the price of legacy, as it was referred to in the *National Law Journal*, being somewhere between $3 million for Nova Southwestern University to an asking price of $100 million for the University of Minnesota Law School. Deeper pockets still are needed for medical schools. For the UCLA David Geffen School of Medicine, for instance, the movie mogul paid a handsome $200 million in 2002.

attach name to something ✓

More realistically, however, you could name an award, a charity you started, a scholarship you could award every year, or an annual event you sponsor. You could promote it on your website, share it on your social media profiles, and post videos on YouTube to let your followers know it's not just a gimmick but a real effort to bring value to a group of people. The bigger the event and the more people who are affected, the more likely it is that you'll create an online buzz that elevates your personal brand above the noise.

Keep the Brand Alive

Once you've established your online presence and developed relation-ships with your followers, you need to maintain those relationships. If you become known for red-hot takes on emerging markets or your in-depth assessments of the latest tech products, you have to reliably deliver those takes. If you trained people to expect your weekly podcast with interviews of other thought leaders, don't surprise them with unexpected gaps in your schedule. There may be times when you want or need to step back, but if you keep your followers in the loop about why you're taking a break, they'll welcome you back when you do return. Just don't stay away too long, or you'll find yourself starting over in a whole new world.

In Chapter 13 you'll learn how, in this era of transparency and tech-nology, your reputation is unavoidably tethered to Google and other search engines. We will explore how, if trouble arises, you can avoid sabotaging the public perceptions you've worked hard to create.

13

You've Been Googled

What's the Verdict?

"CONSUMERS ARE MOVING their lives online," said Google's former CEO Eric Schmidt in an interview with *Fortune* magazine. To put the Google chief's statement into perspective, consider the bizarre story of Hasan Elahi and a life "gone online."

Elahi, a Bangladesh-born U.S. citizen and a professor at Rutgers University, had an unexpected run-in with the FBI in 2002 just after returning from a trip to the Netherlands. He was arrested and detained at the airport in Detroit before learning that he'd been placed on an FBI terrorist watch list after someone sent a tip to the feds alleging that he was stashing explosives somewhere in Florida. Although Elahi was cleared in the subsequent investigation, he was worried that this might happen again and that, before he was again cleared, he might be sent to Guantánamo as an enemy combatant.

Not wanting to take that chance, Professor Elahi took transparency to the extreme and started posting his entire life—moment by moment— online, leading *Wired* magazine to call him "the Visible Man."

Elahi figured that to neutralize further meritless government inquiries into a travel schedule that has him jetting around the world, he would turn his life into a real-life version of the Jim Carrey movie *The Truman Show*. He launched a website called trackingtransience.net, onto which he constantly uploads snapshots of his surroundings (Elahi is still posting his whereabouts). Among the tens of thousands of images of airports he's in, meals he consumes—on planes and on the ground—restrooms he uses, highways he travels on, and coffee shops he sits in, the professor can be tracked in real time via a GPS device he carries with him at all times. This way, he figures, the FBI or Homeland Security can log on and watch him shopping at a Safeway in San Francisco, sipping an Americano at a Starbucks in Midtown Manhattan, or snacking on peanuts aboard a United flight across the ocean. According to *Wired*, which interviewed the professor, his server logs show hits from a number of government buildings, including the Pentagon and the Office of the Secretary of Defense.

All these years later, and still his technotransparency has kept him in the clear and out of Homeland Security's interrogation rooms. He certainly doesn't think he'll be hassled again.

Hasan Elahi is unusual in going to laborious extremes to prove his innocence online. But he is not unusual in being accused wrongly. Plenty of other innocents have taken a hit to their reputation because of something posted online.

How the Innocent Can Take a Beating on Google: Some Examples

For a money management firm, nothing says "You can trust us with your money" like a reference to a major lawsuit it is involved in with a high-profile client that pops up on the first page of Google search results when people type in the firm name.

This firm is real, and it was a client of mine. An executive at the firm called me up one morning and said, "Harrison, do you think you could help us with a reputation issue we're having because of one of our clients?"

The client's fear centered on a business wire posting that reported a lawsuit the firm had filed against a well-known recording artist in 2005 for extortion and civil conspiracy. The ugly post showed up on page 1 of the search—and apparently had been there for years—whenever anyone searched for information about the company on Google.

Even though the client was the one doing the suing, management [be securely] concluded, correctly, that it looks terrible when the first fact someone gets [w/ info] about a firm is its involvement in a contentious legal case. Management [posted] kept putting the uncomfortable issue on the back burner, and the [online] reputation-dinging search result was still being displayed prominently [or] four years after the report surfaced. If you or your company faces a similar [financial] threat to your reputation, don't delay in hopes that it will go away. It won't. [reports] Instead, flood the search engines with up-to-date blogs, news, and articles about your company, its products and services, and its executives or leadership. That onslaught of information will push the damaging entry to the hinterland of search results—at least five or six pages down—where most people won't venture.

Another client of mine, an accomplished entrepreneur who planned on entering the political arena as a conservative, once asked me for my input on a political consultant he'd planned on hiring. The consultant seemed to have excellent credentials at first glance, but a three-minute Google search produced a dating advertisement he had posted on a message board that went into great detail about the qualities and physical traits he desired in a date. My client rejected the consultant, considering it extremely poor judgment for a professional to share this type of personal information so openly. After all, a consultant's job is first and foremost to manage the professional reputation of his clients; if he can't do that for himself, it's probably tough for him to do so for others.

Then there's the story of a female CFO candidate, as reported in a *U.S. News & World Report* article, who was in the job market. The woman—a Harley rider—had posted photos of herself on a motorcycle, wearing little clothing and a whole bunch of tattoos. Kathy Simmons, the CEO of Netshare, a job-hunting website, was interviewed for the article and said she would question the woman's professional judgment if she was considering hiring her and found those photos.

Unfortunately, it's very difficult to always keep one's personal life and professional image separate online. It's not just the growth of social networking sites like Facebook, Twitter, Instagram, and Snapchat; it's also that almost everyone these days has a smartphone, capable of capturing, uploading, or livestreaming any public humiliation or outburst to millions of people in seconds.

Twenty years ago a Manhattan lawyer screaming at restaurant staff to "speak English" and threatening to call the immigration authorities would simply have become yet another story of a jerk customer. But in the age of social media, a video of such vitriol in Manhattan quickly made its way online, where it went viral and spurred complaints to the bar association, an avalanche of bad reviews on Yelp, the discovery of other, similar videos of the lawyer, and the eviction of his law firm from a midtown building. Six days later he offered an apology, but the damage was done. As the social media cycle is speeding up, the reputational harm that occurs from even a week in its glare demonstrates that the need for keeping a check on self-disclosure has become a matter of astute reputation management.

Why Search Engines Can Make or Break Your Reputation and What You Can Do to Influence Public Perception

"Google is not a search engine," says *Wired* magazine. "It's a reputation management system. Online your rep is quantifiable, findable and totally unavoidable." Google doesn't give specific numbers—for competitive reasons, it says—but estimates put the number of Google searches at over 3.5 billion per day and 1.2 trillion per year. Chances are that someone is Googling you right now.

That's especially true if you're in the job market. Whether you're a recent college graduate or a C-level executive, you have a bull's-eye on your application that says "Search me." That's the case because potential employers are concerned about skeletons in your closet and about the things you're not telling them, particularly since the average curriculum vitae is a hyped-up, highly biased description of oneself, mixed with a few half-truths and the occasional outright fabrication. Even though many states now limit what online information employers can use in deciding whether to interview someone, 70 percent are searching social media for information on potential hires, with over half finding something that turns them off the candidate. To proactively manage their reputations, ambitious professionals and executives have the following three strategies at their disposal.

1. Mind Your Website

First of all, it's important to have one. If you are one of the few holdouts who think that your customers don't look for you online, get with it. When someone types your name into a search engine, you want that website to be the first line of defense in the reputation game. A site says who you are and what you do and—by design—how you think of yourself. At the very least your site will take one of the top spots on the coveted first page of Google's listing that provide a reference to your name. You get to decide the message your brand sends here. Add to this the fact that, according to research by Weber Shandwick on online reputation, 99 percent of executives consider corporate websites their prime source of information about a company, whether they seek data on competitors, vendors, suppliers, or business partners.

Once you have a website, make sure it shines. Weber Shandwick's finding that top executives place high value on a well-designed website—I talked about this in the previous chapter on online branding—should induce every corporate stakeholder or executive decision maker to log onto his or her online domain to reevaluate the message it sends to people who are dropping in to find out who you are and what you're all about.

2. Jump Online

You could do worse than emulate the online habits of Brian Chesky of Airbnb, John Legere of T-Mobile, or Marc Benioff of Salesforce. A recent study by BrandsEye showed that these three ranked at the top of CEOs on social media, "viewed positively for being leaders of successful companies but more interestingly, as being accessible communicators that displayed leadership on social and political issues." Legere and Chesky in particular liked to engage their customers and critics on Twitter: Over half of Legere's Twitter interactions were with T-Mobile customers.

When it is necessary to handle negative news, being transparent and disclosing bad news online immediately can be a tremendous asset in influencing public perception. In an article titled "In Era of Blog Sniping, Companies Shoot First," the *New York Times* reports on the strategy of Loïc Le Meur, founder of the video blogging site *Seesmic*, who had to let one-third of his staff go in October 2008. Rather than wait for others to break the news online, which would have invited negative reaction by the blogging masses, Le Meur got in front of a camera and posted an emotional video announcing the layoffs on his site. The comments he subsequently received were largely positive and supportive. Given how quickly news moves these days, getting in front of bad news requires a lightning-quick response. Another example: ANZ Banking Group CEO Shayne Elliot responded to an elderly woman's complaint about a dirty ATM by uploading a video showing him cleaning the ATM himself. Tens of thousands of people watched him mop out the ATM, commenting that he was an "awesome role model!" and "This guy inspires through action!"

Whether you make announcements on Twitter or on your corporate website, the goal is openness and transparency as opposed to hiding and whitewashing. The great thing about Twitter is that it allows you to respond quickly to a wide audience about any emerging story. Smart executives take advantage of this powerful weapon in their battle for an unblemished reputation.

3. Launch a Good News Assault

The Internet is patient and welcoming of the good, the bad, and the ugly. Why not tip the odds in favor of the good? To boost your executive presence and manage perceptions, consider becoming an author. You don't have to occupy space on the *New York Times* bestseller list to flood Google with favorable mentions of your writing on all kinds of websites. Authoring blogs along with professional articles, white papers, reviews, and news releases can all crowd out the reputation busters that fight for space on page 1 of Google. Similarly, offering your expert commentary to mainstream media journalists and pundits will get you quoted online in more places than one. "Help a Reporter Out" has its own acronym (HARO), hashtag, and Twitter account; in it, reporters look for quotable sources and information on everything from mosquito swarms to adjustable rate mortgages to party planners.

As noted above, although the immediate goal of these efforts is to boost your reputation online, the strategies can also keep potential dings to your reputation safely tucked away on page 6 of the search results.

The Seven Most Common Mistakes That Sabotage People's Reputations Online and How to Avoid Them

1. Careless Social Networking

Accept the reality that the Internet is open to everyone and that pictures, video clips, online profiles, and other personal information will often be seen by people to whom you wouldn't show them in the offline world. Posting unguarded images and content on sites such as Facebook, Twitter, and Instagram tends to inflict harm on people's reputations when they least expect it. If you decide to create your own pages and profiles on any of the social networking sites, consider the fact that even the profiles of your friends and others you link to can have equally embarrassing consequences by association, whether or not you monitor your own content closely. It's time to ax the drunk-friends-partying pictures, delete the tweets of you trolling celebrities, athletes, or other public figures—and watch whom you retweet. Politicians of all stripes have had to apologize for liking obnoxious Twitter personalities or retweeting messages from hateful organizations. If you're unfamiliar with faddish memes or odd emoticons, take a moment to find out what they mean before spreading what turns out to be offensive material.

2. Compromising E-mails

Research by Weber Shandwick and the Economist Intelligence Unit has revealed that 87 percent of global executives have sent or received an electronic message (private e-mail, text, or Twitter) by mistake. The research further states that although some e-mails are sent by accident, about one in four executives report that they've forwarded a private e-mail to someone else on purpose. Not all errors are as dire as the one in which some-one at the Hawaiian Emergency Management Agency mistakenly sent a text warning of an incoming missile attack, but considering the millions of e-mails and billions of texts that are sent daily, the potential for reputation-harming fallout is disconcerting, to say the least.

The solution, besides making doubly sure you don't accidentally hit the "reply-all" button, send e-mails in a heightened emotional state, or share confidential information with unauthorized others, may be adding more technology. You can install outbound e-mail monitoring software—if you're working for a larger organization, chances are that it's already in place—or rely on your colleagues to monitor your e-mails for you. The e-mail security provider Proofpoint commissioned a study by Forrester Research that found that 41 percent of organizations with 20,000 or more employees have staff on payroll that either read your e-mails, with their attention trained on confidential information you may be leaking intentionally or by accident, or analyze them automatically via e-mail auditing technology.

When you're the boss, even that technology may not help. John Mackey, the CEO of Whole Foods Market, had a major lapse in judgment when he wrote an e-mail to his board about the potential acquisition of Wild Oats Markets, labeling the move "the elimination of a rival." That kind of language violated federal regulations and promptly landed Mackey in hot water, primarily because the errant e-mail made its way onto the desks of the Federal Trade Commission. However, this was not Mackey's only blunder, as you'll see below. There are clearly a number of ways in which you can harm your reputation via e-mail, and the higher your place on the food chain, the bigger the pickle you could be in.

3. Controversial Blogging and Tweeting

It's bad when a line employee does it—companies frown upon this, frequently firing the offending blogger—but it's a bona fide reputation killer when a top-level executive does it. Back to Whole Foods chief John Mackey. He turned out to be the person responsible for years of anonymous blog postings that, among other unflattering things, questioned the value of competitor Wild Oats's stock and predicted the company's impending bankruptcy—all with the intention to buy Wild Oats once the shares hit rock bottom.

The NPR program *All Things Considered* reported on its website that Mackey's blogging was considered "unethical and embarrassing" by business and legal experts. The controversial blogging also earned Mackey an SEC investigation and a permanent stain on his reputation. Similarly, Elon Musk had to step down as chairman of the board of his car company for tweeting that he was going to take Tesla private and had investors lined up to pay $420 a share. The SEC determined there were no such investors; in addition to his removal from Tesla's board, Musk agreed to pay a $20 million fine.

Advocating what you believe in your blog postings is a good way to build your reputation, but engaging in sock puppetry or manipulating information about your business can end up burning your company and your reputation and landing you in hot water with the authorities.

4. Leaked Memos

Leaks to the media, often in the form of memorandums, are unintended disclosures that can have embarrassing consequences for their authors. Of course, the likelihood that they'll end up online with the author's name in boldface is as certain as an eastern sunrise. Leaked memos have long been weaponized by politicians to tarnish opponents—see this week's or any week's news for the latest bombshell—but disgruntled employees revealing confidential information in the business world is increasingly common as well. Journalists and news sites actively solicit such information from their readers and have created secure online drop sites where whistleblowers can deposit memos, videos, and other data without fear of discovery. Even if the information is old, as with the case of a two-year-old memo by Facebook VP Andrew Bosworth, it can be damaging if it drops during a related ongoing crisis. Back in 2016, Bosworth wrote a memo in which he defended the company from any bad consequences of its business practices by arguing, "The ugly truth is that we believe in connecting people so deeply that anything that allows us to connect more people more often is *de facto* good." In other words, he seemed to be saying, the (business) ends justify the (unethical) means. Given that this memo was published when

Facebook was struggling with a scandal involving data collection by one of its clients, Cambridge Analytica, it deepened the sense that Facebook cared little about its users' privacy and would do anything to grow.

In other cases, corporate attempts to deal with scandal forthrightly can be undermined by private correspondence in which the writer shifts blame. United Airlines CEO Oscar Munoz tried to rise above the outrage following a viral video in which a man is shown being dragged off a UA plane, but in a disclosed company memo he contradictorily blamed the customer: "This situation was unfortunately compounded when one of the passengers we politely asked to deplane refused and it became necessary to contact Chicago Aviation Security Officers to help." As customers are crammed into ever-smaller seats, worrying about being bumped from that tiny seat *after* they managed to board (much less before), an airline CEO's memo blaming customers for problems will only stoke the flames of outrage.

On a different but equally embarrassing note, an Apple memo threatening leakers not just with firing, but with jail and lifelong exile from the tech community—those caught "can face extreme difficulty finding employment elsewhere"—was itself promptly leaked, much to the derision of Silicon Valley.

5. Misstatements and Fabrications

One of the most reputation-damaging mistakes executives make that inevitably get plastered all over the Internet is an outright lie often about their education or credentials. "Claiming to be a Harvard graduate when you really have a degree from a no-name state school is one of the worst things you can lie about on your résumé," noted one survey of hiring managers. Not only does such a fabrication reveal a lack of ethics, but it strongly suggests a dearth of intelligence too, since all it takes is one phone call to set the record straight.

A bunch of high school journalists demonstrated how easy it was to out a fibber when they dug into the background of their new principal, Amy Robertson. The editor of the student paper, Trina Paul, explained the students' motivation, which sounds an awful lot like the motivation of a corporate personnel officer: "She was going to be the head of our school and we wanted to be assured that she was qualified and had the proper credentials." While Robertson had claimed to hold both a master's degree and a doctorate, the student journalists discovered that not only were those degrees bogus, but there was no evidence she had earned a bachelor's degree either. Robertson resigned. But as CNBC reporter Abigail Hess noted, that didn't fully resolve the matter: "The ordeal does raise questions as to how Robertson's résumé fib could have slipped past the adult members of the school board, whose job it was to thoroughly vet principal candidates." Even if you can bluff your way past a hiring manager, don't forget that there are plenty of interested stakeholders who could burrow right past that bluff.

Charles Elson, director of the University of Delaware's John L. Weinberg Center for Corporate Governance, weighed in on a similar case in which a CEO lied on his résumé, noting that distrust is a big part of the damage from such fabrications: "It's not the degree, or lack thereof, it's the misstatement to the board and the public that's the issue."

6. Slow or No Reaction to Rumors and Criticism

The C-suite will again supply us with a case study in what not to do in an era in which everyone has a voice and everything is uploaded. This particular C-suite belongs to Starbucks, whose leaders took more than a day—which is a year in social media time—to respond to an incident in Philadelphia in which an employee called the police on two African American customers waiting for their friends. A fellow customer videoed the encounter, which showed the men handcuffed by the police, and posted it on Twitter. Not only was Starbucks's initial response slow, but in the word of media communications expert Nora Jacobs, it was also "tepid." The company said it was "reviewing this incident with our partners, law enforcement and customers to determine what took place and led to this unfortunate incident." Jacobs noted that "the next day, the company tweeted a bit more abject response, but by then public sentiment was turning against the company." Later that same day, Starbucks finally managed a more comprehensive response, one that seemed to strike the right tone, with the CEO taking full responsibility. But until it did so, the company and its management were scorched for racial insensitivity and customer maltreatment.

Equifax was considerably slower than Starbucks in responding to a crisis, waiting six weeks (!) to reveal a data breach in which customers' driver's licenses, social security numbers, birth dates, and other information were exposed for 76 days. Since data on more than 143 million Americans were out there for the taking, Congress got involved; then-CEO Richard Smith testified that the breach was due to a single employee. Senator Elizabeth Warren berated Smith, stating that "at best you are incompetent; at worst you were complicit. Either way, you should be fired." Other executives *were* fired, but Smith himself was allowed to resign with a compensation package of over $90 million. In the wake of this scandal, a number of states now require disclosure of data breaches and fines for delays.

Stonewalling or hoping that bad press will die down is wishful thinking, particularly when shareholders, interest groups, and the media are keeping ever-closer tabs on executive compensation and wheeling and dealing on Wall Street. A clear, transparent, and swift communication strategy is crucial to protecting one's own reputation and that of the organization one represents.

7. Lack of Executive Presence on the Web

Earlier I pointed out that a clear and compelling website is your first line of defense to keep your reputation safe. But it's equally important to be proactive online as well as defensive, engaging those whose hearts and minds you'd like to capture. Otherwise your executive presence will have nowhere to go. Therefore, turbocharge your efforts and get on Twitter, especially if you are in the media, retail, tech, or entertainment business. A recent report quoting the website CEO.com concluded that "social media . . . has a major impact on brand reputation. A CEO can either participate in the discussion and influence it, or risk the implications of allowing his or her corporate image to be decided in the court of public opinion." A study by opinion-mining company BrandsEye agreed: "The lowest-ranking executives' sentiment scores were driven by a perception that they were inaccessible, running underperforming companies, and were not speaking out on social and political issues." Twitter gives you instant access to customers and potential clients around the globe; by allowing you to respond to events in real time, it lets your followers know that you are out there and engaged with the world.

This chapter has focused mostly on the defensive management of one's online brand and reputation, and given the perils of the web, that focus is vital. But don't let the existence of a downside blind you to the upside or make you shy in embracing it. As CEOs Brian Chesky of Airbnb and John Legere of T-Mobile have persuasively demonstrated (see above), the web offers rich and unprecedented opportunities to engage a huge audience, build a brand, and establish executive presence. Grab it and go.

In Chapter 14 we will delve deeper into the art and science of reputation management and tell you which types of crises represent the biggest threats to your organization and, by extension, to you. We'll wrap it up with tips to navigate a reputational crisis and several strategies to protect your good name and keep your executive presence intact.

14

Reputation Management 3.0

*Understanding Threats to Your Reputation and
Planning Strategies to Protect Your Good Name*

ONE OF THE biggest challenges—and opportunities—that can befall a business executive is a crisis that tests his or her leadership and decision-making skills, with the outcome hanging in the balance. This is not only where the company's products and reputation and even market value may be at stake, but also where one's executive presence is put on trial, asserted, or destroyed. If you haven't learned how to deal with a crisis, your first experience probably will be an unpleasant surprise. Many people harbor misconceptions about what a crisis looks like and how to deal with it, which hobbles their ability to respond effectively. By the time they understand where they've gone wrong, it's too late. Fortunately, you can avoid that fate by understanding the truth about crises and the most common myths surrounding them.

The Top Five Misconceptions About a Crisis Situation

Myth 1: If You Ignore the Media People, They Will Move on and Forget About It

Ignoring the media is the worst thing you can do. Reporters tend to be inquisitive, and when they don't get answers to their questions, they ask more questions. A small crisis, if properly handled, frequently becomes a nonissue, but if handled improperly, it can balloon into a big story, with every reporter asking, "What are they trying to hide?"

A recent example involves Facebook and one of its clients, Cambridge Analytica. In March 2018 both the *New York Times* and the *Guardian* reported that Cambridge Analytica had unauthorized access to the data of 50 million Facebook users. Facebook tried to preempt the stories with a letter saying that the data breach was not really a data breach and announcing on the company's website that Facebook was suspending its relationship with Analytica.

As Bloomberg reporter Sarah Frier put it, "Both moves backfired."

In that website announcement Facebook said it had "received reports" about Cambridge Analytica's misuse of data, implying that Facebook had conducted its own investigation. But as Frier explained, "In fact, the company's decisions were stemming from information in the news reports set to publish the next day, and it had not independently verified those reports, according to a person with knowledge of the matter. By trying to look proactive, Facebook ended up adding weight to the news." Frier observed that Facebook compounded the error when it was revealed that the company had sent threatening prepublication letters to the *Times* and the *Guardian*, actions that were almost guaranteed to heighten media interest in the story.

Facebook's errors didn't stop there. "Silence on the part of Chief Executive Officer Mark Zuckerberg and Chief Operating Officer Sheryl Sandberg didn't help," Frier noted, nor did ongoing reports of management conflict over how Facebook dealt with Russian disinformation efforts. That Facebook executives hadn't engaged the press was also highlighted by media observers, which led to questions about the company's efforts to respond to growing concerns over privacy and media manipulation. Further actions to tamp down the crisis were also ineffective, feeding into the perception that Facebook was slow-walking disclosure, much as it had with the previous year's stories on Russian media manipulation. Frier concluded that "the Cambridge Analytica saga is the latest in a series of bungled Facebook responses, often reactionary and sometimes unintentionally stirring public outrage instead of resolving concerns."

The moral of this story and many others like it is that if the media people do not receive what they consider adequate closure on a question, scandal, or event, they will cite the issue in every story they publish on you and your organization until the matter is resolved—and any further scandals will lead them to resurrect the previous missteps. The solution is transparency. It is key in dealing with the media.

Myth 2: Real Crises Are Sudden Disasters That Immediately Make Headlines

Executives who've never been in a crisis may be lulled into a false sense of security—"Hey, we're careful. This will never happen to us"—unaware that a crisis may be developing behind the scenes. For example, automobile recalls are not uncommon, and most car companies have learned to deal with them quickly. Toyota, however, which had long enjoyed a sterling reputation, reacted slowly to reports in 2009 of a "sticky gas pedal" even after a number of reported deaths. When the company finally began recalling affected cars, it sent a vague letter to owners insisting that "no defects exist." But Toyota eventually recalled millions of cars and, in March 2016, settled with the U.S. Department of Justice to the tune of $1.2 billion.

The takeaway: Don't think you're safe just because your organization hasn't been in the news. A crisis may be festering backstage.

Myth 3: Admitting Culpability Will Make Things Worse

Faced with a crisis, some leaders mistakenly adopt a purely legal strategy. Perhaps they think they'll fare better if they avoid admitting fault. This may be a good strategy to follow in a court of law, but it's usually the wrong strategy in the court of public opinion. Let's recall Starbucks's initial response when a store manager in Philadelphia called the police on two African American customers. One communications expert called that response "tepid," but when CEO Kevin Johnson finally stepped up with a more comprehensive one, he was widely praised for taking direct ownership of the problem, personally apologizing to the men, the Philadelphia community, and all of Starbucks's stakeholders. He also refused to put the blame on the store manager, stating instead that "I own this"—a statement that far more CEOs could use to demonstrate their leadership.

Taking responsibility often saves a company from a PR disaster. Not only that, but this strategy may head off legal problems before they begin. By establishing a strong, supportive relationship with stakeholders in the crisis, a company can frequently avoid the adversarial mindset that leads to lawsuits. In contrast, failure to accept responsibility or apologize has taken many companies down a long, nightmarish road of extended lawsuits and damaged reputations.

Myth 4: "Employee Error" and "Natural Disaster" Are Adequate Explanations of a Crisis

These types of crises are often highly publicized. Their simplicity and controversy make for good headlines. However, the most common and crippling crises generally stem from internal conflicts or management problems. Again, think back to the Equifax scandal in which then-CEO Richard Smith blamed a data breach affecting over 140 million Americans on a single (unnamed) employee; Smith was berated by members of Congress and forced to resign. The fact is, even if the immediate cause of a crisis is an employee mistake or a natural disaster, blaming those factors is a nonstarter; people will still hold management accountable for not properly supervising the employee or not having prepared for the natural disaster. And as noted in Myth 3, shirking responsibility is not likely to mollify either stakeholders or the public, and the fallout from the blame game can do more harm than simply cost you your job. It can erode any credibility you have as a leader.

Myth 5: Only Big Corporations Need a Plan for Crisis Communication

Leaders at small and even midsize corporations often persuade themselves not to worry about a plan for a crisis. They tell themselves that it won't happen to them, and if it does, they'll deal with it then. This "cross that bridge when we come to it" syndrome can be dangerous for long-term survival. Pigalle owner Mark Ofaly learned this lesson the hard way when he unloaded on a customer who posted a scathing review on his restaurant's website. He cursed her out repeatedly, insulted her looks, mockingly offered to return her money, and then, not content simply to respond to her initial bad review, wrote up an entirely new post in which he raged, "It is hard to believe that in this day and age there are still uneducated, unintelligent, unpolished human beings out there that still go out to eat." He did, eventually, apologize, but it would have been better had he been prepared to deal with the (inevitable) bad reviews in the first place.

A popular saying in crisis communication management circles goes: "When it's raining, it's too late to build the ark."

Crisis Intelligence 101: How to Recognize the Many Faces of a Potential Crisis

Being aware of the five biggest myths about crises doesn't mean you will recognize one when it happens. Crises can come in many different flavors, and many executives fail to respond effectively to a crisis because it's not the one they expected or doesn't fit their frame of reference for what a crisis is. For this reason, strive to keep an open mind and fine-tune your perceptual acuity and crisis radar. Realize that reputation crises can sneak up on you in many forms. The sections below explore some of those many shapes.

1. Accusations Spread by a Customer, Whether True or False

In today's world, many potential customers consult review sites for information about a company or product, and that means that one disgruntled customer can have tremendous reach. A diner at a Popeye's restaurant in New York City claimed to have found a rat in her chicken and shared the image on Facebook. Although a Popeye's spokesperson suggested that the "rat" was actually a misshapen chicken organ and promised to test its DNA, the story, with the pictures and gut-wrenching customer descriptions, was picked up by the media and spread as far as the United Kingdom. Depending on the size of your business, this could pose a serious problem.

2. A Damaging Story by a Journalist or Influential Social Media Personality

Sexual abuse scandals are dismayingly common. The *Boston Globe*'s investigation into the priest abuse scandal and cover-up by the Catholic Church hierarchy (which was turned into the Oscar-winning movie *Spotlight*) has led to millions and millions of dollars in victim payouts, the closing of parishes, the disgrace of bishops and cardinals, and the enduring loss of moral authority for the church. Similarly, the series in the *Indianapolis Star* on the assault claims against former Michigan State University sports doctor Larry Nassar led not only to his imprisonment, but to the firing and resignations of multiple MSU officials, investigations of improper and criminal behavior, and continued upheaval at USA Gymnastics, which also employed Nassar.

3. New Government Regulations That Affect How You Do Business

Gig economy businesses like Uber and Airbnb, which entered the market under the maxim "Act now, apologize later," have had to adjust their business models as cities and states update their regulations dealing with the informal economy, lest they lose access to the market entirely. For example, New York City, Uber's largest market, is proposing to put a cap on the company's growth in order to limit the number of ride-hail cars in the city. Such a law would seriously dampen Uber's plans to go public in the near future—particularly as this may set a precedent for other cities.

4. Confidential Information Leaks

All it takes to spark a crisis is one angry employee leaking closely guarded trade secrets, either for revenge on the company or for cold, hard cash. Even more common, however, are unintentional leaks, such as data breaches caused by employees clicking on a malware-infested link or a simple software error leading to the exposure of all sorts of sensitive records. For example, Level One Robotics and Control, which worked with Ford, GM, and Fiat Chrysler Automobiles, inadvertently exposed contracts, work plans, blueprints, and other information as was discovered by security researchers from UpGuard Cyber Risk. Level One's server, which required neither a password nor any other security clearance, contained over 47,000 files and 157 gigabytes of data.

5. Serious Injury to an Employee

A California plastics plant was shuttered and two supervisors pled no contest to felony charges following an explosion that killed two workers. Managers at the plant, owned by Solus Industrial Innovations, had modified a residential boiler rather than install an industrial one in order to avoid the high cost and extensive certification required for an industrial installation. The explosion was so forceful the two workers were decapitated.

6. Serious Injury or Accident Caused by an Employee

Let's say you run a business where deliveries are common. Your employee, a delivery driver, could get in an accident in a company car, fatally injuring others, as was the case when a UPS driver in Clinton County, Pennsylvania, collided with a horse and buggy, killing a woman and her eight-year-old son. The UPS driver was found to be at fault.

7. Criminal Trials and Legal Proceedings

Following a scandal in which Volkswagen rigged engine software to cheat on emissions tests, the company pled guilty in a U.S. federal court to a variety of criminal charges and agreed to pay $2.5 billion in criminal fines and $1.5 billion in civil penalties. Additionally, former CEO Martin Winterkorn was charged with a number of felonies, including wire fraud and conspiracy; and while Winterkorn, a German citizen, could not be extradited to the United States, a criminal investigation in Germany is ongoing. Volkswagen is also facing a multibillion-dollar lawsuit by investors over the software scandal, and the company has set aside over $30 billion to deal with recalls, fines, and other related expenses.

8. Civil Lawsuits and Legal Proceedings

After the boiler explosion at Solus Industrial Innovations, mentioned above, state lawyers pursued a multimillion-dollar fine against the company. Solus initially won relief at the lower court level, but in February 2018 the California Supreme Court ruled that officials could levy stiff fines for workplace violations.

9. Organized Demonstrations or Protests Against Organizations

Because smartphones have made it a snap to take and post videos, misconduct has been democratized. Every week, it seems, there is a new video of a police officer tasing, beating, or shooting suspects who were either clearly under control or running away, which has in turn led to protest after protest and vows not to call or cooperate with police. Any dust-up at your business may also be captured by a phone and, as happened at that Starbucks in Philadelphia, uploaded and spread quickly across the country. While the local Philadelphia protests were small, they were covered widely and required a response from the Starbucks CEO.

10. Chemical or Environmental Accidents

The granddaddy of this type of crisis is the Exxon Valdez oil spill in 1989. Between 10 million and 30 million gallons of oil poured into Prince William Sound on the Alaska coastline, and it long was the standard against which other man-made environmental disasters were measured. Then came the BP Deepwater Horizon explosion in the Gulf of Mexico in 2010. It was initially compared to the Exxon Valdez spill, but it was so much worse that it may have overtaken it as shorthand for environmental catastrophe.

11. Death or Illness of a Key Executive

It was a jolt when Fiat Chrysler CEO Sergio Marchionne took a leave of absence to deal with a previously undisclosed illness—and even more of one when he died shortly thereafter in 2018. Marchionne was so vital to the company that, as Bloomberg reported, its "annual report included a risk disclosure" on him; his leave of absence, in fact, caused Fiat Chrysler's market valuation to drop by 10 percent. While Fiat Chrysler initially claimed ignorance of his illness, it later admitted that "it wasn't forthcoming with some information it now says it knew," according to Bloomberg. Former SEC chairman Harvey Pitt has said that as a general rule, "While everyone is entitled to privacy, companies should make it a condition of the appointment of the CEO that he or she will keep the board fully apprised of any potential health issues" that may affect company value.

12. Unfounded, Untraceable Rumors

Food products are so liable to unfounded rumors that the debunking site Snopes.com has a tag specifically for "contaminated food." This category includes claims that workers deliberately infect products with HIV (Cadbury, Pepsi, various fruits, ketchup, etc.), claims of insect infestation, and allegations of microbial contamination, among others. For example, in 2017 a social media post falsely claimed that "paracetamol" (aka acetaminophen) was contaminated with Machupo, or Bolivian hemorrhagic virus. The allegation became so widespread in Indonesia and Malaysia that health authorities had to issue official proclamations debunking the hoax.

13. Natural Disasters

Untold numbers of businesses across the United States were either destroyed or severely impacted by Hurricanes Maria and Florence. Their assets were literally washed away, and many lost their customer bases because a good number of their customers were impoverished or forced to relocate to other parts of the country. Sanderson Farms in North Carolina, which is the nation's third largest poultry producer, reported that 1.7 million of its broiler chickens "were destroyed as a result of flooding." Both a heartbreaking tragedy and a devastating blow to the business.

14. Allegations of Racial or Sexual Discrimination

If not handled properly, allegations of racism or sexism can evolve quickly into lawsuits. For example, in 2015 Matheson Trucking, along with Matheson Flight Extenders, was ordered to pay almost $15 million to workers for back pay, emotional distress, and punitive damages due to workplace racial segregation and discrimination. Then, in December 2017, the state of Washington also sued Matheson Flight Extenders for employment discrimination. Another expensive example: Fox News settled a $20 million sexual harassment lawsuit brought by former anchor Gretchen Carlson, among others.

15. Strikes or Disruption of Labor Practices

On December 20, 2005, New York City Transit Authority workers went on strike, shutting down the transit system for a couple of days. The crisis for the city was compounded by the fact that local retailers were depending on dollars spent by last-minute Christmas shoppers, many of whom had trouble finishing their shopping without access to public transportation.

I could go on. It should be clear by now that crises can take many shapes and forms. It's practically impossible to anticipate every negative event that may occur, but you should try to anticipate as many different potential crises as you can, particularly the more likely ones in your line of work: A money management business should have a strategy for employee embezzlement; a ride-sharing company needs a plan for clashes between drivers and patrons. Regardless of what type of business you're in charge of, consider how certain circumstances may affect your reputation and how those circumstances should be handled.

Frequently, an incorrectly handled crisis will morph into another kind of crisis altogether. Consider the Solus Industrial Innovations boiler explosion, mentioned above. It may seem to be one protracted incident, but in fact the crisis took place on three levels.

First, the company failed to follow basic industrial regulations. After moving from Pennsylvania to California in 2007, it deliberately scrapped its commercial boiler in order to save time and money; making it operational would have required both installation of a gas line and compliance with an extensive permitting process. At this point, it was a backstage crisis.

Unsurprisingly, the $500 residential boiler that Solus used instead was not designed to handle industrial operations. As a result, according to Josh Cable, a reporter for an occupational health and safety magazine called *EHS Today*, a worker was ordered to "bypass the water heater's automatic shutoff feature by disabling its temperature-control device and installing a new controller to force the heater to operate at higher temperatures needed to melt plastic." As Cable further noted, the temperature and pressure release valve blew; but instead of replacing the valve, the company simply installed a new heat pump motor. "From that point on," the state's complaint observed, "the heater demonstrated daily, obvious signs of distress." Then, in March 2009, the actual accident occurred, killing workers Isidro Echeverria and Jose Jimenez. This is the second step in the saga, when the crisis migrated to center stage and made headlines.

While two plant managers directly involved in the purchase of the boiler quickly reached a plea deal with prosecutors, Solus and its parent company, Emerson Electric, fought the local district attorney over its lawsuit against them. That tough strategy precipitated the third crisis: a hard-fought lawsuit that made headlines years later when the California Supreme Court, in a unanimous 2018 decision, allowed Orange County prosecutors to pursue the case and potentially millions in fines.

The company had multiple opportunities to make different, better choices in this saga. If it had identified and fixed the initial, backstage crisis, it never would have made headlines, and lives would have been saved.

What's the important lesson here? When planning your response to any crisis, keep in mind the repercussions. Ask yourself, will this response create another crisis?

Another important lesson is about backstage crises and live crises. Both deserve your careful attention.

Live crises are the ones that occur without warning, generating immediate news coverage. Often the company and the media will learn about the problem simultaneously. A high-profile accident, an environmental incident, whistleblowing, and a labor strike are examples. These types of crises befall politicians and celebrities, too. A public outburst or a statement taken out of context can become a major story practically as soon as the words are uttered.

Backstage crises, in contrast, fester unseen. For weeks, months, or even years, perhaps only a few members of the company are aware of the issue. However, these issues have the potential to become major crises, and so they should be treated accordingly. Examples include internal allegations of discrimination, operational problems like Solus's residential boiler, and fraudulent accounting practices. When brought to light by the media, these problems can become major corporate scandals, but when they are still backstage, executive presence can be asserted, the problem can be identified, a plan can be devised, and the situation can be corrected. If those steps are taken, the crisis will never see the light of day.

In contrast, you will have little time to devise a plan to deal with a live crisis. For that reason, it is important to have a plan outlined beforehand. With your approach already sketched out and on file, you can summon a quick and resolute response that will give you a much better chance of weathering the storm and salvaging your reputation, perhaps even giving it a boost for making the right decisions under pressure.

The next section offers practical strategies for dealing with both backstage and live crises.

Dealing with Crisis: How to Prevent the Smoke from Becoming a Fire

In dealing with any crisis, your response should always be two-pronged, with an operational response and a communication response.

1. What are you going to do to correct the problem?
2. How are you going to communicate the problem and the solution to your stakeholders and the public?

These two aspects of the plan should be devised, considered, and implemented together in one smooth and powerful response.

Some companies make the mistake of focusing too narrowly on the operational response. They take steps to resolve the issue, but because they do not communicate effectively with the public about their actions, the response fails. The public perceives the company to be unavailable and unaccountable, causing a potentially bigger secondary crisis.

Some companies commit the opposite mistake—focusing too much on the communications response. They offer statements to the public, sounding sincere and concerned, but if their actions fail to support their statements, their words will ring false. In this situation too a backlash against the company can cause a secondary crisis.

The nuts and bolts of an operational response will vary sharply, depending on the nature, technology, and markets in the industry of the company in crisis. Here I will focus on the second prong of crisis response—communications—although there will be some discussion of operational issues.

The following section offers strategies for your crisis communications plan. These steps are necessary elements in dealing with the initial crisis. Think of them as a road map with a series of directions to be followed in the correct order. The playbook steps listed below this road map take individual circumstances into account, offering potential approaches for a variety of situations.

Reputation in Peril: A Road Map for Effective Communications in a Crisis

1. Anticipate the Crisis and Have a Plan in Place Beforehand

Like the Boy Scouts, communications experts have this rule: Be prepared. It's impossible to overestimate the importance of planning for as many different kinds of situations as possible. You never know what scenario the future might throw at you.

Crisis consultant Susan Tellem shared some of the strategies she and the members of her firm use to prepare its clients for possible crises. Not only do they write crisis manuals, but they help their clients rehearse crisis scenarios. One year they conducted a two-day crisis training session with a pharmaceutical company in which they kidnapped the CEO! Senior management (and the CEO himself, presumably) knew that it was a test run, but the majority of the company's employees did not. My colleague said, "It was not a joke, it was serious, and we wanted to make everyone react as they would had it been real, so that they were really prepared." She recounted how thoroughly everyone got into the moment. They wrote mock press releases, spoke with pretend media, and simulated the crisis as accurately as they could.

This story carries two important messages. First, you have to be creative when you are anticipating a crisis. Second, your plan should include as much detail as possible. No matter what size your company is, prepare a detailed, well-considered manual with your crisis plan. "Most of the people I deal with have no idea that something like this is going to hit," this colleague noted. Today's organizations have to be prepared for anything.

2. When a Crisis Hits, Ask Questions—Don't Act Until You Have All the Facts

It's impossible to count the executives who have gotten themselves in trouble by speaking to the media before being informed fully about the situation. As soon as you get your first inkling of disaster, investigate as much as time allows. Only then can you begin to deal with the problem with confidence and accuracy.

Gil Bashe, another colleague, underscored this message. "The first rule is, really analyze the facts. Get details. Any good communication plan, response, activity, starts with the truth and a complete understanding of all the relevant information."

3. Picture the Ideal Outcome

You have all the facts, and now you're ready to start making a plan. Not so fast. Before you reach the planning stage, spend some time considering where you want to end up when the crisis is over. How do you envision your organization once the issue is behind you?

According to Bashe, "It's essential to look at the outcomes, the identity the company wants to create through its communications. . . . We have to act appropriately here, for the outcome."

Among the "outcome" questions to ask are: What impression do you want to leave with your consumers and the public? What relationship do you want to have with your stakeholders? Where do you want to end up in the marketplace? Once you can articulate these goals, you may find that your plan practically writes itself. Striving to accomplish a particular set of goals can make the solution to your baffling problem seem self-evident. But if you have a knee-jerk reaction without having done the homework, you may end up lost and hurting. There's an old expression, "When you don't know where you want to go, any road will get you there." The reverse is true, too: If you know where you want to go, you know what road will take you there.

4. Be Available

In a crisis, many leaders and executives batten down the hatches and stay out of sight. However, the worst thing you can do is say "No comment" when reporters come knocking. Instead, go out of your way to be available to both the media and any stakeholders. Refusals to speak can escalate the initial crisis into a secondary crisis, as was illustrated in our earlier examples. But being open and honest often can defuse a crisis. Human curiosity is a powerful thing; sometimes just answering questions candidly can turn a scandal into a nonstory.

This is what happened to a client of Susan Tellem. The client had been involved in Medicare fraud, and the case went to trial. Although this clearly was a difficult situation, Tellem tried to maintain open communications with the media. She made a list of 20 reporters who covered that kind of story and made a practice of consistently reaching out to them and providing updates. Then, when the verdict was handed down, she immediately called all the reporters to inform them. The sentence, it turned out, was milder than expected, but more importantly, Susan's honesty with the media dampened interest in the case. She said, "Lo and behold, only one magazine reported on it. . . . By being out there and calling them right away, I think we defused a lot of the bomb. Only one publication ran the story, and it ran it in a rather balanced way. So I was very proud of the way it was handled."

5. Every Team Member Should Work on Implementing the Plan

Successful crisis communication is always a team effort. Make sure every team member is on the same page, and assign parts of the plan to as many competent people as you can get on board and move ahead.

These five steps constitute the road map. Make them part of your immediate response to any crisis. Flexible yet crucial, they are the bedrock of a successful response.

The Playbook: Top Strategies for Protecting Your Good Name

The next five strategies are more specialized. They are suggestions for various ways to deal with a crisis and threats to your reputation. Unlike the previous directions, which are intended to be used together to create a total approach, the playbook offers mix-and-match strategies. Their usefulness is highly dependent on the details of the situation. How you use them and when will depend on the specific scenario, your understanding of your market or constituents, and your organizational culture. The goal is to give you an understanding of the different types of strategies available for defusing a crisis.

1. Admit the Problem, Take Responsibility for It, and Correct It

If your organization is at fault for the crisis, frank and full acknowledgment is almost certainly the right course of action. Of course, not all crises involve wrongdoing on the part of the organization. Difficult and confusing new legal regulations and false rumors spread by a competitor are two examples of exceptions. But if the situation is one in which the organization has made a mistake, come clean. You should own up to your responsibility and express your sincere empathy and concern to whoever has been hurt by the mistake. Then do your best to correct the issue and ensure that it never happens again.

It is vital that the organization take responsibility as a whole. Making individual employees into scapegoats frequently will backfire. Instead, the company should coalesce as a team, taking responsibility for what happened and vowing to correct it. If one or two persons were to blame, appropriate action should be taken against them, but the company simultaneously should apologize for the environment and the infrastructure and the procedures that allowed the situation to happen.

Consultant Sarah Spaulding discussed this point in relation to a former client, a medical institution that had experienced a helicopter crash. "The helicopter hit power lines and then crashed," Spaulding recalled. "It would have been really easy to blame the pilot. . . . But instead we talked about the tragedy, we talked about the pilot's good flying record, the safe history of this helicopter service, and how this was just a tragic accident. Then we talked about the crisis procedures that could be put in place so this wouldn't happen in the future."

In a situation like this, your first job is to communicate concern for the victims of the accident, their family members, and anyone else affected by the tragedy. Your second job is to communicate your organization's commitment to ensuring that the situation won't happen again.

Communications consultant Suzanne Bates also expressed the importance of taking responsibility and expressing concern. "This is where the lawyers and communications people get into heated conversations sometimes," she admitted. "The lawyers are never going to want you to take responsibility for anything, yet many times if you take responsibility for the piece you own, it defuses the crisis and in many ways mitigates your risks, even of legal action."

2. Surprise the Media

Sometimes the best way to deflect the attention of the people in the media is by surprising them. Challenging reporters' preconceptions can turn a negative story positive, or at least buy you some extra time.

Public relations expert Ned Barnett helped a client do just that. The client, a college, had just been formed by the merger of two schools. One school paid its employees on a 9-month system, with slightly larger payments disbursed each month; the other was on a 10-month pay system, with slightly smaller payments. When they merged, the new payment system basically offered employees the worst of both worlds—the smaller payments but on the 9-month schedule. The employees decided to sue the college.

However, after investigating the issue, Barnett discovered that the new pay schedule had been mandated by the state. There wasn't much the school could do about it. Rather than being combative about the lawsuit, the school called a press conference to announce that it was filing an amicus curiae ("friend of the court") brief on behalf of its employees, supporting their claims. This turn of events caught the media off guard and helped generate goodwill for the school.

3. Change the Subject

Politicians and celebrities are the acknowledged masters of this strategy. But for companies and business executives, it's touchier; companies and their leaders have much longer reputations to protect. But if the crisis is more smoke than fire or is the type to fizzle out quickly, changing the subject can effectively deflect media attention until the storm blows over. It is a way to get your organization out of the headlines for a few days, and this may be important if your business or cause relies heavily on public opinion.

Media analyst and former campaign advisor Jason Miller decided to "step away" from his job at CNN after salacious details from a child custody lawsuit were published. The married Miller had had an affair with campaign staffer A. J. Delgado, which resulted in the birth of their son; the boy was the subject of the custody suit. Meanwhile, Miller was also alleged to have had another extramarital relationship, this time with an exotic dancer, who claimed that she was pregnant and that Miller had spiked her drink with an abortion pill, leading to her hospitalization. With all this going on, Miller's decision to leave the network both removed him from constant public exposure and saved CNN the hassle of having to either fire him or defend his continued presence on air.

"Stepping away," "not wanting to be a distraction," or "going into rehab" can be an effective way to change the subject when one is caught engaging in bad behavior. Of course, this strategy creates a downside: It offers great fodder for late-night comedians.

Changing the subject has also worked for a huge German company, but the strategy required very deep pockets.

Siemens AG, the German engineering juggernaut, never put too much effort or funding into advertising—until, that is, a corruption scandal rocked the firm in 2006. Its executives were alleged to be paying bribes for infrastructure contracts around the world. To change the subject, the Siemens senior management launched a major global public relations campaign to the tune of $450 million over three years. The campaign was designed to focus public attention on what Siemens does best, by touting its technological advances in energy, industry, and healthcare. The aggressive effort, spanning print, billboard, TV, and online ads, teamed the German conglomerate with the public relations powerhouse Ogilvy & Mather. Whether it all paid off is anyone's guess. After being ordered to pay $1.6 billion to settle bribery cases in 2008, bribery-related trials of former Siemens employees are still ongoing over 10 years later. Yet at the same time, *Forbes* ranked Siemens as #15 among "World's Best Employers" and #7 among "Top Regarded Companies" in 2018.

Changing the subject is a complicated, somewhat iffy, and, as in the example above, sometimes exorbitantly expensive strategy. If a company fails to resolve problems or deflect criticism satisfactorily, eventually consumers will migrate somewhere else. In other words, changing the subject may not be the best strategy for an organization with long-term considerations unless it has the coffers of a Siemens. The same applies to individual business leaders whose executive presence has been damaged by scandal, rumor, or other mischief. Throwing lots of money at a reputation problem can work—if time and money are abundant *and* if the good news about you outweighs the bad.

4. Use Passion to Make Your Case

In the world of business and the world of politics, heartfelt convictions and passionate beliefs often feel like the exception rather than the rule. That may be why passion can be so effective in helping the public understand your side of the matter.

Perhaps this method is best illustrated by a Ned Barnett story. His client, a public hospital in Michigan, had limited funds. One of its most critical services was a prenatal intensive care unit for very fragile newborns and preemies. At one point, however, the underpaid nurses in the unit decided to strike for higher pay. Generally, in a situation such as this, the media folks side with the workers and their union. As for the organization, Barnett said, "The typical thing to do in this situation is to hunker down and not get confrontational."

However, Barnett felt that the stakes were too high to do that in this case, and so he decided on a wholly different strategy. "You're on your own," Barnett remembered his boss saying to him as he went out to speak to the press, because what Barnett was about to do was completely out of line with conventional wisdom. Instead of appeasing the media, he brought some intensely emotional subject matter to display to the assembled reporters: pictures of the intensive care unit and its fragile infants. He explained to the media that these patients required very specialized care. They could not go for a few days without the special help they needed, and nurses or staff from elsewhere in the hospital were not trained to care for the infants properly. Barnett didn't need to say this last part explicitly, but his subtext was clear: If the nurses carried out the strike, they would kill babies. Also, he explained, the hospital did not have the funds to raise the nurses' salaries.

Barnett's passionate approach worked. The media sided with the hospital, the national union disavowed the strike, and the local unions turned against it as well. The crisis was defused.

This approach won't work for everyone or in all circumstances, but if you're in a situation in which the stakes are high and you can claim the moral high ground, don't be afraid to share your emotional investment with the public. Passion is a powerful thing. If you can make your case with sincere emotion, you may find that the public is sympathetic to your cause.

5. Look for the Silver Lining

Great companies can emerge from the trial by fire that is a crisis stronger than they were before. Although that may seem like small consolation in a stressful time, it's worth remembering. In fact, this strategy of looking for the bright side echoes one of the "must" steps listed above: picturing the ideal outcome. It's possible for a company to handle a negative situation with such grace that its response earns the public's respect.

The manufacturer of Tylenol represents a classic and perfect example of such a company. In the middle of a Tylenol tampering scare in the 1980s, the company went above and beyond its responsibilities to its customers, recalling millions of dollars' worth of the product. Despite the scare, those actions earned the company trust. Although the millions of dollars in losses were undoubtedly painful for the accountants that year, Tylenol quickly won back its market share. It continues to be one of the most trusted analgesic brands today, possibly in part because of its responsible actions during the crisis.

For executives who are able to see the bigger picture, a crisis represents a major opportunity to flex their executive presence. Yes, everyone will be focused on the problem. But examples like Starbucks and Tylenol illustrate that smart communication and responsible action during a crisis, when all eyes—the media's, the public's, the stakeholders'—are on the company, can tell a powerful story of redemption to a gigantic audience. And that's not a bad start to reclaim your good name.

In this chapter, you've learned about some strategies for crisis and reputation management. Through the examples of prominent players in business and politics, you've learned what to do and what not to do.

Remember that the number one rule for crisis communicators and executives who are concerned about their reputation is to anticipate and prepare. Your executive presence will be strengthened if you embrace the crisis communication plan discussed in this chapter to maintain your good standing when a crisis strikes. Remember also that you can repair your reputation and restore the luster to your developing executive presence and credibility if it has taken a hit. Just be patient and follow the steps best suited to your situation, and you'll recover in time.

Index

241

About the Author

New York Times bestselling author and executive coach Harrison Monarth is a leader in the field of developing key leadership competencies, executive presence, effective communication, and leadership influence. Harrison has held senior leadership positions in manufacturing, marketing, and organizational development in Europe and the United States.

He and his team of executive coaches at GuruMaker Executive Development work with global leaders at all levels, in a range of organizations from Fortune 100 corporations to entrepreneurial high-growth companies and nonprofits.

Harrison helps managers and leaders develop better self-awareness to understand their impact on others, engage effectively with stakeholders at all levels, strengthen key relationships, change unhelpful behaviors, and accomplish their most important development goals. He has helped leaders facing a range of challenges such as:

- Improving executive presence
- Stepping into a more senior role
- Developing emotional intelligence

- Managing emotions under pressure
- Building strong teams and inspiring people
- Becoming a leader coach who develops others
- Thinking strategically and operating at a higher level
- Increasing strategic influence with colleagues and clients
- Communicating up, down, and across organizational boundaries

Harrison has personally coached leaders from major organizations such as Fujitsu, Procter & Gamble, NASA, Northrop Grumman, PepsiCo, Deloitte Consulting, American Airlines, Baker Hughes, Hewlett-Packard, Standard and Poor's, GE, Intel, General Motors, IBM, Cisco Systems, Deutsche Bank, MetLife, The Nature Conservancy, and many other leading organizations.

Known for his intensive and caring coaching style, Harrison easily gets clients to open up and embrace the powerful leadership behaviors and communication strategies and techniques he coaches. He gently pushes his clients to excellence, as he partners with them on the journey of personal development, acting as a thought-partner, sounding board, champion, and guide who helps clients generate important insights and stay on track in the pursuit of their most important and challenging leadership goals.

Harrison is an adjunct professor at Externado University in Bogota, Colombia, Latin America, where he teaches a popular executive education program on Executive Presence and Leadership Communication to graduate students and executives. He has also lectured at Cornell's Executive MBA program and other universities across the globe.

His books include the *New York Times* bestseller *The Confident Speaker* (McGraw-Hill 2007), *Breakthrough Communication: A Powerful 4-Step Process for Overcoming Resistance and Getting Results* (McGraw-Hill 2014), and *360 Degrees of Influence* (McGraw-Hill 2012), which Stanford Graduate School of Business professor, Jeffrey Pfeffer said is "must reading for everyone who needs to build their personal brand and sell themselves."

Harrison is also a contributor to *Fortune, Harvard Business Review,* and Entrepreneur.com.

Printed in the USA
CPSIA information can be obtained
at www.ICGtesting.com
JSHW010306270124
55889JS00010B/100